# The Films of
# HOWARD HAWKS

by

## DONALD C. WILLIS

# The Scarecrow Press, Inc.
# Metuchen, N.J.    1975

Library of Congress Cataloging in Publication Data

Willis, Donald C
    The films of Howard Hawks.

    Includes index.
    1. Hawks, Howard, 1896-        I.   Title.
PN1998. A3H354        791. 43'0233'0924            75-17724
ISBN 0-8108-0860-9

To My Parents
and My Sister

## CONTENTS

# INTRODUCTION

Howard Hawks is my favorite American film director. He has been since 1969 and Theatre Arts 198K at UCLA-- Seminar in American Motion Picture History: Howard Hawks, a course taught by Peter Bogdanovich. (Bogdanovich chose director and films very well, if he was a bit defensive presenting this "unknown" director to skeptical students.) I'm not saying that Hawks is necessarily the greatest American director, but I do think he's one of the very few great ones we have--in the company of Orson Welles, Buster Keaton, and perhaps one or two others. I don't even insist that he has an obvious masterpiece or two, as Welles (The MAGNIFICENT AMBERSONS, CITIZEN KANE) and Keaton (One Week, The GENERAL) do. But if Hawks has no single, unquestionably great movie to his credit, I think he has more near-misses than just about any other American director:

BRINGING UP BABY, RED RIVER, ONLY ANGELS HAVE WINGS, I WAS A MALE WAR BRIDE, SCARFACE, The BIG SLEEP, RIO BRAVO, HIS GIRL FRIDAY, The THING.

And many of the best performances on film are in Hawks movies:

Cary Grant in HIS GIRL FRIDAY, I WAS A MALE WAR BRIDE, ONLY ANGELS HAVE WINGS, and BRINGING UP BABY; Katharine Hepburn in BRINGING UP BABY; Montgomery Clift in RED RIVER; Humphrey Bogart in The BIG SLEEP; John Barrymore in TWENTIETH CENTURY; John Wayne in RIO BRAVO and RED RIVER; Paul Muni in SCARFACE; James Cagney in CEILING ZERO; Jean Arthur in ONLY ANGELS HAVE WINGS; Walter Brennan in RIO BRAVO and RED RIVER.

Hawks' accomplishments with actors range from stray, dull-film-redeeming performances (Marilyn Monroe in MONKEY BUSINESS and GENTLEMEN PREFER BLONDES; Joel

vii

McCrea in BARBARY COAST) to entire, self-contained worlds (ONLY ANGELS HAVE WINGS, RED RIVER, BRINGING UP BABY, SCARFACE, RIO BRAVO); from virtual one-man shows (Grant in HIS GIRL FRIDAY and MALE WAR BRIDE; Barrymore in TWENTIETH CENTURY; Cagney in CEILING ZERO) to random groupings of almost anonymous actors, for comic and dramatic effects (in BALL OF FIRE, The THING, EL DORADO, AIR FORCE, and the non-Grant parts of HIS GIRL FRIDAY, which in effect is two different movies).

That this superb director of actors usually worked with pulp subjects is what is most fascinating about Hawks. It makes his best movies difficult or impossible to categorize neatly as art, trash, or entertainment and throws critics who attempt to define them strictly in terms either of art or trash. The best criticism of Hawks--Manny Farber's, Otis Ferguson's, James Agee's--is by those who don't insist that he's either a genuine artist or a mere entertainer. The worst Hawks criticism is by those critics who automatically take a film inside out, pretending to see into its hidden depths (whether or not it has any), leaving the surface to the audience, the "groundlings," as if a film didn't at least reveal itself through its surface. Such an approach to a Hawks movie is suicidal for a critic. ONLY ANGELS HAVE WINGS, RED RIVER, and RIO BRAVO are built on actors and actions, not on plots and themes. When you read about Hawks and his "themes," he sounds like the dreariest direc- tor imaginable. What he did was employ his actors' talents to the fullest.

His best actors--Grant, Wayne, Bogart, who were at their best for him--didn't just put in time in his pictures. If Wayne and Bogart hadn't worked for Hawks, I don't think we would have discovered how good they could be. If Grant hadn't, we might not have seen how many different things he was good at. Hawks may appear to begin with less worthy material than other good directors if you consider the plots of his films, rather than his actors, his basic material. This isn't to say that he doesn't need a good script to make a good movie, but his scripts aren't valuable for revelation of character or relevance to life, but for the opportunities they afford actors like Jean Arthur and Montgomery Clift to make their physical presences felt. The scripts open outward rather than inward. Hawks' best films are simply "escape" if you just want to get them out of the way of serious con- sideration. They're legitimate other worlds if you don't have constricting, preconceived ideas of what's art and what's not.

PART I

COMEDIES

## BRINGING UP BABY

In BRINGING UP BABY Katharine Hepburn does "any crazy thing that comes into her head" and, with help from Cary Grant, turns it into one of the great comedies. Just as the basic joke of Frank Capra's film of ARSENIC AND OLD LACE is that Cary Grant, who's supposed to be the sane one in the story, is actually the craziest one of all, so the basic joke of Hawks' BRINGING UP BABY is that Katharine Hepburn, who's supposed to be the crazy one, isn't much crazier than anyone else. Hawks has said that he thinks that it's a mistake that there are "no normal people in it," but that's no more a fault than that everyone in SCARFACE is a bloodthirsty killer. Everyone in BRINGING UP BABY is crazy or at least susceptible. Miss Hepburn will be practicing flipping olives into her mouth while a psychiatrist (Fritz Feld) tells her about mental disorders ("All people who behave strangely are not insane"), his eyeballs spinning around alarmingly as he concludes. Charlie Ruggles, nervous about the strain of insanity in her family, has to ask May Robson, "But you're all right, aren't you?" Near the end a jail comes to resemble an insane asylum as the characters file one after the other into cells. The only trouble is that, in the movie's insane world, there's no obvious difference between attendants and inmates. The one subtle distinction is that some of the characters think they're normal and the others don't worry about such things.

Which is all to say that the movie is about nothing at all. It's not about the tragedy of humiliation or the lure of irresponsibility or the muddleheadedness of scientists or the filthiness of the rich. It's just about Katharine Hepburn, Cary Grant, and some other memorable screwballs. She's an heiress, and he's a zoologist. She takes his golf ball. She takes his car. He, in turn, takes a lot from her. She gets a leopard (Baby) and, since he's the only zoologist she knows, she asks him what to do with it. He doesn't know for sure. A dog (George) takes an intercostal clavicle (a bone) from Grant and buries it. The leopard escapes. They look for the dog, the leopard and the bone. Meanwhile, an-

3

other, less tame leopard escapes from a circus. Everything
and everyone but the bone winds up in the jail. At the end
Miss Hepburn returns the bone to Grant, and he saves her
when the reconstructed skeleton of a large dinosaur collapses
under her weight. She sees it's love, and the movie might
be called a test of love, but nothing worse than that.

BRINGING UP BABY is about Katharine Hepburn and
Cary Grant the way other great comedies are about W. C.
Fields, Buster Keaton, and the Marx Brothers. It's based
on actors and movement and sound. There's no story, play,
or message to get in the way. It's sloppy, meandering, episodic, awkwardly "developed." It jumps around arbitrarily
from location to location, and the camera doesn't always seem
to be in the one, right, perfect place. The pace is spasmodic. Grant and Hepburn advance through underbrush, slide
down a hill, sit still for a minute, jump up, and rush off
again in search of George and Baby. It's not the well-made
comedy HIS GIRL FRIDAY is, with its "balancing" strain of
seriousness. Its gags are often timed wrong, one getting
lost in another, passing unheard or unseen by the audience.
Laughs come in un-uniform clusters. The movie doesn't
build, but depends on the inspiration of the moment. Fortunately, almost every moment is inspired.

At the time probably nobody working on the movie
thought that they were making "art," but they were (I insist),
and accidents like this help make up for all the times somebody thought he was making "art" and wasn't. Where most
movies put actors at the service of inferior material, BRING-
ING UP BABY puts everything at the service of the actors.
And when you have actors like Grant and Miss Hepburn, that
amounts to a stroke of genius. The two rarely had compar-
ably gifted co-stars--Grant did with Jean Arthur in ONLY
ANGELS HAVE WINGS and TALK OF THE TOWN, Ingrid
Bergman in NOTORIOUS, Irene Dunne in The AWFUL TRUTH,
and Eva Marie Saint in NORTH BY NORTHWEST; and Hepburn with John Barrymore in A BILL OF DIVORCEMENT,
Ralph Richardson and Jason Robards, Jr. in LONG DAY'S
JOURNEY INTO NIGHT, Spencer Tracy in ADAM'S RIB. And
sometimes even when they did, the actors in question weren't
at their best--as in the case of Hepburn with Tracy in most
of their other films, or Grant with Marlene Dietrich in
BLONDE VENUS or Jean Harlow in SUZY. And the other
times they co-starred with each other they always seemed to
be stuck in a Philip Barry play--HOLIDAY, The PHILADEL-
PHIA STORY. 1 They're two of the most fascinating people

just to watch, and in BRINGING UP BABY our view is unob-
structed. (Even the other actors don't interrupt too often,
and, in this special case, "interrupt" is the word, even for
actors as good here as Charlie Ruggles, May Robson, and
Walter Catlett.)

Grant and Hepburn don't assume characterizations
here so much as attitudes toward each other. Hepburn, unintentionally, keeps making Grant look ridiculous and she
likes him so well that she knows he won't mind if she laughs
at the spectacle. He's not so sure he doesn't mind. She
even finds funny his statements that he's getting married and
that his fiancée thinks he has some dignity. The fact that
he takes a pratfall immediately after such pronouncements
also helps undermine them. Hepburn is always making herself look ridiculous, too. She also takes pratfalls, but she
doesn't have as far, psychically or physically, to fall. The
same things that happen to him (ripped clothes, near-com-
mitment to mental institution, incarceration in jail) happen to
her, but they don't faze her. She's evidently used to such
temporary setbacks and actually enjoys them. ("Isn't this
fun, David? Just like a game.") Grant doesn't seem to enjoy them, except in retrospect, but he doesn't laugh at her
out of spite when she accidentally follows him in a slide down
a hill and stops in sitting position beside him. One reason
he doesn't is that the net she's holding ends up over his head,
and she's laughing at _him_ again. He's never in any position,
psychically or physically, to laugh at her. He's always at
least vaguely annoyed with her--more often distinctly--but
never enough to do more than feign strangling her (like Keaton with Marion Mack in The GENERAL) or to make him
forget that he's a gentleman and she's a lady, or at least
that he's a gentleman.

His annoyance with her occasionally irks her, as if
she thought he were trying to spoil the fun they were having.
But she comes right out and says she likes him. He shows
that he likes her by not strangling her or letting her fall
from a scaffold or hitting her with an old, just-unburied
shoe. Anyone with less affection for her _would_ have let her
fall, strangled her, or hit her with the shoe. To anyone
who can't understand why Grant doesn't--that is, to anyone
who sees Miss Hepburn as only the obnoxiously affected little darling she indeed is and not as the genuine knockout she
also is--the film must seem baffling. She recognizes these
signs for what they are, if he perhaps doesn't, lets him know
she does, and he accepts her interpretation.

Her heiress and his scientist are appealingly helpless
without each other. The difference is that when he gets into
trouble, he doesn't know how to get out, and when she does,
she can cope. In a wood, she starts to walk away from him,
bravely declaring, "I can take care of myself," and presently
trips over a log. She can handle an un-housebroken leopard
fine until Grant informs her that it's the wrong leopard and
her screams bring him to her rescue with a chair. She's
dependent on him because she wants to be; he's dependent on
her because she wants him to be. It's love by intimidation.
Grant's mind may be on the intercostal clavicle throughout--
a typical shot has him looking at the dog and her looking at
him--but Hepburn's assaults have a cumulative effect on him:
"In moments of quiet I am strangely drawn to you. But there
haven't been any quiet moments." Like most of Hawks' best
films, BRINGING UP BABY is noisy and fast, and love has
to compete with the racket. (To overlapping dialogue among
Grant, Hepburn, Robson, and Ruggles, Hawks adds overlapping barking from George and overlapping yowling by the
leopard.)

Grant is usually aloof and withdrawn, or as aloof as
he can be with Hepburn besieging him. When he wants to
get in a word he has to step on her foot. Her perpetual
motion sometimes overwhelms him and at other times spurs
or startles him into activity. But his customary position is
sitting (Hepburn: "He has to take frequent rests"), with his
elbows on his knees, as if he's waiting for something or
waiting out something. He seems to regard the dog, George,
as if the latter were an active and malign intelligence, and
he seems to be correct. He's stiff and reserved and moves
in starts and stops, as if his mental impulses were sporadic
and non-continuous; as if he were an automaton operating on
hundreds of separate, successive instructions, and with each
new instruction, forgetting the previous one. His attention
doesn't so much wander as lose itself entirely to each new
object it focuses on. He's not absent-minded so much as
single-minded, and his body just seems to hang there, incidental to his mind, or to the idea in it at a particular point.

Miss Hepburn races around the sets, breathlessly
rushing up to Grant or Miss Robson (her aunt), then spring-
ing back, like a ball in a pinball machine; shadowing Grant
as she alternately cries, "What did I do? What did I say?";
running after him calling "Nice George!" as he calls
"George!" after he has asked not to echo his "George!" with
her own; or just running around, unable to check her own

BRINGING UP BABY: Ruggles, Robson, Hepburn, Grant, and George.

momentum.   At one point Grant tells her, "You do every crazy thing that comes into your head, and you don't tell me," and the movie, concisely, is Katharine Hepburn doing every crazy thing that might enter a madcap heiress' head, with Cary Grant reluctantly joining her.   An accurate picture of the movie might be simply a catalogue of crazy things, like Miss Hepburn playing "He loves me, he loves me not" on her toes, or throwing Grant's sock into a bonfire after she has accidentally burned his other one, or repeating, "I was born on the side of a hill," as she walks, after losing a heel.   But Miss Hepburn is charming even when she's not doing something crazy, when she's just tugging at Grant's robe trying to get his attention, or giving him a hurt, dirty look when he says something about putting her "in a padded cell," or wiggling her fingers as she says, "It'll make your hair curl."

Most performances have blank spots in them (even
Grant's does here--fortunately; it's hard enough deciding
which one to watch), as if the actor had temporarily shut
down, but every moment and piece of Hepburn's here is
memorable, loudly or quietly--an eager, fast walk up to
Grant; a look of sly, sensuous submission under his imperfectly impervious gaze; a contented purr as she stretches out
after luring him to her apartment.   Her physiognomy is in-
credibly malleable--she finds a striking new angle, position,
movement, look, or voice for each scene.   It's the greatest
comic performance that I've seen by an actress, endlessly
watchable and fresh.   She keeps saying that Grant is "so
good looking" without his glasses, while she is just beautiful.
But there's a big difference between something like BRING-
ING UP BABY and something like A WOMAN REBELS, a
tear-jerker made barely bearable more by her beauty than
by her talent.   Her beauty and her talent, well-employed,
are a formidable combination.   (And why didn't she work
with Hawks again?   Perhaps Grant had more sense or taste
than she did.)

The dialogue in BRINGING UP BABY takes imaginative leaps with its play on words--they go by so fast that
audiences, as with a Marx Brothers comedy, sometimes
don't even notice.   Miss Hepburn leads Grant around to the
side of a mansion in the dead of night, and he objects, "You
can't just go climbing into a man's bedroom window."   "I
know," she replies, "it's on the second floor," and begins
picking up stones to throw at it.   There's a leopard in her
bedroom, and Grant cries, "You've got to get out of this
apartment!"   "I can't.   I have a lease," she answers with
a straight face.   And she doesn't pause to make it clear
that something has been left out.   The film's mixture of
subtle and blatant humor keeps one off balance, and the
comment on it I recorded when I was thirteen and less dis-
cerning--"Loud but fair"--is an understandable reaction to
the more obvious blatancy.   I still think it's loud, but I
now think it's great too. [2]

## Notes

1.   Logically, The PHILADELPHIA STORY should be one of
      my favorite movies since it has my three favorite
      actors--Grant, Hepburn, and James Stewart--in it.
      But it has also got "ideas" which are talked to death
      and a shallowness where there is supposed to be depth.

2. I have a similar initial resistance to Preston Sturges'
   frantic comedies, which usually wears off pretty
   thoroughly by the second viewing.   However, even
   after acclimatization, I don't think that the best
   Sturges--HAIL THE CONQUERING HERO, The LADY
   EVE, The MIRACLE OF MORGAN'S CREEK--are up
   to BRINGING UP BABY.

# HIS GIRL FRIDAY

The Ben Hecht-Charles MacArthur play, "The Front
Page," is a laugh machine.  It's all surface and no sub-
stance; at its best it simply captures a spirit, creates an
ambience.   Tough, no-nonsense attitudes toward love and
romance and toward newspaper reporting camouflage sentimental attitudes toward romance and reporting, though the
play takes Hildy Johnson's rhapsodizing over his life and
escapades as a reporter more seriously than his mooning
over his fiancée.   It tries to balance cynicism and sentimentality, but the two attitudes cancel as often as they balance each other, or simply fail to connect, either with each
other or anything else.   The play falters when it pretends
that its sentimentality is its depth, or that it has depth.
It's a series of comic situations, sometimes ingenious,
invariably amusing, but (to quote BRINGING UP BABY)
"There's nothing there!"

Hawks' HIS GIRL FRIDAY, which is based on "The
Front Page," doesn't transcend its origins, but it's a machine of a somewhat higher order, thanks primarily to Cary
Grant, who is even better in this film than he is in BRING-
ING UP BABY.   It's still all surface, but Hawks and Charles
Lederer got at least halfway in reshaping the material into
a great comedy vehicle for Grant.   The play is finally as
much a limitation as an inspiration, a leash for Grant, but
at least a long one.   The added scenes with Rosalind Russell,
Ralph Bellamy and Grant are inspired comedy, clearly superior to the original material, though comparing the movie's
new scenes with those which were originally in the play isn't
entirely fair--the screenplay does seem to retain many of
the play's weaker scenes and to drop some of its better
ones.

Grant is perhaps the only American actor outside the
great comedians who could have sustained a series of comedies tailored for him:   BRINGING UP BABY, HIS GIRL
FRIDAY, and I WAS A MALE WAR BRIDE constitute, in

effect, such a series.   The greatest comedies--The CIRCUS,
The BANK DICK, The Music Box, ANIMAL CRACKERS--
were, I believe, those fashioned around the talents of one
actor (or one comedy team), and if Cary Grant never got a
nice, long series all to himself, he at least got one comedy
(I WAS A MALE WAR BRIDE) to himself and one (BRINGING
UP BABY) which he shared with Katharine Hepburn--and it's
arguable whether Hepburn stole it from him.

      "The Front Page" is all energy, a well-oiled machine
for generating and channeling energy.   In HIS GIRL FRIDAY
Grant is not just an energy machine; he's a thinking machine,
a computer that's always on.   He can slow down, unlike the
play, and you don't ask questions, as you do when the play
stops to make one of its furtive, humanistic points.   When
he's not on the attack, he's thinking, and not about the consequences of his words or actions, just about his next move.
There isn't a trace of sentimentality to his character.   He's
thoroughly despicable, as inhuman as W. C. Fields in YOU
CAN'T CHEAT AN HONEST MAN.   He's callous and couldn't
care less, unlike the original play, which is callous but
nervous about it, pausing every once in a while to worry
over itself.   Its concern for Earl Williams and Mollie Malloy
and its nostalgia for the old-style, freewheeling journalism
seem to be signs of the authors' guilty consciences, efforts
to proclaim itself socially redeemed, which it isn't.

      Having read the play, seen it performed, and seen
two film versions of it, I am pretty thoroughly convinced
that there is just no way to take "The Front Page" seriously,
not even the Hawks version.   The execution-eve setting,
with its undercurrents of feeling and references to death,
would seem a natural for Hawks.   The reporters' glib dis-
missals of Earl Williams' imminent hanging echo the fliers'
superficially unfeeling reaction to Joe's death in ONLY AN-
GELS HAVE WINGS.   But there's actually less feeling beneath the surface of Hawks' film than beneath the play's,
and it's just as well.   The Williams-Mollie Malloy relationship is just a pretext for laughs at best, and the noise it
generates doesn't compensate for its hollowness.   In the
movie John Qualen is calculatedly pathetic, and Helen Mack
is a screaming banshee of a nagging conscience.   It would
be better if we could just assume that the reporters aren't
really indifferent.   The doomed lovers are there for comic-
dramatic balance and for kicking off the comic mechanism.

      Grant, as bullying Morning Post editor Walter Burns,

is funny even when he isn't doing or saying anything.  The
play dies temporarily whenever there is no laugh line or
when one doesn't click, because there's nothing else to back
up the dialogue--the dialogue is its own excuse, an attempt
to recreate an atmosphere and a setting; the reporters are
fairly anonymous.  It's superficially expressive and fails
when it tries overtly to express any underlying factors, such
as the raptures of journalism or the presence of death.  The
lines are everything.  When the play gets self-conscious, it
falls apart.  Grant's Walter Burns doesn't seem to be con-
scious of anything.  He acts only instinctively as he manipulates people and situations to get his way.  Grant backs up
his lines.  The other actors depend on their lines; Grant's
depend on him.  He manipulates words as he manipulates
people.  He attacks people almost physically with words,
pushing Miss Russell before him around the press room as
he unleashes a barrage of words, pulling Ernest Truex up
by his coat and directing him out of the room in a single
movement.  In the middle of a speech he'll imitate a statue

HIS GIRL FRIDAY:  Cary Grant, Frank Jenks, Roscoe Karns,
Gene Lockhart, Porter Hall, Rosalind Russell and Regis
Toomey.

("Hildy Johnson statues") or Hildy as an old woman ("See her, Bruce?  She's <u>old</u>, isn't she?"), without stopping for breath.  In a scene lasting several minutes a cigarette that he holds in his hand seems to dance crazily around the room in the background, as if powered by the energy generated by his words and thoughts.

As in ARSENIC AND OLD LACE, the authority of a strong assertive characterization backs up his dialogue.  As in that other movie, everything he does seems right because he's so assured, forceful, self-confident.  He's so good in both movies that he makes one impatient with the rest of the movie, however good <u>it</u> may be.  (The rest of HIS GIRL FRIDAY is decidedly better than the rest of ARSENIC AND OLD LACE.)  "The sardonic and quick-witted" (in Manny Farber's phrase) in HIS GIRL FRIDAY use words as weapons, but most of the characters cease to exist when they stop talking.  Grant's Walter Burns is the ultimate refinement of this idea of verbal dueling.  Nothing hinders him.  Every word, gesture and thought is directed toward the battle at hand.  His only considerations are strategy and timing, not conscience, decorum, or common decency.  A Richard III without blood (or at least with less blood) on his hands.  Waggling his eyebrows hopefully, he asks Diamond Louie, "Was she dead?  Huh?" after Mrs. Baldwin is injured in a car crash.  He's always on the offensive, even in the worst spots.  Handcuffed, he still contemptuously barks at Sheriff Hartwell, "Make up your mind!" when the latter fails to come up with a witty retort at one point.  He intimidates, badgers and accosts everyone, from the mayor to his ex-wife Hildy Johnson to her fiancé.

The movie, unfortunately, is less a matter of team-work between Grant and Miss Russell than of his leaving her far behind and of her trying to catch up with him.  She's not a complete drag, like poor, beset Pat O'Brien's Hildy in the Milestone movie of the play, whose insistent glumness is a real wet blanket.  But at times she's almost babyish when she's just supposed to be flustered and she can't make much sense of her difficult role of mediator between Grant's consciencelessness and the play's conscience.  She's more of a square in her yearning for "respectability" than she's intended to be.  It's hard to see what the two see in each other.  Miss Russell is a competent actress--and at times better than that, as in the scene with John Qualen in his cell--who's just out of her league with Grant.  The movie, which improved on the play by switching the Hildy role from

male to female, would have been further improved with
Katharine Hepburn, Jean Arthur, or possibly Margaret Sul-
lavan in that new role.

The two chief comic modes of the movie are the bla-
tantly unfair and the comparatively fair verbal duel.  It's at
its most delightfully, smirkingly inhuman when it opposes a
markedly inferior and a superior duelist; when, that is, it
pits someone (Ralph Bellamy, Billy Gilbert) who not only
does not know how to duel, but who does not even know that
there is such a thing as dueling with words, against someone (Grant, Clarence Kolb) who uncharitably disregards (even
exploits!) his opponent's ignorance.  What makes these encounters so hilarious, yet oddly un-brutal, is that the victims
are so naive that they don't even know that they've been dis-
patched (though they sometimes have a vague glimmering).
Defeats are marked by the shrinking or dwindling away of
the victim's voice or by the unparalleled vacuity of his subsequent statements.  (The light dawns slowly in Bellamy's

HIS GIRL FRIDAY:  Ralph Bellamy, Cary Grant, Rosalind
Russell.

face--"Then Mrs. Sweeney <u>didn't</u> have twins!"--and Grant
turns an incredulous, questioning face to him, as if to ask,
"You can't be <u>that</u> slow?")   After Grant, Gilbert and Bellamy
give the two funniest performances.   Their characters have
unknowingly strayed into enemy territory, and what they
don't know can't hurt them.   Gene Lockhart's Sheriff Hartwell is an intermediate character who knows what's going
on but who can't do anything about it.   He relies on charity
and luck rather than on his wits.   The other newspapermen
and officials--Grant, Porter Hall's Murphy, Kolb's mayor,
Roscoe Karns' McCue, Frank Jenks' Wilson, Regis Toomey's
Sanders--are pretty evenly matched, though Grant always
seems to win no matter who his opponent is; he just never
concedes.

          The movie is primarily Grant plus myriad stunts with
words, and it's very nearly a great comedy in spite of its
flaws.   Hawks puts two, three, four, or ten people into the
frame and has them cram as many words as possible into
very small spaces of time.   Actors overlap each other's
speeches, match each other in vehemence and volume, toss
in words offhandedly, mangle them (Abner Biberman:   "She
ain't no albino.   She was born right here in this country."),
snap in-jokes ("Archie Leach," "Ralph Bellamy"), and
threaten and curse those who get in their way.   The overlapping itself sometimes generates a gag:   Kolb asks Gilbert
his name, and the latter replies, "Pettibone," as Gilbert in
turn asks, "What's yours?"   Kolb considers Gilbert's answer
out loud--"Pettibone"--and Gilbert, delighted, splutters,
"No!  Not really?"   Hawks condenses and concentrates by
occasionally shooting two conversations at once, as when
Miss Russell grabs two phones, or when she takes one and
Grant takes another, or when Grant takes one while she and
Bellamy rage at each other.   The Hawks-Lederer version
of the play, like the Milestone-Lederer-Bartlett Cormack
version (Adolphe Menjou:   "Son of a...!" under the screech
of a typewriter carriage's return), has fun with forbidden
words:   Miss Russell:   "Shot him right in the classified
ads....   No, 'ads'!"   The Milestone film has more tricks
with the camera--some of which work, some of which don't--
and occasionally poor sound recording, but it's quite good
too, with its own set of top character actors as reporters
(Walter Catlett, Frank McHugh, Matt Moore, Edward Everett
Horton).   But Hawks has Grant, and that makes most of the
difference.

# I WAS A MALE WAR BRIDE

I WAS A MALE WAR BRIDE is Hawks' most disreputable comedy, and you don't have to go much further than the title to guess why. [1] The most obvious kind of situation comedy, wholly unbelievable, even though it's based on a true story, it's a sort of true-life fantasy. In her famous essay-attack on Andrew Sarris and company and the auteur theory, "Circles and Squares," Pauline Kael fired one of her main salvos at MALE WAR BRIDE:

> These movies soak up your time. I would suggest that they don't serve a very different function for Sarris or Bogdanovich or the young men of Movie-- even though they devise elaborate theories to justify soaking up their time. An educated man must have to work pretty hard to set his intellectual horizons at the level of I WAS A MALE WAR BRIDE (which, incidentally, wasn't even a good commercial movie). [2]

Sarris was perhaps intimidated--he didn't put I WAS A MALE WAR BRIDE in italics for the year 1949 in his The American Cinema. Hawks, however, has called it one of his favorites among his films, and Peter Bogdanovich listed it as one of his 13 favorite Hawks movies in an article for Esquire. It was one of my early favorite Hawks films, too (along with The THING), when I first saw it on television in the early Sixties. But I too was perhaps intimidated by Kael and the title, for when I saw it again, for the third time, in Bogdanovich's Hawks class at UCLA in 1969, I didn't like it as well. (It was a bad print, as I recall, but I'm beginning to rationalize.) Even so, I thought it was funnier than any film with a title like that deserved to be, and I still liked the line, "Any identifying scars on my second cousin's clavicle?!"

There are perils beyond the title and the wrath of Kael. The movie looks as though it was made very economically

on location in Germany and England.   Most of the bit actors'
voices sound hollow and wrong.   Ann Sheridan is pleasantly
exasperating, but a little pushy with the fond-indulgence-of-
male-quaintness stuff.   And, as in BRINGING UP BABY
(perhaps thanks to Hagar Wilde, who was also on that film),
a lot of the lines and words are unexpected and fanciful, but
are delivered so straight, almost deadpan--they're not subtle,
just delivered subtly--that they slip by most of the audience:

> Sheridan:  We're lost.   We're absolutely lost.
> Grant:  Is there a difference?
>
> Grant:  You're subnormal.
>
> Sheridan:  You unspeakable weasel.
>
> American consul (registering Grant as Sheridan's
> bride; to Sheridan):  Well, obviously these appli-
> cations are intended for the <u>husband</u> to fill in.
> This doesn't apply to you.   You'll just have to make
> the proper adjustments.
> Grant (startled):  What?!
> Sheridan (clarifying):  On these papers.

The movie is indeed about a male war bride, no getting around it.   Now it might sound, considering all the ob-
stacles, as though it's no use going any further.   But Cary
Grant happens to be the male war bride, the movie is wonderfully well written and directed and often hilarious, and it
definitely belongs in italics.   In fact, it's pretty nearly a
great comedy.

I WAS A MALE WAR BRIDE is a situation comedy,
but Cary Grant is the one in the situation.   If any other
actor around at the time had been put into the same situation
and film, you probably could have stopped right at the title. [3]
But the person sitting at the bottom of the hill, pointing out
to Katharine Hepburn the net that she just dropped over his
head (in BRINGING UP BABY), is just the one to play a
male war bride.   Grant is one of those rare actors who
knows when the humor in a situation is implicit and who doesn't
have to thrash around to find it.   Grant plays straight man
to the comedy that's already there in MALE WAR BRIDE,
and by so doing heightens it and gives it point.   As with
Buster Keaton, his deliberately minimal expressiveness here
allows the viewer to read in his various reactions to the disasters that befall him.   But, also like Keaton, he's not a

blank--he just doesn't have to go very far to get the look or tone he needs for a line or scene.  He doesn't maintain his reserve perfectly.  When he breaks it, though--as in a playful knock-knock routine with a maid on the other side of a bedroom door--he's still controlled, and the mixture of exuberance and self-restraint is delightful.

The sense of detachment from other actors and from his surroundings that Grant has in his Hawks movies is perfect for this one- or two-note comedy of indignation, and his performance as Henri Rochard is a strong candidate for his best.  He appears determinedly above it all, as if he were objectively witnessing his own humiliation and not liking it one bit, but realizing that there is nothing he can do about it.  He's right:  there isn't.

Things begin badly for him and get worse and worse, until he's forced into transvestism to get aboard a ship to go to America with his (female) bride.  Finally, things get so bad that they can't possibly get any worse.

It's basically a one-gag comedy, like Keaton's SEVEN CHANCES, with Grant suffering at the hands of one woman rather than hundreds and getting tangled up in the snarls of military red tape that marrying her entails.  I WAS A MALE WAR BRIDE is, in fact, somewhat like a silent comedy, or a long pantomime with Cary Grant suffering in more or less silent indignation.  There are no musical cues to tell you when to laugh or when to expect a laugh.  A simple shot of a doorknob coming loose in Grant's hand is the quiet punchline to a sweet, silent, tucking-girl-into-bed scene.  Sometimes Grant doesn't even have to move.  As Sheridan notes, he looks "so funny just sitting there" in a collapsed jeep, and all Hawks has to do is keep the camera angled slightly down on him.  The movie has an unusual, disjointed rhythm, not just attributable to sloppy editing.  At first, it seems to have no rhythm or pace at all, until you realize that Hawks is taking his cue from Grant, letting him decide how long to take on a scene; that is, letting him decide how thoroughly a fool he wants to make of himself.  For the one sure thing in each new scene is that Grant will be made to look silly, even if it takes a little time.

The picture is drab-looking.  It's just Grant and a lot of space.  But it's not necessarily dead space.  It's Grant and however much space Hawks thinks is necessary to best set off Grant.  There's a medium shot, from a jeep,

Ann Sheridan and Cary Grant in I WAS A MALE WAR BRIDE.

of Grant, at night, returning to Sheridan in the jeep after he
has climbed up a pole to read a sign.  The sign is in German, and he has held his lighter up to it for her to read
from the jeep.  As he returns, he asks her what it means.
When she says, "Wet paint," Grant is close enough for us to see
for ourselves, and he looks down at himself.  The gag is in her
words and his movement and in the interval between her answer
and his movement.  In another medium-far shot, Grant, at a
railroad crossing, is caught on the safety bar as it slowly
rises.  We see him through the last passing boxcars of a
train, and at each gap between cars he's a little higher.
It's like the last, driest refinement of a basic gag.  (The
later and similar MAN'S FAVORITE SPORT? returns to the
basic gags, but with no refinements.)

The choicest example of the movie's dry, deliberate
humor is a close or medium-close shot of Grant trying to
find a comfortable sleeping position in a chair.  He folds
himself up in it, prepares to drift off, then notices a leftover hand just sticking out in front of his face.  He vainly
tries to tuck it in somewhere or to push it to one side, then
reluctantly unfolds himself and tries another position.  There's
still an extra hand.  He stares at it, but it doesn't go away.
Later in the movie he's forced to sleep in a bathtub and
again ends up staring balefully at his hand.  ("What a place
to put a faucet--in the middle of my back.")  Hawks gives
Grant all the time and space he needs to develop the gags
to the point of maximum humor.

In the first half of the movie, Grant's humiliation is
courtesy of Ann Sheridan; in the second half, courtesy of the
U.S. Army and Navy.  In the first half, military orders
force him to stay with her.  Later, after they're married,
by his church, her church, and the military, she says, "I
don't see how we could ever get a divorce.  It would be
something like unwinding the inside of a golf ball."  In the
second half, the whims of billeting force him to stay away
from her.  Hawks once observed that comedies sometimes
make the mistake of beginning by promising, 'Now we're
gonna be funny," then fail to deliver.  With I WAS A MALE
WAR BRIDE he was burdened with one of the most unpromis-
ingly promising titles a movie ever had to survive.  But,
surprisingly, the idea of a male war bride turns out to be
an inspiration rather than a handicap.  It's a little difficult
to explain, but Grant winds up as Sheridan's bride, or, as
he tells someone who wants to see his wife: "According
to the war department, I am my wife."

He can't find a place to sleep anywhere on the post all night, at one barracks because he's a man, at another because he's a woman; one time because he's a dependent and not an American officer, another time because he's an alien, and it doesn't matter whether he's a man or a woman. He's just the right combination so that he can't find a place to lie down.   When a guard makes a passing reference to the "weaker sex," he rejoins, "I believe they're stronger, and you know why?  'Cause they get enough sleep, that's why."

By the end of the film he's so used to the runaround that he just speaks his piece about being "an alien spouse of female military personnel" and leaves everything up to the official or sentry to sort out.   ("There will be a moment or two of confusion....")  He's dead on his feet and can only mechanically repeat "Hello.  Goodbye," to Sheridan's friend as she passes by saying "Hello, Henri.  Goodbye, Henri." When, earlier, Grant asks Sheridan what she means by "sex antagonism," she answers, "I think it means just the opposite of what it sounds like."  He admits, "I can't even think what it sounds like."[4] He later finds out that it doesn't really pay to think.   He simply does what they tell him to do in order to get what he wants.   It's a good compromise: he does what they want--he becomes a male war bride--and he gets what he wants--Ann Sheridan.

### Notes

1.   At that it's a better title than "I Was an Alien Spouse of Female Military Personnel En Route to the United States under Public Law 271 of the Congress," which is what Henri Rochard was officially.

2.   I Lost It at the Movies (Little, Brown, 1965), p. 307

3.   Rex Harrison was the studio's first choice for the role.

4.   It means the same thing as Fritz Feld's line in BRING-ING UP BABY:  "The love impulse in man frequently reveals itself in terms of conflict."

## MONKEY BUSINESS

MONKEY BUSINESS belongs to what might be called Hawks' George ("Foghorn") Winslow period. Or his Charles Coburn period. Or his Marilyn Monroe period. But no matter what you call it, it was bleak. Fox did for Hawks what Paramount did for Frank Capra--it straitjacketed him. In the early Fifties, both directors were making feature-length, TV-style situation comedies and both proved that they didn't do their best work in a box. MONKEY BUSINESS and GENTLEMEN PREFER BLONDES are not Hawks' worst movies but they are close enough; they share a basic ugliness and crudeness with Capra's RIDING HIGH and HERE COMES THE GROOM that seem partly studio-induced. There's evidently a point at which a good director gets so far "within the system" that he just cannot operate. Except for I WAS A MALE WAR BRIDE, Hawks' pictures for Sol C. Siegel, Hal Wallis, and Samuel Goldwyn are impersonal technical exercises on which he acted as traffic director. The best he could do (BALL OF FIRE, AIR FORCE) was keep the traffic moving.

I suspect that the real authors of MONKEY BUSINESS were Ben Hecht and Charles Lederer. Hecht and Lederer also did the script for a pitiful little Columbia comedy of 1947 called HER HUSBAND'S AFFAIRS, about an inventor's lather which provides instant shaves or grows hair on its users. As with MONKEY BUSINESS and its rejuvenation serum, use of the lather leads to a variety of outlandish (and totally unfunny) situations. The lather was actually a by-product of an embalming fluid, and the youth serum in MONKEY BUSINESS might be a leftover from the lather. Both movies are vaguely recognizable as descendants of screwball comedy (neo-classic screwball comedy, as it were). But they employ fantastic science-fiction devices instead of imagination, and standard, dull husband-and-wife teams (Franchot Tone and Lucille Ball in the earlier movie, Cary Grant and Ginger Rogers in the later) instead of original characters.

22

The informing idea of MONKEY BUSINESS seems to be that rejuvenated adults would act like idiots. The movie conforms neatly to Professor Grant's description of youth: "maladjustment, near-idiocy, and a long series of low-comedy disasters." It's for people who adore chimps and babies and actors and actresses being cute all over the place. It never gets its premises and its exposition cleanly out of the way but constantly changes direction. The script keeps returning to "Go" and struggling through more strained explanations to get to brand-new "comic" situations. In early scenes it looks as though Grant will bumble, rather ingratiatingly, through the movie as an absent-minded professor. Later, after he first samples the serum, the script falsely promises to turn him loose on another mad ARSENIC AND OLD LACE-type binge. But he's never out of the clutches of the script for long, and it keeps funneling him into variations on his two basic roles. After his first transformation and a marvelous, tricky little Grant bit with arms and knees, the movie becomes a series of mechanical sight gags, then runs out of them and begins setting up the next act. Grant has a few other bits (the way he says, "What's the vulture doing?" Charles Coburn: "It's a phoenix." Or the way he, sans glasses, explores Hugh Marlowe's face), but the tortuous script gives him little latitude, and he doesn't really develop any firm characterization, only fragments of characterizations.

Grant rarely gets going, and when he does he never gets very far. Ginger Rogers, on the other hand, never stops. She's always pouring on whatever she thinks needs to be poured on--solicitude for Grant in the early scenes, aggravated pixyishness during her reversion to youth. Her ideas of youthfulness and wifeliness are gratingly artificial. Her brand of infantility is embarrassing rather than amusing, like Joan Collins' reversion to babbling babyhood at the end of LAND OF THE PHARAOHS, when she panics at learning that she has been sealed up in a pyramid. Away from Fred Astaire, in movies like TOM, DICK AND HARRY and ROXIE HART, Miss Rogers was self-indulgently cute as a comedienne and MONKEY BUSINESS plays right into her weaknesses. She and Coburn are at times almost unbearable, although he has some good lines.

Robin Wood's analysis of the movie in his book, Howard Hawks, shows how distorted a picture of a movie a critic can draw if he really puts his mind to it. He begins calmly and reasonably by picking out key plot points ("stable

marriage, " "suppression, " "'B-4' releases all the things
they weren't"), then says, "The comedy of the first half of
MONKEY BUSINESS is so fast and funny that we scarcely
have time to realise what is happening. " This sentence
doesn't appear to refer to the MONKEY BUSINESS he has
been describing (maybe it refers to the Marx Brothers'
MONKEY BUSINESS, which is fast and funny), which is a
rather dull-sounding, improbable combination of science
fiction and marital drama. In fact, this line and one or
two others are the only hints he drops that the movie is supposed to be a comedy. For himself, Wood admits, it isn't
a comedy. It's the movie in which Hawks "moves closest
to tragedy. " He takes it for granted that it's a laugh riot--
an assumption which indicates to me that he's not going to
deal with the movie at all--then moves on to the implications
of the real MONKEY BUSINESS, which concern "the savagery that underlies civilised life. " He drops in words like
"subversive, " "disturbing, " "ferocity, " and "dangerous" in
describing a comedy with rather hackneyed attitudes toward
marriage, love, and jealousy. He grotesquely inflates the
movie's significance: "In fact, more even than their marriage
is in question: the whole basis of their lives ... the formula ... undermines the whole of civilized existence. "

Wood's distortion of the movie, which is about as
tame a comedy as there is--thematically if not physically--
becomes ludicrous when he describes Miss Rogers and Grant
just before their second reversion to youth: "A moment, for
the audience, of extreme panic: a world of subversion and
disruption opens up before us: what further can the drug
reveal about the Fultons' lives--about our lives?" These
ruminations make no sense in connection with the movie, only
as support for the rest of Wood's argument.

That moment is one of "extreme panic, " if for anyone, for Robin Wood alone. Nothing could be further from
the viewer's mind than considerations of his life or possible
terrifying consequences for Grant and Miss Rogers. The
audience is only anticipating (or perhaps dreading) another
merry spree. Wood's words have no meaning when held up
to the movie or the experience of the movie. I find it hard
to believe that even he panicked at that point. Perhaps he
panicked in retrospect, while writing on the film, the better
to support his claim for the movie's "subversive" qualities.
Wood writes like most auteurist critics, who don't seem to
experience art so much as hear about it second-hand. Most
of them sound as though they "learned" what art was from

their English professors and from other critics, not from
art itself, which is really the only way in.   They pick up
the necessary terms and ideas and apply them to works of
art, without understanding, or at least without illumination.
Wood is at his worst on movies like MONKEY BUSINESS
and HIS GIRL FRIDAY, which resist analysis in the kind of
critical terminology which can be mechanically applied to
most other works of art--to some of Hawks' films like
SCARFACE and CEILING ZERO, for example--without sounding obviously inane.   In his better moments, as in his put-
down of LAND OF THE PHARAOHS, Wood correctly observes
that Hawks' "art lives, not on the level of ideas or themes,
but in the flesh-and-blood process of mise-en-scène...."
Why then does Wood attack Hawks' art where it doesn't live,
where he admits it doesn't live?   Perhaps Wood decided not
to go into the mise-en-scène of MONKEY BUSINESS because
it's such a visually lifeless, if frenetic, picture, to use
a neutral term.   Repulsive is closer to the truth.

# TWENTIETH CENTURY

TWENTIETH CENTURY is less a movie than it is a stage, constructed and designed for John Barrymore. And Barrymore's maniacal stage director Oscar Jaffee is less a character than a quick-change artist who sheds roles and adopts new ones in mid-sentence and mid-gesture. All that the director, the writers, and the other actors had to do was provide Barrymore with as many pretexts as possible for mock-swoons, fits of rage, somber preludes to suicide, and impersonations of camels and signs of the zodiac (e. g., Sagittarius, the Archer). TWENTIETH CENTURY is virtually all Barrymore's. The gears of the plot fail to engage when he's not on the screen, certainly not when he's off it for long. Roscoe Karns floats amusedly and amusingly through the movie, his hands undulating hypnotically before him, but his role of aide to Oscar Jaffe leaves him little else to do. Walter Connolly, as Oliver, another aide, is present only to be pulled by the lapel into rooms or sat down peremptorily or fired by Jaffe. Only Carole Lombard as Jaffe's protégée, Lily Garland, has a semblance of a life of her own, and even she is, at her best, a replica of the master, molded in his image, as she carries on grandiosely before Jaffe or before her dull boy friend ("Would you mind letting me in on some of these trade secrets?").

Like Cary Grant's Walter Burns in HIS GIRL FRIDAY, Hawks' other adaptation of a Hecht-MacArthur comedy, Barrymore's Oscar Jaffe compulsively manipulates those around him to serve his own ends. He's a tyrant, though less callous and violent than Walter Burns. He's essentially harmless but, like Burns, he preys on the weaknesses and illusions of others. Unlike Burns, though, he seems subject to some of those same weaknesses and illusions, at times appearing to be almost human. Generally, however, he only affects human guises and attitudes for nefarious purposes

Like Grant, Barrymore can turn a scene inside out, changing directions and immediate objectives at whim. Like

Grant also, Barrymore is a master of the visual aside, drop-
ping an imitation of a camel into his spiel as one might slip
an odd, foreign phrase into a conversation, then immediately
going on to the next matter of stage business.  Like Grant,
he's not at all averse to prodding his audience when he
thinks it's not paying proper attention to his theatrics, as
when (twice) he holds up his arm and points to the sling for
the benefit of Lombard's boy friend.   (In HIS GIRL FRIDAY,
Grant wipes a fake tear from his eye with a handherchief
when Ralph Bellamy doesn't happen to be looking.   He nudges
the latter into looking up and repeats the action for him. )
And, like Grant, Barrymore pulls people around and up and
down to get them into the most receptive position for his
little acts.   He physically manipulates them as he manipulates
props like a lamp, a handkerchief, or the sling, and he
takes every advantage of the theatrical possibilities of the
setting at hand--a stairwell with echo potential, cramped
train compartments with captive audiences and an atmosphere
of intimacy, the stage itself.   Miss Lombard or Connolly can
stop him for a few minutes or divert his attention momen-
tarily, but his energy and ingenuity cannot be dammed up
or re-channeled for long.   Once he jerks spasmodically back
to life, throwing back his head or hopping crazily into the
air as if he has just been electrocuted, it takes him only a
few seconds to gain momentum again.

    Barrymore meets his match in histrionics in later
scenes with Miss Lombard.   Though he created her, his
control of her is sporadic and tenuous.   She alternately ig-
nores him, falls in with him, and engages in competitive
swooning.   She plays for him; he plays for her; or they,
rather aimlessly, play simultaneously for each other and,
consequently, for no one.   He is again the master at the
end, after conning her into signing a contract with him by
feigning slow death by gunshot-wound.   On her own, Miss
Lombard tends toward a monotonous whine, and she depends
on Barrymore for her presence somewhat as Lily Garland
owes her existence to Oscar Jaffe.   She's better fending off
Barrymore than conducting her own comedy-dramas.   He has
more shticks and more to work with, more colorful language
and more garish epithets--"You amoeba!"; "Anathema--child
of Satan!"; "It's Waterloo, with General Sheridan 30 miles
away!"; "The Old South does not yodel!"

    If, as Otis Ferguson suggested, the movie TWENTI-
ETH CENTURY did not do very well on its initial release,
it's not surprising.   The theatre background of the movie is

John Barrymore as Oscar Jaffe in TWENTIETH CENTURY.

rather alien, and I suspect most non-theatre people feel a
little uncomfortable with it.    (I get a little more comfortable
with it each time I see it. )   I don't understand exactly how
Oscar Jaffe fits into The Theatre, how and where The Theatre and Oscar Jaffe intersect.   I read him only as an isolated character, not as a product of any environment, and
Lily Garland only as a product of Oscar Jaffe.   How could
anyone get anywhere directing the melodramas he apparently
exclusively directs?   Is this puzzling element part of a sa-
tire on The Theatre or stage directors?   Oscar Jaffe is
more comprehensible to me as a caricature of John Barrymore and of Barrymore movie roles like Svengali.   ("I'm
no Trilby!" fumes Lily Garland, and we cut to Oscar Jaffe
entering à la Svengali. )   Oscar Jaffe at times appears to be
a caricature of a particular director, but I've never heard
who it might be.   The movie ultimately doesn't make sense
to me.   A vital link seems to be missing.

Parts of the movie, however, make a lot of good,
hard, comic sense, and I would guess that, as with HIS
GIRL FRIDAY and "The Front Page," Hawks' movie of
"Twentieth Century" is superior to the play, however strong
its ties to the theatre.   Some of the best moments are quick
cuts, little cinematic coups, like the "Trilby" bit, or the
cut from Jaffe chalking a line on the stage for Lily to follow
to the one of the stage covered with chalk lines.   It may
have begun as Hecht and MacArthur's "Twentieth Century,"
but it's now Hawks' and Barrymore's as well.

BALL OF FIRE and A SONG IS BORN

Like BRINGING UP BABY (two leopards, a dog, and
a mad heiress on the loose), Hawks' BALL OF FIRE sounds
like just another strained situation comedy. Eight professors
(read "dwarfs") who are compiling an encyclopedia put up a
night club dancer (read "Snow White") who gives them some
non-intellectual insight into the more arcane subjects to be
found in their "S" volume--sex, slang, etc. Only very occasionally, however, does the movie remind you of the painful
comedy it might have been, particularly when it gets a little
too hectic or cute; for instance, when the seven older professors (Gary Cooper is the younger one) do the conga with
Snow White (Barbara Stanwyck) for the second-easiest laugh
in movies. (The easiest--patented by John Ford--is any gag
about drinking.) Otherwise, snappiness and sentiment, both
exaggerated to just the right degree, prevail.

BALL OF FIRE is kind of dull-looking, but it sounds
as good as almost any Hawks film, thanks to everybody
involved, from Billy Wilder, Charles Brackett, Thomas Monroe and Hawks to Cooper, Miss Stanwyck, Allen Jenkins,
Elisha Cook and Richard Haydn. Where it could have been
coy and cute about Topic A, it's verbally and emotionally
forthright. It could have been a real wheeze about seven
dirty old men, just too adorable for words, but the script
is too smart to get stuck at the obvious level of innuendo;
it takes for granted the professors' (most are aging bache-
lors) interest in the foreign country and goes on from there.
As a fairy tale set in New York, in this century, it's almost
as winning as Frank Capra and Robert Riskin's LADY FOR A
DAY; not quite as sure or funny, but not too much less.

It's an ideal minor project for Hawks. There's a lot
of solemn nonsense about Hawks and the theme of The Group, [1]
when the truth is that he seemed to work best and least
self-consciously when he had a half-dozen or so voices,
faces, and bodies to orchestrate. It's the fact of the group,
not the idea, that inspires Hawks here. He skillfully builds
up vocal rhythms with four, six, nine actors--one taking one

line, the next another, the next another, with no pauses,
then the last (sometimes Haydn) breaking the pattern with a
deliberate, carefully enunciated "Hoi toi toi." The rhythm
matters more than the meaning. The actors' voices (except
for Haydn's, which is always unmistakable) don't seem to be
connected to particular actors. The professors are so much
a group that they seem to belong to a single body with mul-
tiple voices and limbs. But their perfect solidarity has
little thematic resonance; it is employed for comic sight and
sound effects, as in their mad scattering at Miss Stanwyck's
approach or their dispersal when they enter a room. BALL
OF FIRE resembles HIS GIRL FRIDAY (and also Sturges'
The PALM BEACH STORY) in this relegating of actors to
almost anonymous voices and movements. It has pauses for
the actors to breathe, a little heart, although (however good
Cooper and Stanwyck are) none of the brilliance of Cary
Grant's Walter Burns. It may not be as fast either, but it's
fast enough. Artificial, a concoction, it is nevertheless certainly not dull, not the way Wilder and Brackett wrote it or
the way Hawks directed it. There's no special brilliance to
it, but it has a great deal of energy and invention.

It's a messy movie, mostly intentionally, as if everything everybody happened to think of had been approved and
used. Wilder and Brackett juxtapose comically conspicuous
slang with scholarly speech in the dialogue (Stanwyck: "I'm
a pushover for streptococci"), and Hawks keeps the two
worlds of words and their denizens jostling against each
other. When Stanwyck tells Cooper, in several different but
equally colorful ways, to get out of her dressing room, he
has just time enough to add, admiringly, "The complete
conjugation!" before she shuts the door on him. Later, after
they're better acquainted, Cooper, very staid, proper, and
respectful, asks Miss Stanwyck for another sample of "yum
yum" (kissing). The script kids both worlds--inside and
outside. It doesn't take sides, but plays one off against the
other.

The verbal comedy is solidly grounded in the well-
judged contrast between the two leads, the exaggeratedly
knowing, worldly Stanwyck and the exaggeratedly prim, care-
ful Cooper. All the word tricks in the world would be of
no use if the two stars weren't just exactly wrong for each
other at the beginning. (That same year, 1941, Miss Stanwyck took two other men for similar rides, in MEET JOHN
DOE and The LADY EVE--Cooper again and Henry Fonda,
respectively. It must have been her best year, as it was

Cooper's, though more for this film and for MEET JOHN
DOE than for his Oscar-winner, SERGEANT YORK.  Right
year, wrong movie. [2])  Both are slightly, but not wholly,
ridiculous.  Stanwyck is always loose and loud and slinky;
Cooper always straight and tall.  He never unbends, even
for a kiss or a fight.  At the end he skitters back and forth
erect, with arms out straight, as he challenges gangster
Dana Andrews.  When Queensberry rules fail, he runs at
him like a windmill, his arms rotating crazily.  The fight
itself is shown as just a flurry of lanky arms and legs that
doesn't violate the Cooper image of literally stiff-necked
respectability.

    The Cooper-Stanwyck romance takes most of the usual
romantic-comedy turns (including the one, also in MEET
JOHN DOE, in which a disillusioned Cooper confronts Miss
Stanwyck), but Wilder and Brackett fill it in with simple,
satisfying details--the books she stands on to kiss him; the
wet rag to cool the back of his neck, then hers; Andrews'
ring which she returns to him, accidentally or not; and Miss
Stanwyck's eyes, luminous in the dark motel room as Cooper
unknowingly reveals his full feeling for her, not to his col-
league Haydn, as he believes he's doing, but to her.  Cooper
and the other professors are never made to seem such hope-
less cases that they can't be taken seriously at odd moments,
and the movie touches unexpectedly with the most unexpected
characters--Cooper's, Haydn's Professor Oddly, Henry Travers' Professor Jerome, Miss Stanwyck's.  For all its comic
fluttering about the subject of sex, the movie is concerned
finally, almost endearingly, with the mysteries and inequities
of sex.  It doesn't solve the mysteries, but it appreciates
them.

    A SONG IS BORN is instructive, if nothing else--it
helps to clarify what made the original, BALL OF FIRE,
good.  In and of itself it's of little interest. [3]  It's mostly
repetition and minuscule variations of BALL OF FIRE.  It
does manage to work up a few good jam sessions with Benny
Goodman, Louis Armstrong, Lionel Hampton, Louis Bellson, Tommy Dorsey and Mel Powell.  In fact, the guest-
star musicians so take over the first half of the movie that
the real stars begin to look like guest stars.  When the
nominal leads (Danny Kaye and Virginia Mayo) step in midway, towing the BALL OF FIRE plot along with them, it's
almost an intrusion.  And Benny Goodman (as Professor
Magenbruch) pretending that he never heard of Benny

Goodman is such a pleasant conceit that you wish the old
plot and old lines would go away.   But the movie rarely
breaks away from the original to do something on its own.
The professors here are composing a musical encyclopedia
rather than researching slang, but the scriptwriter didn't
bother to pursue the switch; what music material there is
just constitutes an addition rather than a new translation.

Half the fun of BALL OF FIRE is its spirit of verbal
free-for-all.   The comedy is based on words--types of, uses
for, sounds of, games with.   And the words give some
structure and style and meaning to the plot and characters.
Without the Tinker-to-Evers-to-Chance wordplay, the older
professors (now six rather than seven) in A SONG IS BORN
are just lovable old fuddy-duddies.   Hugh Herbert has one
"woo woo" at the end; Benny Goodman is cute learning to
play the clarinet; and O. Z. Whitehead in the Richard Haydn
role is as touching as Haydn when recalling his mild, pas-
sionless marriage.   But, with those exceptions, the professors are wasted, as a group and as individuals.   Gone with
the professors is a sense of the story as a fairy tale.   The
subject of music isn't re-woven into the plot in place of
words.   Leftover slang ("yum yum") from the first script is
without a context.   Since there's no gap between the hero's
and the heroine's vocabulary for them to bridge, the two
are never even really introduced to each other.   They're just
thrown together arbitrarily.   And writer Harry Tugend didn't
come up with many music gags to replace all the word gags
he couldn't use.

A SONG IS BORN is most instructive where it most
resembles BALL OF FIRE--in the central comic-romantic
plot.   It's unnerving to see the same romantic elements that
are affecting in BALL OF FIRE scattered ineffectively through
A SONG IS BORN, as if what was magic once couldn't be
magic again, or what seemed magic wasn't really after all.
The rag, the books, and the eyes in the dark figure in
the remake too, but there's nothing to back them up.   They're
still magic touches, but they were part of a more inclusive
magic in the first film, growing as they did out of script,
direction, and performances.   Here, like the leftover slang,
they have no context.   The Kaye-Mayo romance takes many
(not all) of the same turns as the Cooper-Stanwyck romance,
but it's not the same comic love story, not with a different
set of actors.   The trouble is that Hawks saw it as the same
one, and Kaye and Miss Mayo end up playing Gary Cooper
and Barbara Stanwyck rather than Professor Robert Frisbee

and Honey Swanson.   The names are different, but the basic
style and mannerisms are the same.   Kaye and Miss Mayo
don't match the original couple or make the roles their own.
Kaye is so retiring that Goodman and the other musicians
dominate the first half of the movie, and Miss Mayo doesn't
even end up where Miss Stanwyck, with her comically affected swagger, began the earlier movie.   Neither comes
close enough to creating a character for the question of a
contrast between them to arise.   And you can't have a romance without a romantic couple.

A plot may be thin, but a director can make it into
something more by telling it as best he can visually, through
his actors, by finding its worth in the dramatic, comic or
emotional points he can make vivid through his actors.   The
right expression on an actor's face or his movement, or con-
trasts of expressions and movements can be the movie, as
when in BALL OF FIRE Cooper comes up behind Stanwyck
after he has proposed to her and asks to speak to her "Dad-
dy" (Dana Andrews, her boy friend), who's on the phone.
The situation is vivified and clarified by the deft balancing
within the frame of the "uh-oh" look she hides from him
and his look of aggressive, wide-eyed innocence.   The scene
derives its humor less from Andrews' gulling of the gullible
Cooper than from the latter's comic eagerness and sincerity
and the way Stanwyck, at his side, guiltily watches him as
he talks to Andrews.   In A SONG IS BORN Kaye and Mayo
return the story back to the unembellished plot.   To make
the scene in BALL OF FIRE Hawks had to have the fairy-
tale background, the relationship as developed between the
two leads up to that point, the specific situation, the look
on Stanwyck's face, and the look on Cooper's face and his
stumbling speech.   In A SONG IS BORN Hawks has only the
situation.   In BALL OF FIRE, the situation is beautifully
crystallized in the Cooper-Stanwyck chemistry.   In the one,
the couple "makes" the scene; in the other, the scene is
made for them.

Color makes A SONG IS BORN ugly where the original
was just visually dull.   There should be a credit for Special
Technicolor Consultant for Lips.

Hawks has said that he found he didn't know what he
was doing remaking a movie he had made just seven years
earlier, and the remake looks as if it were copied frame
by frame from the original rather than shot from a script,
as if he had someone run him a scene from BALL OF FIRE

in one room, then ran out and transferred it intact into A
SONG IS BORN in the next.   He also throws in variations
on gags from BRINGING UP BABY and HIS GIRL FRIDAY--
Kaye shielding Miss Mayo's exposed derrière with a suitcase
and Bubbles (of Buck and Bubbles) greeting Hugh Herbert's
"Bach.   Johann Sebastian Bach" with a "How do you do?"
The movie answers the question, What does a director do
when he has nothing to do?  Very simply, nothing.


## Notes

1.   "The sensitivity with which Hawks treats culture in this
       film is related to his response to the idea of the
       group. "--Robin Wood, Howard Hawks.

2.   There's an in-joke in BALL OF FIRE about SERGEANT
       YORK.   Dan Duryea says, "I saw me a picture last
       week, " and moistens his gun sight.   The gag pops up
       again in The THING.

3.   When asked once what prompted him to remake his own
       film, Hawks replied, "A lot of money. "

## FIG LEAVES

Since The ROAD TO GLORY (1926) has evidently disappeared, FIG LEAVES (also 1926) is now Hawks' "first film," and, considering the number of silent films lost, we're lucky to have even one Hawks of this early vintage. It's a fairly auspicious beginning, too. It's a slight and silly little comedy, but lively and visually attractive (thanks in part to Joseph August's photography and William Cameron Menzies' art direction). It's smoother technically than Hawks' first talkies, which seem stodgy by comparison. There isn't even a story; there are just a few, basic cliché attitudes toward the battle of the sexes, with resolute husband George O'Brien reduced to jelly in his wife's presence and acquisitive wife Olive Borden stifled by marriage but loyal nonetheless. It bears some superficial resemblance to The WOMEN (1939) in the analogy it draws between women and animals--a neighbor lady is seen as a snake tempting Eve, the wife--and in its obsession with women's fashions and its actual fashion show. (Both fashion show sequences were evidently originally in color.) But it's a comedy through and through, not a soap opera masquerading as comedy.

The basic familiarity of the situations would be grating if the actors weren't so physically aggressive. It's as if Hawks weren't sure whether he was directing actors or a troupe of acrobats, or as if irrepressible, bouncy Clara Bow were playing all the parts. The points are familiar, but Hawks makes them visually and vividly. Perhaps the key sequence is one in which Eve reveals that she's jealous of Adam, and Adam twirls around and around drunkenly, shouting, "Li'l Eve's jealous!" The comic kick certainly isn't implicit in such a scene; it's in the husband's crazy, almost grotesque over-reaction. In this movie a girl doesn't just down a shot of liquor--she indicates its swift descent within with a gesture. When Eve tells her neighbor, "Adam's too good," Adam is outside the door self-confidently tapping his fingers on his chest. When she opens a package and can't wait to see what's in it, her fingers fidget crazily, like

36

Katharine Hepburn's in BRINGING UP BABY when she says she knows how to do the olive trick.  Adam's uncouth friend, Eddie, doesn't just ogle the women in their revealing gowns at the fashion show; he breaks out into appreciative, spontaneous applause.  And when Josef André, the lady-killing couturier, jerks Eve by the arm after him, she yanks him right back.

Adam begins his confrontations with Eve as if he were squaring off for a ten-rounder, but her tactic of stepping right up into a clinch instantly confuses and disarms him. The high point of this comic composition with bodies is the scene in which Adam tells Eve off, and she stands at the far corner of the room as he exits huffily in the opposite direction.  A third party, André, hovers uncertainly, half-hidden, behind a chair, counting on Adam's rage to blind him to his presence as Adam stalks out past him to the door. But Eve's tears stop Adam at the door, and he turns around. As he does, André squats down abruptly and ignominiously, behind the chair.  Though FIG LEAVES is trite, its visual hyperbole is redeeming.

A prehistoric prelude to the story has a winning off-handedness to it.  Rube Goldberg props and devices are given added twists.  A brontosaurus sheds tears when scolded by the first Adam.  The latter resets his sand-and-coconut alarm "clock," "plumps" and adjusts his log-pillow, and goes back to sleep.  The insidious snake that aggravates the first Eve's dissatisfaction with her home life has a bewhiskered face out of Dr. Seuss and greets her with an incongruous, "Good morning, Eve."  There's even a pre-King Kong giant chimpanzee.

The titles are as undisciplined as the action.  Adam's friend gives him advice about women:  "Treat 'em rough, but don't kill 'em--you might want 'em for something someday."  Eve's girl friend comments slyly on Eve's new dress: "I knew a girl who used to get her clothes from André's for practically nothing."  The action takes place on the "Rue de la Fifth Avenue," in the couturier's luxurious den of iniquity.

In the opening sequence, Eve breaks into tears, then peeks through her hands at the effect on Adam.  In the "modern" sequences, André starts to swoon with joy or exhaustion and peeks around to make sure he's being watched. John Barrymore's Oscar Jaffe in TWENTIETH CENTURY

and Cary Grant's Walter Burns in HIS GIRL FRIDAY are the
ultimate refinement in Hawks' films of such devious theatri-
cality.

"The Ransom of Red Chief"
(in O. HENRY'S FULL HOUSE)

        The twist in the Howard Hawks-Nunnally Johnson adap-
tation of O. Henry's "The Ransom of Red Chief" is at the
beginning rather than at the end.   Two con men kidnap a
holy terror of a boy, and his parents counter their ransom
demand with an offer to take him off their hands for a price.
The cheerful horror of the initial twist and the integrity of
the film's deadpan style make this short the modest high
point of Hawks' tenure at Fox.   The insolent, deadpan George
Winslow boys of Hawks' two other '50s Fox pictures, MON-
KEY BUSINESS and GENTLEMEN PREFER BLONDES, are
like stray fragments of it.   It has perfect unity and simplicity and looks and sounds so right that it seems like an
original rather than an adaptation, as though it couldn't be
as good in another medium.

        The stylization of the acting makes it look like a
Buster Keaton comedy with Keaton playing all the parts
(which he in fact did do in the 1921 short, "The Playhouse"),
straight-faced, with slight variations.   It's in the tradition
of W. C. Fields' "The Fatal Glass of Beer," with every
role--the charmless rustic parents, the townsfolk, the force-
of-nature boy, the con men--comically stylized.   Fred Allen
(who replaced Clifton Webb) and Oscar Levant as the con
men, Sam and Bill, make an unforgettable pair of voices
and faces.   Their dour mien makes them perfect foils for a
child-monster.   Glum, with black eye (Levant), gloomy, with
Indian war paint and feather (Allen), or simply terrified
(both, often), they're as funny as they always seemed to promise they would be in movies, but rarely were.

        The sober understatement of the dialogue is sometimes
hilarious, as when the mother, casually watching through the
front window as Sam and Bill carry off their boy, says,

"Now they're puttin' a sack over J. B. 's head, " and the father replies, "Must be strangers. "  Or when the men, in a note, threaten to return J. B. and run, and the father writes back that they had better return him after dark, "otherwise, the neighbors, who have been celebrating his loss, may do you a harm. "

Fox evidently cut this section from some release prints of the film, perhaps because it showed up the others. Henry King's "The Gift of the Magi" and Henry Hathaway's "The Clarion Call" (with Richard Widmark calling everyone "Clamhead!") are poor, just the classic O. Henry twist ending and nothing else.  Henry Koster's "The Cop and the Anthem" is slight but pleasant, with Charles Laughton warming his way into your heart just by the way he catches an umbrella tossed to him or bounces along in woe over his lost soul.  "The Last Leaf" (directed by Jean Negulesco) is, even without the surprise of the ending, an intriguing idea, and my liking for it persists after a third viewing, though I could do without Anne Baxter's emoting.  Linking a girl's ebbing life to the decreasing number of leaves on a vine is a delicate proposition, but the short is punctuated by downright eerie shots of leaves (several, three, two...), sunlight on a window shade, and a lantern ("He was a great artist"), which are almost supernatural in tone.

Note on MAN'S FAVORITE SPORT?

Thanks to a local TV station's policy of programming two-hour movies in two-hours-minus-commercials time slots, and to the network's live coverage of our President's return from Russia, I saw only half of MAN'S FAVORITE SPORT? I hadn't much wanted to see it, but I don't thank the network, its affiliate, and the President for keeping it from me.  The selected scenes I saw actually made me want to see the whole thing--or, more precisely, I would like to see Paula Prentiss' entire performance.

Hawks wanted Cary Grant to star in the movie, but he got Rock Hudson.  Maybe he should have quit right there.

MAN'S FAVORITE SPORT? is a sort of sequel in spirit to
BRINGING UP BABY and I WAS A MALE WAR BRIDE, perhaps Hawks' two best comedies, with the hero humiliated
and exasperated by women and other, less persistent factors.
If Hudson had starred in those earlier comedies, there
wouldn't have been much point in talking about them either.
He's just too easily flustered by Miss Prentiss.   He's defeat-
ed at the beginning of SPORT?, whereas Grant's frustration
simmers all through BABY and BRIDE.   There was a sense
of progression, or retrogression, in the Grant comedies, a
sense of things getting worse and worse for Grant and an
ironic sense of this progression on his part.   In SPORT?
things begin pretty badly for Hudson and they stay bad.

        Miss Prentiss slips more agreeably into Katharine
Hepburn's shoes.   Her bass voice is comically imposing.
She's more consciously malevolent-charming than Miss Hepburn in BABY.   She's just terrible to Hudson, and her out-
rageousness almost makes the movie half a good comedy.
(Or half of the half I saw.)   Her peak moment is the accidental flipping of an ashtray halfway across a room into an
aquarium.   The movie, however, generally lacks this quality
of exaggeration.   It's mostly old stuff--trouble with the tent,
the foot in the bucket, etc.   It apparently re-does the scene
from BABY (I didn't see it) that Hawks already had re-done
in A SONG IS BORN, in which Miss Hepburn's dress is torn.
If Grant had been starred with Prentiss--a potentially terrific team--even some of the old gags might have worked.

# PART II

# WESTERNS

RED RIVER

In his book on Hawks, Robin Wood at one point declared:

> RIO BRAVO is the most traditional of films. The
> whole of Hawks is immediately behind it, and the
> whole tradition of the Western, and behind that is
> Hollywood itself. If I were asked to choose a film
> that would justify the existence of Hollywood, I
> think it would be RIO BRAVO.

Hawks' best movies encourage such pronouncements, and
though I might not go quite that far on any single Hawks
film--I couldn't single out any particular one of his best
films as his masterpiece or as The Great American Film--
I think RED RIVER (not RIO BRAVO) is more nearly the
summit of traditional Hollywood film making, of both its epic
and Western traditions. It has everything working for it.
It's what you wish every movie could be and what very few
are: exciting, funny, moving, beautiful, majestic. I think
it's successful on all levels and in almost every area: the
mythic level, the interpersonal level, mise-en-scène, acting,
dialogue, detail, music, characterization, plot, theme, photography, setting, humor. And it's more than the sum of
those parts.

RED RIVER is certainly not just a plot, though it has
a good, sturdy plot--the book proves that. Borden Chase's
Blazing Guns on the Chisholm Trail--the title does not belie
the content--is like a blueprint for RED RIVER. The story
is pretty much the same. The few changes the movie makes
in the story are improvements, but they don't "make" the
film.

In 1851, Tom Dunson leaves a wagon train to begin
his own cattle herd in Texas. On the way down he meets a
boy, Matthew (Mathew in the book) Garth, who has survived
an Indian attack on the train. Some fourteen years later

Walter Brennan, John Wayne and Mickey Kuhn in RED RIVER.

Dunson and Garth begin driving their cattle to Missouri.
Dunson pushes his men, threatening to whip and nearly killing a cowpoke who accidentally starts a stampede. Later,
Dunson, backed by Garth and Cherry Valance, a gunslinger,
shoots three hands who threaten to leave the drive. That
night he sends Valance and another man after three other
hands who desert. The drive crosses the Red River into
Kansas. Valance returns with two of the deserters (the
third died in a gunfight), and Dunson orders them to be
hanged. Garth balks, and Valance and others disable Dunson. They leave him, and Garth heads the drive, taking the
cattle to Abilene on the new Chisholm Trail. They come
across a wagon train, carrying gamblers and women to Ne-
vada, under Indian attack.

          In the movie, Garth and Tess Millay, one of the wom-
en on the train, fall in love, but Garth and his men continue
on to Abilene. Dunson and some hired gunmen spend a night

with the train.  Tess tries to talk Dunson out of revenge but
fails, and Garth faces him in Abilene.  Valance wounds Dunson, and Dunson kills him.  But Garth refuses to draw his
gun.  Dunson knocks him down, and Garth finally defends
himself.  Tess stops the fight, and Dunson accepts Garth as
a full partner.

   In the book, Valance vies with Garth for Tess, staying behind when Garth leaves for Abilene.  Provoked by
Tess's taunts that he's poor "as a beggar," he takes some
gamblers/gunmen with him to kill Garth and take the herd
from him.  But the men are killed, and Valance returns to
the wagon train alone, only to face Dunson.  Tess saves
Dunson by jarring Valance as he fires, and Dunson kills him
but is himself wounded.  In Abilene, Garth draws on Dunson
but can't shoot.  Dunson shoots and wounds him, then collapses.  Garth and Tess carry the mortally wounded Dunson
by wagon back across the Red River, and he dies on Texas
soil.

   Chase writes in a dumb, tough/epic style:

   Such was Mathew Garth.  A male creature, loaded
   with threat in every movement.

   He looked at Dunson with eyes that were focused on
   infinity.

   Guns had spoken on the bank of the Brazos.

   Almost the grasping fingers caught the loop.

Characterization is laughably simple.  Cherry Valance is
just "a mad pair of devils" dancing in the eyes.  Tess appears at the beginning as well as the end of the book--she
begins embittered and she stays embittered.  The movie
doesn't soften or water down the characters so much as it
humanizes them. [1]  Chase's Dunson is totally inhuman, and
his only remotely sympathetic character is Garth.  Chase's
story is the source of RED RIVER as "The Greatest Gift"
is the source of Frank Capra's IT'S A WONDERFUL LIFE.
That is, it's just an idea for a movie and a basic outline,
in terms of quality about on par with the scripts that Chase
worked on for Anthony Mann and William Wellman. [2]

   The key to RED RIVER is, I think, the mise-en-scène,
as I think it is to several of Hawks' movies.  The key to

all movies--good and bad--is, according to hard-line versions
of the auteur theory, supposed to lie in the <u>mise-en-scène</u>--
or, roughly, staging and camera movement and placement.
In actuality this is infrequently the case; rather, the key
usually lies in haphazard combinations of factors, with elements of staging figuring strongly as the informing force only
occasionally.  In RED RIVER Hawks expresses the tensions
of the story in terms of staging, and the movie's spatial excitement constitutes a brilliant application of Hawks' familiar
technique of framing his protagonists within groups, within
their milieus.  Hawks tells the story as several, interrelated
stories, with interrelated tensions: father-son, trail boss-
drovers, cattle drive.  So closely are the stories interrelated,
in fact, by the <u>mise-en-scène</u>, that they don't even briefly
resolve themselves into the one central story--Dunson and
Garth--until the very end, when the drive is over and the
two protagonists are face to face.  Hawks so stages the action that the tensions of the several storylines are constantly,
rather than simply intermittently, present.

In RED RIVER Hawks almost invariably sets foreground action in the context of background or middle ground
witnesses or participants.  The positioning, stances, and
movement of all the actors comment on and intensify the
drama of those in the foreground.  The essence of RED
RIVER is perhaps the gunfight, or the prelude to the gunfight, with everyone ready to draw or be drawn upon.  Duels
between two men turn into combat among three, then four,
then perhaps six.  The movie does not consist merely of
picturesque groupings of cowboys and riders--though it does
do that, almost incidentally, and that's part of its beauty.
Hawks frames the action to involve everyone in it:  the cow-
hands are both part of the setting and part of the action.
They reconcile the epic and the interpersonal elements of
the story.  Hawks refrains from reducing the action to a one-
to-one duel until the end.  The infrequent close-ups are almost shocks.  They mar the film's visual continuity, between
the physical elements in a given scene--foreground action,
middle ground bystanders, background landscape--and from
scene to scene and shot to shot.

Just behind the story, or just inside it, another movie
is unraveling, a picture history of the West, told in terms
of men, clothes, horses, trees, clouds, cattle, sunshine,
shadow, water, and dirt.  There are a few conventionally
striking silhouette shots against the night sky, but Hawks
generally employs the actors, horses, and terrain in original

RED RIVER: Walter Brennan, John Wayne, John Ireland,
Paul Fix, Montgomery Clift, Ivan Parry, Glenn Strange.

compositional ways. It's not something that's announced, but
it helps to explain the resonance of the story. This story-
within-a-story is related by the way the men stand watching
a gunfight, the way they eye Dunson as he strides into camp,
the way they file slowly down sloping ground in search of a
lost cowpoke. It has to do with the way Dunson and his
horse cut a diagonal (bottom left to top right) across the
screen as he rides up (away from us) after the wagons.
Dialogue is fixed firmly in a time and place when it's spoken
by four mounted men (Hank Worden, Noah Beery, Jr., Paul
Fix and Montgomery Clift) sitting facing each other over a
knot of horses. (Almost everyone in the cast learned how to
ride a horse.) RED RIVER loses more than the story when
it goes indoors with Joanne Dru--it loses a special look and
flavor. When the drovers come across a wagon train besieged
by Indians, the film is back in familiar visual territory.

Even at the beginning, before the time gap and the start of the drive, the first confrontation between Dunson and Matt is shot so that it's more than that confrontation. (The boy's drawing on Dunson is rather awkward foreshadowing.) Groot, later the drive's cook, watches the two from a distance. Groot is the narrator, and as the person closest to Dunson, is, along with Matt and, finally, Tess, one of the few who dare tell the boss he's wrong and who are heard. The scene thus establishes more than tension between two fast guns--it establishes a system in which the gun is not the final authority.

The relationship of Matt, and to a lesser degree of Groot and Cherry, to Dunson is based on an attraction-repulsion principle which is responsible for much of the movie's tension. Dunson's defeat is impossible as long as Matt, Groot, and Cherry back him, however reluctantly or indirectly. Cherry backs him when Teeler complains about the rations. Matt, a faster draw than Dunson, wounds Bunk Kenneally by drawing on him before Dunson, who's also

Noah Beery, Jr., Montgomery Clift and Walter Brennan in RED RIVER.

faster than Bunk, can draw on Bunk and kill him.   But Matt
doesn't go so far as to disable Dunson.   The extent of Matt's
feeling and respect for Dunson is measured by the difference
between the tentative acts of defiance he does commit and
the absolute acts he could and probably should commit.   His
action here is little more than the equivalent of Groot's "You
was wrong, Mr. Dunson."  Matt and Groot disagree with
Dunson but, unlike him, aren't so sure of themselves that
they want to interpose their own will.

Matt, Groot, and Cherry come to Dunson's aid again
when he takes on the three mutineers in a gunfight, but only
because the other three force the issue.   Groot, the comic
chorus, expresses his dissatisfaction with Dunson's tyranny
by relishing the opportunity to pour whiskey on the wound
Dunson gets in the shootout.   Dunson knows he can't rely any
longer on Matt, so he has Cherry go after the deserters instead.   Dunson's revelation that, despite his wound, he's
staying awake all night to make sure that no one else deserts
while Cherry is gone, makes the split between Matt and Dunson more pronounced.   Matt sees that Dunson is killing himself bit by bit--integrity of purpose is becoming insanity.
Dunson's announcement that he intends to hang the two deserters rather than take them on in a fair fight makes the
split complete.   Matt turns on him and Cherry follows his
example.   But Matt's respect for Dunson is implicit in the
action even as he goes against him.   He nearly kills Teeler
for threatening to kill Dunson during the mutiny.   Hawks and
Charles Schnee construct each scene so carefully that Matt's
actions are as much acts of allegiance and loyalty as of defiance.   It's a beautiful balancing act.

There's much feeling in RED RIVER, but it's usually
expressed obliquely and imaginatively.   Manny Farber called
the story of RED RIVER "romantic, simple-minded mush,"
but I think RED RIVER is one of Hawks' least mushy pictures
and possibly (as the other Farber, Stephen, thinks) his best.
I believe I realize when a Hawks film is corny but terrific
(most of ONLY ANGELS HAVE WINGS and RIO BRAVO),
when it's just corny and not so terrific (parts of RED RIVER,
mostly with Joanne Dru, ANGELS, RIO BRAVO), and when
it's just terrific and not corny at all, and I think most of
RED RIVER (like most of SCARFACE, The BIG SLEEP, and
his best comedies) belongs in the last category.   It's generally neither pseudo-tough nor soft.   It's moving but only, it
seems, incidentally, because the film has so many concerns
and doesn't labor its points.

When Dunson can't bring himself to request Matt to buy Dan Latimer's widow the shoes Dan was going to buy her, Matt says the words for him. When Matt takes over as trail boss, he leaves Dunson behind alive, even though he knows it may mean his own death. (Cherry's comment is "You're a little soft.") Later he tells an edgy drover who is standing guard, "He wouldn't pick you off in the fog."

In ONLY ANGELS HAVE WINGS, there's no tension to the Thomas Mitchell-Cary Grant relationship, which borders on the sentimental and didactic (e. g., Jean Arthur watches Mitchell to see how she should act toward Grant). Mitchell's allegiance to Grant is a given that's neither tried nor tested. It's a near-dormant narrative point. In RED RIVER, Dunson gives Matt every reason in the world to stop liking him--that's what makes Matt's implicit, crazy devotion to his mentor so admirable. Matt knows that he's faster than Dunson--Groot tested them at the beginning of the drive--so he refuses to draw on him in Abilene and at first won't even defend himself.

As for Dunson's reasons for stopping the fight (once Matt starts it), I'm not as confident as Wood that the Coleen Gray-Joanne Dru associations in his mind would overpower Dunson's sense of humiliation and outrage at being robbed of his cattle. But perhaps the partial lack of credibility of the much-discussed climax (I half believe it) is more a matter of the weight of the immediate images than of any illogical development of the script. On the one hand, there is, as Wood notes, the image of Dunson striding inexorably through a sea of cattle toward Matt;[3] on the other there's the image of Tess scolding them as they sit, looking amiably foolish, beside each other. I believe the first one most--it is tremendous--and the one of Tess least, regardless of its associations with earlier events.

Joanne Dru doesn't fit. I don't know what actress would have.[4] (What was needed perhaps was a combination of Jean Arthur and Lauren Bacall.) She's too insubstantial a character and actress to override Wayne's authority as Dunson, and her glossy look and voice are jarring. She and Coleen Gray are verbally aggressive embarrassments, unsuccessful attempts by Hawks to repeat his casting coups with Arthur and Bacall. Miss Gray merely provides an echo for Miss Dru, and Miss Dru merely officiates at the reunion of Wayne and Montgomery Clift. There's no depth to either of them, as there is, say, with Zita Johann's Quita in TIGER

SHARK, a basic integrity and presence that makes what she
says secondary to what she is.  Miss Dru provides the overt,
verbal expression of the bond between Dunson and Matt, a
bond expressed more laconically and affectingly in the rest
of the movie.

Wayne and Clift give perhaps their finest film performances in RED RIVER, which (despite the presence, or
lack of presence, of the two women) can be defended as the
best-acted of all Westerns, and perhaps the best Western.
(I think the Arthur Penn-Leslie Stevens THE LEFT-HANDED
GUN is about as fine, but it is also badly flawed by the
muddling of the Pat Garrett role.)  Wayne is required to do
more than usual, but not more than he can do (as in some
Ford films like The LONG VOYAGE HOME, The QUIET
MAN, and The SEARCHERS).  His Dunson is one of the few
later examples of Hawks' monomaniacs, like Scarface and
Walter Burns.  (Khufu in LAND OF THE PHARAOHS is
another.)  He's mean but he's not the monster of Chase's
book.  Wayne moves slowly and deliberately, and his delivery is forceful but not exaggerated.  Clift's self-consciously
controlled delivery--the intentional edge on his voice--makes
you listen to him and lets you know that he is thinking about
what he's saying, as the way his arms hang loosely and con-
spicuously at his side lets you know that he's thinking about
what he's doing.  He always seems to be watching, holding
back and waiting.  As played by Clift, the character of
Matthew Garth is at once exciting and affecting--and one of
the greatest characters in Hawks' or anyone's films.  The
potential for violence in Wayne is on the surface, immediate;
in Clift it's just underneath, but under his control.

The movie, unfortunately, retains traces of the book's
cornball epic style, in the acting and in the dialogue, in
silly flourishes like Tess's striking a match as she gives
Dunson her name ("Tess Mill-ay!") or Dunson's handily
catching a knife Groot tosses him as he wrestles an Indian
in the river. [5]  They mar the surface of the film.  Some
lines--Dunson's comment on the boy, Matt, "He'll do," or
his "I'll put a mark on 'em"--carry a faintly foolish, built-
in epic echo.  The introduction of Cherry Valance and his
subsequent personal/professional competition with Matt is
prime terrific-corny Hawks.  Clift's and John Ireland's
style and nervy masculinity and Walter Brennan's comic
asides keep the proceedings from inflating into dull who's-
top-gun? bravado.

Despite the temporary lapses RED RIVER has a solid
core--the Wayne-Clift-Brennan-Ireland relationship--and a
genuine epic resonance, with some event of epic stature
every fifteen minutes or so--a storm, a stampede, Indian
attacks, the crossing of the Red River, the meeting of the
herd and a locomotive, the arrival in Abilene.    The measure
of Hawks' achievement is that he maintains a balance between
the epic events and his epic characters.    One half of the
movie is never lost in the other; each lends authority and
meaning to the other.

I prefer, if only slightly, Hawks' super-Western to
the broken eloquence of John Ford's The SEARCHERS.    The
latter also has scope, power and beauty, but the strain on
the actors to live up to the themes and setting sometimes
tells:  they shout a lot, but usually to no good end, as if
they were trying to fill up the epic spaces with words.    And
though the central character of the Indian-hating Ethan Ed-
wards is powerfully conceived and often powerfully developed,
the script fails, when it tries, to find expression for his
hate in words.    Even John Wayne isn't as tough as the Frank
Nugent script requires him to be, and he's unconvincing just
when he should be most ferocious.    (Humphrey Bogart is
similarly feeble in similar scenes in TREASURE OF THE
SIERRA MADRE.)    Andrew Sarris may be correct when he
says that Hawks' movies lack the memorable images of
Ford's--The SEARCHERS undeniably has many; RED RIVER
has an uncustomary number for Hawks--but movies are more
than images, and on the level of actor-to-actor, The SEARCH-
ERS is often weak.    RED RIVER sustains and reinforces its
imagery with the tension of the central relationships, through
staging, acting and dialogue (the last is Ford's particular
weak spot).    In The SEARCHERS the only actors who don't
sound as though they're reading a script are Hank Worden,
Ward Bond and Ken Curtis.    RED RIVER is superbly acted,
not only by Wayne and Clift, but by Brennan, Ireland, Noah
Beery, Jr., Ivan Parry, Paul Fix, and, again, Hank Worden.

Max Steiner's score--one of the most moving on film--
may be partly responsible for the upward reevaluation of the
Ford Western.    It's always jumping in to help when the
actors get in trouble with words.    Although it suffers from
some of the same excesses as Dimitri Tiomkin's otherwise
fine score for RED RIVER--needless beefing up of dramatic
scenes, underlining of specific actions--it's a great score,
and the gap between it and the movie, itself very good, is
narrow enough that it may not seem to exist.

I don't want to conclude leaving Hawks' power as an image-maker entirely undefended. The shot of Coleen Gray left isolated by Wayne in the middle of the plain, with the wagon train not far off in the background, is unforgettable and alone almost compensates for all the empty chatter from Misses Gray and Dru.

## Notes

1. The script also cuts references to Dunson's English origins and to Matt's fighting for the South.

2. The Chase-Wellman THIS MAN'S NAVY is an incredible combination Navy recruiting poster-Wallace Beery vehicle.

3. In The WILD BUNCH Sam Peckinpah, using the telephoto lens, creates a comparable image of inexorability and imminent violence as the Wild Bunch marches to the final showdown--similar dramatic effect, different visual means.

4. Miss Dru replaced Margaret Sheridan in the role when the latter became pregnant. Hawks rewrote Miss Sheridan's scenes to fit Miss Dru, and there, apparently, went part of the film. Miss Sheridan later starred in Hawks' The THING.

5. This anticipates Groot's toss of the rifle he defends himself with against the quitters, but that's no excuse for it.

# RIO BRAVO

RIO BRAVO forces me into the uncomfortable position
of challenging as much as championing a movie which many
think is great and which I in fact consider very good.  Although RIO BRAVO has to be defended against the same basic objections that can be made against ONLY ANGELS HAVE
WINGS--cliché characters, situations, and attitudes--the
inferiority of RIO BRAVO to ONLY ANGELS HAVE WINGS
has little to do with the clichés the two films share.  Robin
Wood solves his problem with the film by stating flatly, almost defiantly, "There are no clichés in RIO BRAVO, " after
he lists the cliché characters and magically transforms them
by calling them "entirely and quintessentially Hawksian. "
The main thrust of Wood's argument is that the Dean Martin
character, Dude, the drunk, the friend of the hero (John
Wayne) who "used to be good, " "exactly reverses" the stock
Western figure of the "Fallible Friend. "  Actually, he's the
reverse cliché, the once-good man redeemed.  Wood gets
silly when he thinks he's getting to the heart of the movie:

> There are those who can see no more to this theme
> of close friendship between men in Hawks's films
> than the endorsement of a hearty, superficial ma-
> tiness:  nothing could be further from the truth.
> These relationships in Hawks almost invariably em-
> body something strong, positive, and fruitful:  at
> the least (The THING) a warmth of mutual response;
> at the most (RIO BRAVO) the veritable salvation of
> a human being. [1]

Wood, however, is helpful in that, unintentionally, he clearly
shows where Hawks' art doesn't lie:  in themes or characterization.  That RIO BRAVO is indeed about "the veritable
salvation of a human being" has next to nothing to do with
its being a smashing movie, the best late Hawks and a
reawakening after the relative failures of The BIG SKY and
LAND OF THE PHARAOHS and the outright failures of MON-
KEY BUSINESS and GENTLEMEN PREFER BLONDES.  The

basic "relationships in Hawks" are often at best a pretext, at worst a handicap.   Where his films live is on the surface, and in films the surface is arguably the most important level.

RIO BRAVO is not, however, what I would call super-ficial, not in terms of its use of actors, if it is in terms of thematic development and characterization.   When critics talk about Hawks' "machismo" and "male chauvinism," I get the feeling that they're talking mainly about ONLY ANGELS HAVE WINGS, RIO BRAVO, and EL DORADO.   But I think these critics are taking Hawks too "seriously" or at least "seriously" in the wrong way, using his themes against him rather than citing them in mistaken support of him.   The element of machismo in his movies is incidental to the fact that they're mostly high-adventure stories, that there's just no real place for a woman in most of them (even in RED RIVER, which challenges the myth of machismo).   The fact that Hawks' actors are generally better than his actresses also makes for imbalance in the films.

RIO BRAVO is based on two words in RED RIVER: The boy, Matt, fresh from witnessing an Indian attack, meets and impresses Dunson, and the latter tells Groot, as the boy walks away:   "He'll do."   The operative word in RIO BRAVO is "good."   Hawks says he got the idea for his movie from HIGH NOON, in which the marshal and his wife are the only two people in a Western town "good" enough to face the gunfighters.   In HIGH NOON the marshal goes around asking for help and doesn't get it; in RIO BRAVO help keeps coming to the sheriff, and he refuses it or dis-courages it.   He is trying to hold the brother of the local war lord in jail on a murder charge, and he doesn't want amateurs or cripples to get killed by the enemy's hired, professional gunmen.   The film is like an extension of the Montgomery Clift-John Ireland competition in RED RIVER, with Sheriff Wayne testing, proving, and judging everyone else and, in turn, being tested, proved, and judged by them. This is, of course, a Limited Conception of Life and won't help you through the next day, but it's a damn good way to make a movie, to make characters larger-than-life, heroic.

When Dean Martin asks Wayne if Ricky Nelson, the newcomer, is as good a gunman as he, Martin, used to be, Wayne replies, "It'd be pretty close.   I'd hate to have to live on the difference."   The script makes fine judgments like that seem very important and valid as an index of char-acter.   A sort of professional hierarchy, based on skill,

judgment, and character, evolves in the course of the movie.
Wayne says that Nelson is so good "he doesn't have to prove
it. " And he asks his wagon-master friend Ward Bond why,
if he's so good, he had to hire Nelson.  But the order is
unstable.  On the basic fact (or cliché) of Martin's deterio-
ration from top gunfighter to drunk, the film constructs elaborate, interrelated systems of mutual evaluation and of
mutual concern and caring, and the movie gets its rather
specialized excitement from the state of flux of the interre-
lationship.  You can forfeit your claim to others' respect by
not getting involved when you should, even if you are "good. "
Nelson minds his own business while his boss (Ward Bond)
gets shot minding Wayne's, and he's temporarily denied
entry into the inner circle.  Wayne, sometimes arbitrarily,
decides who's acceptable and who isn't, but his decisions
aren't binding--the other characters keep proving him wrong
about them.  His initial reaction to Nelson's declaration of
neutrality was that he "showed good sense.  I'd like to have
him. "

     But he generally establishes the terms of acceptability,
and his judgments are like prods.  Martin asks Wayne if
they're going to trail a gunman into a saloon.  Wayne point-
edly replies:  "We used to. "  Martin proves himself equal
to the task, but when the two get back to the jail, Wayne
warns him, "You surprised 'em. "  When it comes out that
Martin actually wounded the man--on the run--before the latter went into the saloon, Wayne quickly deflates his ego by
reminding him, "You had to go in after him. "  Wayne tells
Walter Brennan that, good as he is at guarding the jail, his
game leg will put him and others in danger in an open-air
fight.  Brennan tags along anyway and helps by tossing
sticks of dynamite for Wayne to explode with rifle fire over
the enemy's stronghold.  (Wayne, of course, as he tells
Brennan, could have done it all himself. )

     The script takes its hierarchy seriously, but not so
seriously that it forces the viewer either to take it seriously
too or to reject it.  The movie is not self-parody, but it's
not an existential statement either.  You enter its world; it
doesn't enter yours.  Almost every scene has a comic edge,
evidence of Hawks' and his writers' (Jules Furthman and
Leigh Brackett) willingness to kid themselves and, at the
same time, evidence of their confidence in the fantasy world
they're constructing.  When Brennan complains, half in jest,
half in earnest, "You've got to be drunk to get any attention
around here, " the construct doesn't collapse.  The comic

vein of self-consciousness reinforces it.   It enables the
viewer to suspend disbelief.   The hierarchy is more a means
than an end--a string on which to bead several fine performances, or actor-actor relationships.

RIO BRAVO is almost the same movie as ONLY AN-
GELS HAVE WINGS, only longer, more loosely structured,
and imperfectly cast.   It's a fine variation, with the Cary
Grant, Jean Arthur, and Richard Barthelmess roles cleverly
re-written for John Wayne, Angie Dickinson, and Dean Martin.   Wayne and Dickinson express their affection for each
other through comic belligerence.   She always chatters on
and on, leaving him speechless.   When Wayne finally comes
right out and says, "I'm glad you stayed," he flusters poor
Miss Dickinson, who isn't used to direct statements from
him.   She cries helplessly, "Now, why did you have to go
and say that?"   That's the only way she can say she's glad
he said what he said, but he of course doesn't get the message.   She, however, gets <u>his</u> message at the end when he
threatens to arrest her if she wears her scandalous costume
before the saloon public.   Her warm response surprises and
disarms him, and it's love for sure.   The most memorable
romances in Hawks' movies proceed by comic indirection and
non sequitur.   His characters generally don't blurt things
out, except for comic effect.   They express emotion through
action, inaction, hesitation, or outright silliness:   for example, Wayne reassuring Brennan that he's wanted by planting
a kiss on his forehead when he isn't looking.

Like ONLY ANGELS HAVE WINGS, RIO BRAVO has
a strong, Hitchcock-like underpinning of suspense, and it
packages comedy within drama within suspense, like Chinese
boxes.   A suspense situation--inexplicable offscreen gunfire
draws Wayne to the jail--becomes comic:   Wayne finds that
Brennan has fired out on an unrecognizably clad Martin at
the jail door, then affecting:   when Martin complains about
Brennan's garrulousness, Wayne informs him, "That old
fool's talkin' 'cause he nearly killed you."   That one line
turns the scene inside out and dexterously alters the relationship among Wayne, Martin, and Brennan.   It's a stinger
for Martin, but it's also an economical, shorthand way to
reveal feeling (on the part of both Wayne and Brennan).
Only rarely does the movie turn simple and sappy, as for
instance in the song sequence involving Martin, Nelson, and
Brennan.

This interlocking suspense-comedy-drama is weakened

by the virtual separation of the Wayne-Dickinson story from
the Wayne-Martin-Brennan story.  Late in the movie Wayne
even has to explain to Dickinson who Brennan is.   There
seem to be two different movies which occasionally overlap.
Wood explains this away by saying:

> ... there is a certain unobtrusive symbolic oppo-
> sition between [the jail and the hotel where Miss
> Dickinson stays] (women tend to dominate in the
> hotel, and are excluded from the jail, where a
> miniature all-male society develops in isolation). [2]

For a good two-thirds of the movie, the script skillfully in-
terweaves the two stories.  But near the end it strains in
maneuvering them both toward a climax.  Part of the strain
is due to the fact that one story has already climaxed in the
song sequence.  The "climactic" gun battle is really just a
working off of accumulated tension or, at best, an affirmation
of the Wayne-Martin-Brennan-Nelson union.  The final scene
between Wayne and Dickinson ends the other story, almost
as an afterthought.  Between the two endings there's still
action, suspense, and comedy, but no drama, and it's missed.

Wayne, Brennan, and Martin are at their best; that's
the strength of the film.  Wayne's and Brennan's best performances (that I've seen), in fact, are in RED RIVER and
RIO BRAVO.  Even if you don't think Wayne is an actor
(and he isn't in some movies), you have to grant that he has
presence, and it's not just a matter of size.  But when he's
rushed through a movie and a plot, his presence is more
than half-wasted.  It's just taken for granted by his directors
in many of his movies, or established at the beginning (as
in BIG JAKE and TALL IN THE SADDLE) and then left virtually forgotten and unused.  RIO BRAVO is built around
Wayne, spatially as well as dramatically, as it's built
around all the actors.  Hawks keeps reestablishing, as it
were, Wayne's authority physically and dramatically, as in
the scene in which he simply stands behind the enemy sentry
posted on the walkway across from the jail.  He addresses
him gruffly, "Good evening!" and stands there until he edges
away nervously.  Even in simple transitional shots, Hawks
makes use of the authority of Wayne's presence, as when,
upon hearing the enemy's "Alamo" challenge, he shifts his
stance uneasily, or when, forced by one of the enemy to
make a difficult decision ("What'll it be?"), he simply takes
a deep (noncommital) breath.  His imposing presence is used
ironically, for comedy, in the scenes with Miss Dickinson.

Ricky Nelson, John Wayne and Dean Martin in RIO BRAVO.

In almost any Wayne movie, Wayne gets a few lines which seem to have been written specifically for him even if the role doesn't appear to have been. They usually come just before he poleaxes someone, as, for instance, in RIO BRAVO, when he threatens a thug, "We'll remember you said that," after the latter makes the mistake of denying that any-one has just run into the saloon. In RIO BRAVO, every one of Wayne's lines seems tailored for him, partly because his delivery is considered, unhurried. Each one comes directly from the character, is an expression of his character. He doesn't have any empty talk. The excitement Wayne can generate at stray moments in almost any film he's in is sustained throughout RIO BRAVO.

Walter Brennan has the time of his life as Stumpy, in a classic use of an actor's voice. Half the time he's just a loud, disembodied, offscreen yowl that finds hilarious just about any kind of situation--comic, dramatic, or neutral.

When Wayne asks to be let into the jail's inner sanctum,
Brennan calls out playfully, "What's the password?"  When
Wayne warns John Russell, the enemy, that in case of an
attack on the jail, the latter's brother, Claude Akins, will
get shot, Brennan cackles confidently, "I can practical
guarantee that!"  Thanks to him, RIO BRAVO almost qualifies as one of Hawks' comedies, and one of his best ones.
Brennan's performance is the classic example of a Hawks
film expressing feeling through comedy.  There's a sense of
continuity rather than dichotomy between the broadness of
the comedy and the core of feeling.

Martin is good too, offsetting the pathos inherent in
the role of a drunk with a brash defensiveness and a painful
sensitivity to the concern shown for him by others.  He
fights himself and everyone else, and makes his too inevitable
triumph believable through his character's innate aggressive-
ness.  His role may amount only to a remarkably well developed stereotype, but Martin injects conviction into it.

One not too serious weakness of the movie is Angie
Dickinson.  She's not nearly as good as Jean Arthur was,
and her voice is not in the least distinctive, as Lauren Bacall's was, in analogous roles in earlier Hawks movies.
But the role of Feathers[3] is so well written that it covers
for her deficiencies.  She's not really a bad actress, just
dull and flavorless (though not in this film).  She doesn't
act in RIO BRAVO so much as loll around in her role and
bask in John Wayne's presence.  She tries to make herself
striking or sensuous or at least un-monotonous, but I think
most of the credit for the character's qualities goes to Furthman, Brackett, and Hawks.  She's actually pretty good--
better than Bacall in TO HAVE AND HAVE NOT--but it
seems more a coaxed than a felt performance.

The more serious weakness in the film is Ricky Nelson as Colorado, a role derived from Clift's and Ireland's in
RED RIVER.  He's supposed to be larger-than-life too, but
it's painfully obvious he's a size or two smaller.  There's
just no actor there, only bravura mannerisms--a finger
placed beside the nose, a slow, deliberate walk--that are
comically unrelated to Ricky Nelson's non-presence.  The
movie's epic style more or less fits everyone except Nelson.
Wayne, Martin, and Brennan, in forging their roles here,
make you forget their other film and non-film roles, but you
never forget that Ricky Nelson is Ozzie's son, the singer.

## Notes

1. <u>Howard Hawks</u> (Doubleday & Company, 1968), p. 50.

2. <u>Ibid</u>. , p. 38.

3. The name goes back to Josef von Sternberg's UNDER-
   WORLD (1927) and Evelyn Brent.   Jules Furthman
   worked on that screenplay too, and, according to
   the May-June 1974 issue of <u>Film Comment</u>, so did
   Hawks.

EL DORADO

## The Stars in Their Courses

In the course of making EL DORADO, Hawks forgot
all about the book he began with, and it's just as well.
Somewhere along the line he and/or scriptwriter Leigh
Brackett junked Harry Brown's solemn, pietistic bloodbath,
The Stars in Their Courses, and started all over again.
Fate is really the only character in the book, though there
are a lot of names in it too.  Brown's so-called characters
are defined solely by their submissiveness to fate or, to be
more specific, to Brown's small-minded conception of fate.
Everyone's caught up a little too easily in Events:

> It was a plumb easy thing to start a big rock rol-
> ling down hill, but once it was given that first
> shove, no man alive could stop it.  A wall of dead
> men might, though.

There's a heavy, heavy sense of inevitability and of
the senselessness of the inevitable, and nothing else.  And
the violence is carefully planned to appear senseless:  in the
most striking instance, a gunman does his best to keep a
boy out of the big showdown, and the boy ends up in it--and
in the man's saddle, dead in his place.  Calculated senselessness is something of a contradiction.  The book is
fraught (and "fraught" is the word) with premonitions and
portents:  dreams, prophecies by a mad girl, and plain
flash-forwards.  It's decked out with Biblical references
(including the title), "epical" identifications of characters
with the land and the elements, and other estheticizing devices.  But the lapses into epic language are as laughable as
Borden Chase's in the book RED RIVER is based on:

> Tall Arch Eastmere rode with the thunder.

> Ann Randal sensed that she had already become her
> husband's living urn...

62

> Arch Eastmere was a tall man abroad on the earth.
> As he wandered the earth he was long and lonely.
> He could teach the tiger to be more deadly.   The
> crouching lion would flee his face.   He rode as a
> king on a saddle of silver.

All the characters' worrying over the inevitable violence
seems less a qualification of it than an excuse for it.   The
somber, melancholic overtones seem to be a rationalization
of the book's gory payoff rather than the characters' ration-
alizations of the parts they play in it, since there are no
characters.   The book has a little authentic humor in it, but
not much--it's generally self-righteously self-pitying over
what it knows must be.

If the above-described work sounds familiar, that may
be because, as noted in reviews of it in 1960, The Stars in
Their Courses is a revamping of The Iliad.   The reviewers
also noted that that fact didn't make much difference.


## EL DORADO

> ... and there are home remedies for alcoholism,
> vomiting scenes that are supposed to be hilarious,
> and one of those girls who hide their curls under
> cowboy hats and are mistaken for boys until the
> heroes start to wrestle with them.  --Pauline Kael
> (in Kiss Kiss Bang Bang)

Kael's comment proves that though it's difficult to dis-
like as likable a movie as EL DORADO it's not impossible.
Depending on whom you listen to--auteurists or anti-auteur-
ists--Hawks movies like RIO BRAVO and EL DORADO are
either the work of someone getting more and more mature
and wise or someone who's just getting old and tired.   But
both characterizations sound inaccurate.   Hawks' late Westerns (even RIO LOBO) seem more like the work of someone
in his second childhood, someone who really enjoys what he
does and who transmits his enthusiasm to his cast and crew.
"Mature" and "reflective" might be how one would want to
characterize Hawks' later films if one saw his work in terms
of a struggle between maturity and immaturity, but any dis-
interested party can see that they're about as reflective as
the later works of W. C. Fields.

EL DORADO is good-natured, easygoing, and rather

undisciplined, though it occasionally surprises with a stunning
bit of acting or violence--Chris George's and James Caan's
introductions (in the same scene), the shooting of Johnny
Crawford (the only scene remaining more or less intact from
the book)--that seems to belong to some other, more ambitious, less relaxed movie.   Hawks sometimes falls back on
the above-listed reliables (Kael forgot to mention the bathtub routine) and he sometimes even resorts to uncustomary
zooms, spectacular camera angles, and comic special-effects
violence.   The wild violence at times threatens to take over
here, as it does in RIO LOBO.   But this Western at its
best is, like The THING, an essence of Hawks' movies, in
its natural, unforced sense of camaraderie and in its lived-
in atmosphere.

The material in EL DORADO may be tried and true,
but there's no law that says a director can't tell an old
story a little differently or say the same thing two different
ways.   Women are still betraying men as they always have
in Hawks' films (or as they always seem to have before the
film picks up the story), and there are tense street patrols,
as there were in RIO BRAVO.   As Robert Mitchum enters a
saloon, John Wayne tells James Caan, "They laughed at him--
that'll make the difference"; afterwards, Wayne tells Mitchum,
"They'll be ready next time," just as Wayne warned Dean
Martin in RIO BRAVO.   And EL DORADO amounts to an en-
forced sobering up of Mitchum, as RIO BRAVO did of Martin.

But not "just as."   This time the participants are
Wayne and Mitchum and James Caan and Chris George.   And
Michele Carey, Charlene Holt, and Arthur Hunnicutt.   And
a Hawks film is as fresh as the matches Hawks can make
with his actors--in EL DORADO, the best matches are
Wayne and Mitchum, Wayne and Caan, Wayne and George.
A reversal on this pattern of pairing has Mitchum every
once in a while ask Caan, omnipresent but unintroduced to
him, "Who the hell are you?"   Wayne, rather obviously, is
the one who makes it all work.   The Caan-Carey match, by
contrast, remains stale and gets no further than the script.
(Miss Carey is the girl in the cowboy hat.)   There's no plot
really, no structure and no suspense; every so often a woman will worry out loud about "those men waiting around,"
but those men never really materialize as a threat.   It's
just cheerful comedy and a concern with the scene and the
actors at hand.

Wayne and Mitchum and Wayne and Caan are essentially comic teams.   Wayne and Mitchum have grown old and
crippled together and find comfort in each other's discom-
fort.   The movie is hardly an elegy.   When Wayne starts to
leave Mitchum's sheriff's office with a crutch, Mitchum
points out, "That's _my_ crutch. "   A doctor tending Mitchum
is called away to Wayne, and Hunnicutt observes, "Reckon
he's got a more interestin' misery. "   Mitchum finds it hard
to straighten up (literally as well as figuratively), and Wayne
suffers attacks of partial paralysis.   Mitchum looks as if
he'd just as soon give it all up.   He probably would too, if
it weren't for the fact that Wayne is around watching and
nettling him and looking in almost as bad shape himself;
Mitchum probably figures that since Wayne hasn't given up,
maybe he won't either.   Mitchum thinks Wayne just wants
to help him, but Wayne really wants him to be self-reliant.
When R. G. Armstrong asks Wayne, "You backin' him up?"
Mitchum answers for him:   "No, he's _not_!"

Mutual irritation brings Wayne and Caan together too.
Caan is at first irritated by, then amused at this old man's
show of independence, and Wayne is amused by Caan's cocki-
ness, his name (Alan Bourdillon Traherne), and his absurd
hat, and is irritated by Caan's amusement at his expense.
The friendship impulse in Hawks' characters "frequently reveals itself in terms of conflict" too.

The Wayne-George relationship is a more serious
matter, a variation on the Clift-Ireland rivalry in RED
RIVER.   They play gunfighters who respect each other, but
Wayne goes to friend Mitchum's aid, and George hires out
to rancher-villain Edward Asner.   They share a basic self-
confidence and enjoyment of their work, but their regard for
each other translates into tension.   Though they're always
smiling, they realize that one or the other will eventually
have to die.   George is the one who dies, of course, but
his death is one of several memorable scenes in the movie.
It's like Hawks' long-postponed resolution to the unresolved
Clift-Ireland relationship in RED RIVER.   (Peter Bogdanovich describes it in a review in Focus on Howard Hawks. )

What makes EL DORADO good are the tensions and
the ties between actors and the details of their performances,
details that can salvage a dull scene or make a good one,
such as Wayne's arms flailing like flippers to underscore a
verbal point or his tacking one sentence onto the end of

another without a break--"I'll decide when and where I risk
my neck.  This isn't it"--or George's eyes following Caan
as Caan circles his table while the other gunmen at the table
are distracted by trivial matters.  Hawks has characterized
EL DORADO as virtual leftovers from RIO BRAVO, and the
movie is a mélange, but of colorful bits of business, anec-
dotes about piano players, and sharp exchanges of dialogue.
It's more than a bunch of actors just having fun, but it does
fall just short of earnest moviemaking.  Occasionally, Hawks
whips up some real excitement, as in a saloon scene where
piano music and words explode into violence, or a scene in
a deserted church with bullets and bodies flying and falling
every which way.  But he seems to be compensating, with
energy, for lack of an informing vision or idea, and the
movie is little more than the sum of its parts, some of
which, admittedly, are terrific.

A final note:  it's odd that two movies (ONLY ANGELS
HAVE WINGS and EL DORADO) which so resemble one other
movie (RIO BRAVO) should be so dissimilar.  But EL DORA-
DO dispenses with most of RIO BRAVO's love interest and
thus any real link to ONLY ANGELS HAVE WINGS.  (RIO
LOBO goes on to dispense with actors.)


RIO LOBO


It's ironic that Hawks, usually a fine director of
actors, is responsible for RIO LOBO, one of the worst-acted
movies in recent years.  But here he was working with
amateurs in spirit if not fact, except for John Wayne, who
walks through as if he were just chaperoning the kids in the
cast, and Jack Elam.  Along about the time you begin won-
dering wistfully, "What was acting like in movies?" Elam
enters and reminds you, even in an irritating, one-note
comic role, what an actor can do for a line.  He gives more
inflection to a cackle than the other actors do to a whole line
or speech.  Hawks has Wayne again, as in EL DORADO, but
he can't make any actor-actor matches with him since there
aren't any other actors except Elam, who pretty much keeps
to himself.

There's crude, gratuitous, laugh-getting violence, elaborate, strained comic dialogue, and one good, big action set-piece.  The plot, developed in the dialogue, in dull monotone, is unfollowable.  The few, patented Wayne lines ("You'd a been sorrier if you hadn't") stick out obtrusively from the generally colorless dialogue.  There are embarrassing coincidences in the plotline, and the characters are given to startling emotional outbursts which are so unjustified in the context of the film's lax narrative that they seem grotesquely comic.

There are thematic resemblances to RIO BRAVO, EL DORADO, and even ONLY ANGELS HAVE WINGS.  (Yes, this is "quintessentially Hawksian" as well as terrible.)  But the resemblances don't help this film any more than they hurt those earlier ones.  Hawks wasn't too happy with RIO LOBO either, and it qualifies as his TOPAZ, Alfred Hitchcock's late contribution to amateurishly-acted films by highly professional directors.

THE BIG SKY

## The Big Sky

> It was as if a man couldn't get free from what he
> had been and done.  He couldn't be himself alone;
> he had to be all the other men he was, in the sea-
> son before and the season before that and the seaso
> before that. --The Big Sky.

The title of A. B. Guthrie's book contains two ironies,
one intentional, one unintentional.  The intentional irony is
that no matter how big the sky above a man's head he's still
not free, not entirely, from the consequences of his actions.
He may be free of the constricting effects of civilization, as
Guthrie's mountain men Boone Caudill, Jim Deakins, and Dick
Summers are, free of unwanted responsibilities and ties with
other men, but he's answerable to himself, to his past, and
ultimately, to other men.  The book at its most imaginative
celebrates the strength of the few ties between men in the
wild regions of the West and Northwest in the 1830s and
1840s.  It's nearly as skillful as Mizoguchi's film SANSHO
THE BAILIFF at showing how echoes of its protagonists' past
linger on in the present.  Boone's early attraction to Teal
Eye, an Indian princess, grows into a love that, seven years
after they're separated, draws him back to her.  His recol-
lection of Dick Summers' words about a "game high up that
a hunter hardly ever saw from below," an observation made
in passing many years before and many miles away, saves
Boone and his party from starvation.  And his blind killing
of his friend Jim leaves Boone an outcast from civilization
and wilderness at the end of the book.  Links between men
are few but powerful in Guthrie's West.

The unintentional irony is that The Big Sky almost
loses itself in a mass of minute detail.  At its least imaginative, the book is a catalogue of Western flora and fauna.  As
with Moby Dick and whaling, the effect of the volume of detail is finally trivializing rather than intensifying.  The first

68

two (of five) parts of the book consist of conventional "action"
set amidst endless trees, bushes, rivers, animals, and
sounds of birds, wind, and water.  Nature is less magnificent than monotonous:  how many ways are there to describe
the sun rising, crossing the sky, and falling?  How many
ways to describe a campfire and cooking?

The sun also rises in the latter half of the book, but
the seven-year gap between parts two and three adds the
dimension of time to the narrative.  Guthrie is aware of the
difference:

> There was the first time and the place alone, and
> afterwards there was the place and the time and
> the man he used to be, all mixed up, one with the
> other.

It's a long time getting there, but hunter Dick Summers'
memories of mountain men and "rendezvous" and exploits of
the past in chapter 23 signal the real beginning of the book,
when naturalistic detail becomes subordinate to themes of
time and aging and love and friendship, and the arbitrariness
of the first half's violence, gamy humor, and endless trees
and berries is absorbed into the fibre of the story.  Once it
gets started, it's a good book.

## The BIG SKY

Hawks' version of The BIG SKY never does get
started.  This is one of the few occasions when Hawks'
source material was superior to the finished film.  It's
partly a picturization of Part Two of the book--the dullest
section of the book, the keelboat expedition up the Missouri--
and partly its own concoction.  Hawks and Dudley Nichols
threw out just about everything of value in the book, and,
in view of what was kept and what was added, this clearly
wasn't a wise decision.  They didn't compensate for the loss,
as Edward Paramore and Frank Capra did when they tossed
out most of Grace Zaring Stone's material in making The
BITTER TEA OF GENERAL YEN.  The BIG SKY is a long,
rather dull, but also rather likable movie--not good, but not
bad either, moderately entertaining but trivial.  It's like
leftovers from RED RIVER. [1]

Again the title is ironic.  The BIG SKY makes little

use of its epic spaces.    Instead,  nature dwarfs the movie and
its concerns.    In Guthrie's book,  distances in time and space
help create a deep sense of kinship between people.    The setting gives the characters stature:    "It made a man little and
still big,  like a king looking out. "    In the movie,  the setting
is just a scenic backdrop,  well-employed in shots of the fur
trappers pulling the keelboat up the river or of Indians riding
along the shore on horseback.    But a comparable movie on
the subject of fur trapping and mountain men,  ACROSS THE
WIDE MISSOURI (1951),  based on the history-book counterpart to Guthrie's novel by his friend Bernard DeVoto,  has
more of a feeling of having been worked out around its epic
setting and better captures the sense and spirit of a lost way
of life.    The plot of The BIG SKY seems to have been just
plunked down on the Missouri.    The William Wellman movie,
which resembles the latter half of the Guthrie book,  is finally insubstantial too,  just moderately good,  but it doesn't
seem tied to a puny plot as The BIG SKY does,  and its
Indian beauty (Maria Elena Marques) seems a real part of
frontier life rather than simply a staple of action melodrama,
as Elizabeth Threatt is in The BIG SKY.

     Some of the names are the same as in the book,  but
Hawks and Nichols discarded virtually all its characters.
Summers,  the hunter,  the "old-timer," becomes Zeb Callo-
way (Arthur Hunnicutt) in the movie,  but without the dimensions the term "old-timer" implies in the book.    Jim Deakins
(Kirk Douglas) is pared of his religious musings and his significance as a link between civilization and wilderness.    But
the difference between the book's Boone Caudill and Dewey
Martin's version is crucial:    Guthrie's violent,  impulsive
near-savage,  who almost kills his father and regrets that he
didn't,  is barely recognizable in Martin's comically brash
young punk.    The real achievement of Guthrie's book lay in
his getting the reader to accept,  or at least not to reject,
his man/beast hero,  a man on the fringes of civilization,  by
locating his savagery within the man's own value system and
qualifying it with civilizing taints (for example,  his love for
Teal Eye).    Martin is just small as a hero.    He begins by
not liking people much,  especially Indians,  and then gets to
like them.    Perhaps Hawks toned down the character and
altered him because he had already more or less told his
story in SCARFACE.    Guthrie's Boone and Hawks' Tony
Camonte,  in fact,  both kill their best friend over a girl.

     The character relationships with which Hawks and
Nichols replace Guthrie's are at best tenuous.    Douglas and

Martin give each other big, broad smiles every once in a
while and always seem on the verge of doubling over with
laughter at nothing.   Even Hawks had to admit that The BIG
SKY was "very much of a failure on my part in telling the
story of friendship between two men. "  Neither the bonds
nor the tensions between the two men are very well realized.
The narrator (Zeb) even has to come to the story's aid near
the end to explain what's happening.   The narration tries to
supply what the movie doesn't, a real sense of comradeship
between Boone and Jim.   Instead of developing that sense,
the script shoves one of the book's peripheral concerns--the
fur company's attempts to sabotage Jourdonnais' expedition--
into stage center in the movie.   The script might better have
forgotten all about plot and been a documentary of men and
keelboats and sky and river.   At times it almost is just that,
but it keeps dwindling into conventional heroes-and-villains
melodrama.

     Arthur Hunnicutt gives the best performance, out-talk-
ing everyone else in true Hawks spirit, and the movie, again,
might have been better off shutting up about fur company
hirelings and Indian girls and listening instead to his tall
stories and backwoods wisdom.   Most of the movie's atmosphere is in his stories and phrases, and it might have made
it pretty far up river on just the material that was so dull
in the book--campfires, men, the river, and the sun--going
nowhere in particular, but getting in as much detail in a
minute as the book took several pages to cover.   As it is,
the better scenes are simple ones around the campfire, with
the trappers wistfully talking about women or cutting off useless fingers.

     Dimitri Tiomkin's score has a lovely theme or two,
but he drags out the heavy artillery for the "dramatic" episodes and kills any sense the movie might have had of the
strangeness and suddenness of an Indian attack, in the middle
of a seemingly empty wilderness, or of the hazardousness of
a keelboat broken loose from its cordelle.   He and the plot
should have been left back at RKO.


                              Note

1.   There's an Indian girl (well, she's supposed to be a girl)
     who maliciously pours whiskey on an open wound and
     who gets left behind, standing isolated in the middle
     of her village, and there's a five- or six-man gun

battle that breaks up a lot of accumulated and immediate tension.    (A jabbing firebrand rather than a tossed
shotgun precipitates this one. )


Note on VIVA VILLA!


Erratic, but sharply written historical comedy-drama.
A lot of fun with firing squads, bank robberies, and yellow
journalism.    Florid titles ("Hate came thundering out of the
cactus") and bad back projection, but Wallace Beery as
Villa, always blushing and childlike, is endearing, and Stu
Erwin's journalist is the more certainly written equivalent
of Arthur Kennedy in LAWRENCE OF ARABIA (which, otherwise, is a much better film).    Erwin:   "'Mexico forgives
me'. "    Beery:   "Those are my last words?"

# PART III

## ACTION DRAMAS

# ONLY ANGELS HAVE WINGS

Childish, banal, phony, and enjoyable, ONLY
ANGELS HAVE WINGS is the prototype of the in-
side-out Hawks adventure film.  Hawks's story,
dialogued by Jules Furthman, is frankly terrible.
A small group of reckless pilots employed by a
cuddly, impecunious Dutchman (Sig Ruman) faces
death daily in flights over the fog-bound Andes.
Suddenly a New York chorus-girl (Jean Arthur)
arrives in their midst ("I quit a show at Valparai-
so").  The moment she lets slip that her trapeze
artist father lost his life through not using a net,
a bond is forged between her and the disillusioned
skipper (Cary Grant).  When the cause of his dis-
illusion (Rita Hayworth) turns up as the wife of a
new pilot named Bat (Richard Barthelmess) whose
cowardice once caused the death of the brother of
Grant's best friend (Thomas Mitchell), the complications have become as unlikely as their resolution
is predictable.  As the only available flier, Bat
volunteers for a dangerous mission, Kid insists on
going with him, the plane crashes into a flock of
condors and catches fire.  Bat refuses to bail out
and executes a daring landing, allowing the mortally injured Kid just time enough to gasp out the
heroic details.
Inside the big cliché are the small ones:  the
equation of maturity with an acceptance of sudden
death; the heroine playing Liszt in the lounge at
one a. m. ; the stiff-upper-lip inventory of the dead
pilot's belongings; the pseudo-tough byplay accom-
panying the lighting of a cigarette or the flipping of
a double-headed coin; the probing for the bullet in
the hero's shoulder; the nursemaid relationship between him and the old friend too blind to fly, who
insists on coming too. --Peter John Dyer, "Sling
the Lamps Low" (in Focus on Howard Hawks).

All of this is basically true, but ONLY ANGELS HAVE
WINGS is a terrific movie anyway.    For me, it's Hawks'
key film, if not quite his best one.    It's a film which logically, reasonably, shouldn't have been any good at all, yet
it is astonishingly good, a one-in-a-million movie, unique
even among Hawks' films.    It should have been simply a
dumb "B" movie, mildly entertaining at best, and it shouldn't
have been directed by someone as talented as Howard Hawks.
It was, however, and superbly, and it should make anyone
who practices prescriptive criticism uneasy.    I myself might
have advised Hawks against using Cary Grant and Jean Arthur
in the starring roles.    They seem miscast.    But their Jeff
Carter and Bonnie Lee are two of my favorite people in
movies.    On one level, I don't believe a minute of ONLY
ANGELS HAVE WINGS; on another, I believe almost every
moment.    It's the best "B" movie I've ever seen.    I think
it's about as silly as anything I've seen, but I love it as I
love very few movies.

ONLY ANGELS HAVE WINGS is a fascinating problem
for a critic, and critics of it can be pretty neatly divided
into two categories: 1) those, mostly auteurists, who think
it's marvelous, no problem; and 2) those, like Dyer, Manny
Farber, and Pauline Kael, who find it quaint but enjoyable,
who admit it has something, but that whatever that might be,
it's not worth bothering about.    Although I agree with the
opinion of the former group, I identify more strongly with
the latter.    It may be a fine movie, but that's certainly nothing to take for granted.    It's easier to see what's wrong with
it--the plot, the cliché characterizations and attitudes, some
of the dialogue--than to see that there's something else at
work too, something alchemic and extraordinary.    The film
is composed of about equal parts of art, trash, and technical
virtuosity.    Its staunchest defenders don't seem to realize
that it has a lot to overcome; its detractors don't see past
its handicaps to see that they are overcome.    It's as if its
defenders thought that to admit that the material was basically rather shoddy would be to say that the movie couldn't be
good, when that's the sort of contradiction and challenge
auteurists are supposed to thrive on.

Robin Wood comes closest to acknowledging the contradictions of the movie.    He admits right off in the analysis
in his Hawks book that some may find it "corny," "melodramatic," or "banal."    Then he forgets this beginning and
goes on to treat the basically banal material quite seriously,
but despite this approach he is intermittently convincing and

even perceptive. (The different ways critics deal with the movie are almost as fascinating as the movie itself.) There's no reconciliation of the phrases "completely achieved master-piece" and "stock situations" and "far-fetched coincidences" in his argument. He assumes that Hawks transcends his origins, and that's all there is to it--the result is pure, sterling Hawks. Well, it is and it isn't.

Basically it's the same dumb adventure movie it was under the title AIR MAIL in 1932, as directed by John Ford. But Ford was evidently not interested in such recalcitrant material and wisely left it to die slowly by itself. (The Hawks-Wead CEILING ZERO also derives in part from AIR MAIL, which was co-scripted by Wead.) And the coward-- the Barthelmess character in ANGELS--just disappears in the Ford movie, which might seem to be a good way to sweep a cliché under the rug, but which is actually just a cliché unfulfilled, nothing lost but nothing gained.

CHINA SEAS (1935, Tay Garnett) has more direct ties to ANGELS. Jules Furthman, who, with Hawks, wrote ANGELS, co-scripted CHINA SEAS. In this version, the coward (Lewis Stone) dies proving himself, in an hilarious scene in which he crawls on broken ankles along a ship's deck and drops with a bag of grenades onto a pirate boat. Still, it's more amusing than AIR MAIL and more deserving than ANGELS of the friendly but generally condescending comments ANGELS usually receives. ANGELS is essentially CHINA SEAS with superior acting and direction. Robert Benchley and Jean Harlow, as one of captain Clark Gable's old girl friends (Rosalind Russell is another), are amiable, and CHINA SEAS is lively and fast, though thoroughly famil-iar and inflicted with the tacky look of most MGM films of the period when they stepped out of the boudoir. (The same stock shot of the ship turns up in broad daylight and on dark, moonlit seas.) Miss Harlow and Miss Russell are roughly analagous to Jean Arthur and Rita Hayworth in ANGELS.

The attitudes toward death in ANGELS, stoical and otherwise, derive from Hawks' own THE DAWN PATROL (which was remade the year before, 1938). A bit of Hol-lister (Gardner James), a Royal Flying Corpsman who be-rates the others for laughing at death but who later proves himself in battle, turns up in both the Arthur and Barthel-mess characters.

The seeds of ONLY ANGELS HAVE WINGS are in a
hundred grade-B and A-minus movies, and Hawks' film
doesn't let you forget it.   Their claim on it can be seen in
any ill-considered line (Miss Hayworth:   "You were right,
Jeff.   I'm no good"), or wrong turn in the plot (Grant teaching Miss Hayworth how to be a good wife to Barthelmess),
or blatant coincidence (Barthelmess turning up in the same
outfit with arch-enemy Thomas Mitchell and bringing along
his wife, who's Grant's old flame). [1]   And synopsizing the
plot, as Dyer shows, reduces it to just another of those
"B"'s.   Dyer also provides one clue as to why it isn't just
another "B":

> Once one has accepted the reality of an impressive-
> ly graphic flight in bad weather, actually witnessed
> contact between the crashing plane and the palm
> tree whose top it slices off, and a collision in mid-
> air with a condor, one can accept anything. [2]

Hawks has said that some of the incidents in the movie--the
condor, Mitchell's death--are based on real-life incidents.
But the "realness" of the movie is due as much to the naturalness and unphoniness of the actors--to the depth of Hawks'
and the film's conception of what it's possible for actors to
do--as to particular "lifelike" scenes.

Hawks made the movie to order for Cary Grant and
Jean Arthur, which is to say he was given carte blanche to
make a movie with two of the best actors around at the time.
And the movie's basis is as much in Grant and Arthur as in
that slew of "B" movies.   BRINGING UP BABY and ONLY
ANGELS HAVE WINGS as vehicles for actors are so good
that they make one wish that all of Hawks' movies had begun
as assignments to build something around the talents of a
Grant, a Hepburn or a Cagney.   The closest analogies I
know of are to the silent and sound comedies which were
written expressly for Buster Keaton, W. C. Fields and
others, and to Sternberg's best Dietrich films.

"It takes time...," Dunson says at the beginning of
RED RIVER, and that's one secret of Hawks' working method.
When asked about the experience of acting in The THING,
Kenneth Tobey replied:

> It was a great deal of fun....  On most pictures
> you don't have time to work like that; with Howard
> Hawks you have a lot of time....  We all kind of

> fell in love with his style and, as it happens in
> dramas, you get a camaraderie and an essence of
> jollity and fun that comes across very clearly, I
> think.   This happens more on the stage, because
> you rehearse more.   Of course, we rehearsed a
> great deal on this picture ... it takes a lot of re-
> hearsal to get that unrehearsed quality. [3]

The rehearsing shows in ONLY ANGELS HAVE WINGS, as
in The THING.   On the level of plot--or that part of the film
which lends itself to synopsis--it's often silly and juvenile.
But on the more important and immediate level of one actor
confronting another, it has a conviction, credibility, and
fluidity rare in films.   There's no waste motion.   There are
no dead spaces, in terms of screen time or geography.   The
plot is almost entirely subsumed in the physical presence of
the actors.   Unlike the actors in, say, Hawks' CEILING
ZERO, who get lost in the plot and in the author's over-ex-
plicit point-making, the actors in ONLY ANGELS HAVE
WINGS are almost always in control--not the characters, but
the actors.   That might seem to be a fine distinction, but
"character" implies something conceived on paper or in the
director's mind, and "actor" implies a physical presence.
It's in the acting and staging that this movie lives (although
I imagine that almost any competent director could have made
a moderately good movie with the Furthman-Hawks script and
dialogue).

There are few of those ponderous passages that litter
most movies, Hawks' included, in which the actors fail to
register because the plot has virtually gone on without them
or left them with nothing to do but mark time.   It is clear
that Hawks took much time and care on the sets with the
actors, reworking the character relationships as drawn in
the script.   I'm not saying that ONLY ANGELS HAVE WINGS
is the most brilliantly acted movie ever (that's probably
CHILDREN OF PARADISE), but I know of few other movies
in which you get as strong a feeling of living, breathing
human beings acting out a story.   It has a visual authenticity
which gives it much, though not total, dramatic validity.
It's the opposite of a movie like GERTRUD, Carl Dreyer's
fascinating (and I think pretty successful) experiment, in
which everything is in the dialogue (or the subtitles), and
the actors might as well be mannequins.   It's virtually the
reverse of films like Antonioni's and Bergman's, in which
the actors are generally not so much characters as calculatedly lifeless embodiments of the director's bright ideas; movies,

ONLY ANGELS HAVE WINGS:  Victor Kilian, Allyn Joslyn,
Cary Grant, John Carroll and Jean Arthur.

that is, in which what's on the screen is just a backdrop for
the director's ideas and which we value or don't value depending on how we like the way the director thinks (dully,
usually, in the cases of Antonioni and Bergman, imaginatively in the singular case of Dreyer and GERTRUD).  Hawks'
is a physical rather than a cerebral cinema--or it is at its
best.  At its worst--say, SERGEANT YORK or The ROAD
TO GLORY--it's cerebral, in the worst way.

ONLY ANGELS HAVE WINGS is the flip side of
BRINGING UP BABY--a dramatic fantasy world--and as inconsequential and nearly as good in its own way.  What indeed can anyone see in it besides, in Pauline Kael's words,
"the sex and glamor and fantasies of the high-school boys'

universe"?  It's ideal of its kind, but its kind has little relation, or only the most tangential relation to anything outside
it.  It means a lot more to me than most movies that have
more, or more direct, relation to life.  But its inconsequen-
tiality, or rather the high value I place on its inconsequenti-
ality, is harder to justify than that of BRINGING UP BABY
because it is, ostensibly, about something--"the imminence of
death" or the integration of the individual into the group.  It
is also more difficult to claim that its value lies not in any
ultimate meanings or statements, but in Cary Grant, Jean
Arthur, Thomas Mitchell, etc.; that the story and the themes
and the characters are the means and the performances and
the appearance of reality the ends.  It may seem condescending to say that a work that has been praised for its depth
should instead be praised (and just as highly) for its surface
excitement, but I don't think it is.

It's easier to conclude, as Wood does, that the movie's "sense of the imminence of death, of the surrounding
darkness" is what makes it "so modern:  in the world of the
hydrogen bomb, one doesn't have to be an Andes mailplane
flier to feel that one may be dead tomorrow."  (One doesn't,
one might add, need the bomb to feel that.)  Although I believe I like the film as much as Wood does, he takes it
more seriously than I ever could, or at least he takes it
seriously in a different way.  The feeling is definitely there.
ANGELS is "enormously affecting," or at least very involving, but not because what Hawks says is especially new or
profound or important, but because the way he says it
through his actors is so consistently fresh and imaginative.
He's working with genres, stock types, and "far-fetched coincidences" (as Wood admits), as he did in BABY, but he's
also working (in both these films) with some of the best
actors in Hollywood (or the world for that matter), and the
brilliance of the two movies has much less to do with the
fact that one happens to be a screwball comedy and the other
a romantic melodrama than that one is based on the Grant-
Hepburn combination and the other on the Grant-Arthur combination.  What makes them so special is that Hawks didn't
have to squeeze Grant, Hepburn, and Arthur into some dumb,
pre-sold property like a play or a novel; he started with them
and made the film fit them rather than vice versa.

The Grant-Arthur team is a less likely one than Grant-
Hepburn.  They're from different worlds, like Hepburn and
Grant in BRINGING UP BABY, but, although Miss Arthur
enters Grant's world, they never really seem to belong to

Melissa Sierra and Jean Arthur in ONLY ANGELS HAVE
WINGS.

the same one.  She's more out of her element than she's
supposed to be, like a little girl allowed to play baseball
with the Big Boys.  She reinforces female film critics' case
against the film as a refuge of the worst male chauvinist
attitudes.  (She makes Molly Haskell "wince in embarrassment to the tune of woman as second fiddle. ")  But she's
such a good actress that she makes her betrayal of woman-
hood seem less a betrayal than an original, if slightly suspect, definition of it, although her brightness and her awareness of what she's doing may make her capitulation seem
even more objectionable to women--devastatingly effective
male propaganda, in effect.  She throws the whole movie off,
or on, depending on what you think Hawks and Furthman
wanted it to be.  She's not really big or tough enough to be
a globe-trotting "showgirl. "  Her initial naiveté in the Hawks
movie, however, is as believable as her initial cynicism in
her Capra movies, MR. DEEDS GOES TO TOWN and MR.

SMITH GOES TO WASHINGTON. She makes her character believable on the set despite the unbelievability of it in the script. She's not docile or (in Haskell's term) "craven in her availability." She's spunky and forward, and her availability is less a submission to Grant than a demand for reciprocation. She may capitulate, but she formulates the terms of capitulation.

Grant enforces the separateness of their two worlds with his studied aloofness. His Jeff Carter is one of the most successful incarnations in movies of the cynical-sentimental hero, more successful even than the Bogart of CASABLANCA and TO HAVE AND HAVE NOT and the John Garfield of FOUR DAUGHTERS, in part because the role is better written, in part because it's better acted. There is, as Haskell says, "a strong streak of self-pity-disguised-as-tough-indifference" in the Grant character, as there is also in the Bogart and Garfield characters, but I think Grant comes closest to making sense of the contradiction between the surface insulation and the core of feeling in this kind of hero.

Grant's Jeff Carter is at once a romantic and a cynic, not just a romantic pretending to be a cynic. Grant is callous, as he is in HIS GIRL FRIDAY, but he's human too, only the humanness doesn't cancel the callousness, as it usually does (and is rather obviously intended to do) in the cynic-hero. Grant, Hawks, and the script tie both facets of the character to a machine-like super-efficiency in Jeff Carter which is attributable to neither cynical nor sentimental attitudes. His dual attitudes, in fact, seem separate expressions of a deeper, what's-best-for-the-team nature. He has dual reactions to Barthelmess' successful emergency flight to and from a plateau. When Barthelmess radios the news of his success, Grant answers, "What do you want me to do, pat you on the back?" but the expression on his face is one of grudging admiration. When Barthelmess returns, Grant notifies him that he's hired, not unconditionally: "I'm knee-deep in friends around here, but you're one guy I can send out in any kind of weather on any kind of a job without losing any sleep except over the ship." But, after Barthelmess leaves, and Mitchell, having seen the size of the check for Barthelmess' mission, exclaims, "Isn't this too much?" Grant, clearly impressed, replies, "Not for that kind of flying."

Both Grant's imperfect imperviousness and his

vulnerability seem subservient to his devotion to flying, the
latter taking the form of practicality as well as more conventionally heroic forms, like determination to fly the worst
missions himself.  His callousness isn't just a thin, easily-
cracked shell, an excuse for sentiment; it's a necessary part
of him.  It's firmly grounded in the character as developed
by Grant.  It's sometimes so extreme it's breathtaking--
verging on the comical--as when Miss Arthur innocently
picks up an item from among a dead flier's belongings, and
Grant contemptuously compliments her on her "choice":
"You've got a good eye, lady."  (She gives it to the flier's
girl friend.)  Grant isn't simply defensively antagonistic, as
the Bogart and Garfield heroes are, retaliating with adolescent spitefulness against the world for the emotional wounds
it has inflicted on them.  He's genuinely smug and unpleas-
ant, which I think redeems, or qualifies, by complementing
rather than just covering that streak of sentimentality in
him.  When Miss Arthur asks him, "How can you do that?"
when he begins attacking the steak cooked for the man who's
now dead, he looks up in mock puzzlement at such a naive
question.  His passion for flying, for living, overrides petty
matters of politeness, of consideration for others, of his
own feelings.

He expresses his feelings in subtle, unexpected ways.
When Victor Kilian tosses the dead flier Joe's (Noah Beery,
Jr.) possessions on the counter, he recoils slightly.  Just
after Beery crashes, he comments on his recklessness,
"Mr. Wise Guy," but the catch in his voice reverses the
tone of the words.  His "Don't you think I care?" in reply
to boss Sig Ruman's complaint about having to send boys up
to die, isn't supplicating or begging for recognition of his
feelings.  It's querulous, a termination rather than an opening of discussion.  Grant's petulance acts against the sentimentality of his scenes, making them something more than
pretexts for emotional tugs.

The movie is often characterized as an expression of
Stoicism, but to me it seems more an expression of the
impossibility of Stoicism.  For all the talk about not discussing the fact of death, there is a lot of talk about death.
In somewhat the same way, Henry James' advocacy of Stoicism seems an admission of the impossibility of not feeling:

> In other words consciousness is an illimitable pow-
> er, and though at times it may seem to be all
> consciousness of misery, yet in the way it

> propagates itself from wave to wave, so that we
> never cease to feel, and though at moments we
> appear to, try to, pray to, there is something that
> holds one in one's place, makes it a standpoint in
> the universe which it is probably good not to for-
> sake. [4]

What makes the pseudo-Stoical attitudes toward death in the
movie seem of perhaps more moment than they are is the
almost palpable presence throughout of death and danger.
Wood is right when he says that the distinctive flavor of
ONLY ANGELS HAVE WINGS is due to the tension between
background ("the surrounding darkness") and foreground (the
interaction of the characters).

I think Woods' emphasis, however, is wrong.  The
presence of death is primarily an excellent suspense and
action device.  It's a background, not a metaphysic.  The
tension it generates gives the movie the illusion of depth
because Furthman's script sustains it so well throughout.
It's not simply a matter of 1) an action sequence, 2) drama
and comedy, and 3) more action footage.  The "reality" of

Victor Kilian, Richard Barthelmess and Cary Grant in ONLY
ANGELS HAVE WINGS.

the flying sequences that Dyer mentions carries over into the
story.   Scenes of the plane landing on and taking off from an
isolated mountain plateau--with no musical or fancy photographic effects, just slow, breathtaking, continuous movements
of the plane circling the base of the plateau, taking its whole
length to come to a turning stop, then using the drop off the
side to pick up speed--have a residual effect.   Once you buy
them--and you can hardly help but do so--you will buy just
about anything.   Whether the attitudes expressed toward
death in the movie are adolescent or adult (or a little of
both), they're grounded in the movie's own impressive version of the nature of adventure and sudden death.

     The movie has a way of turning the most hackneyed
scenes into memorable, moving ones.   When Grant has to
tell Mitchell that Mitchell's eyes are so bad he can't fly any
more, he leads up to it, tries to get Mitchell to say it himself, then finally turns to him and gets it out:   "You're
through flying, Kid."   Mitchell mumbles, "Yeah," without
even turning around to look at him.   It's a simple line, but
the scene is given impact by the involved process of hesitation, circumlocution, and indirect confrontation.

     At the end, Jean Arthur wants to tell Grant goodbye
before she leaves, but she's not sure that he wants to say
goodbye to her.   She asks Kilian if it's all right.   He says
he thinks it is.   She wants him to be sure it is.   He reassures her, and after starting off and edging back, she finally
gains enough confidence to go right into his office.   After
the crash of Noah Beery, Jr.'s plane, the onlookers stand
still and apart for a few moments not saying anything.   The
scene's focus is in their silence and their stances.   A lesser
director would have kept the thing moving.

     In what should have been the worst scene, Miss Arthur
accidentally shoots Grant in the shoulder when she throws a
gun onto a table, after threatening to shoot him to keep him
from flying.   She runs to him, but he motions her back,
crying, "Go away!"   Everyone runs in, and she has to explain who did it:   "I did.   I didn't want him to go."   An em-
barrassingly obvious plot point--since Grant is hurt, Mitchell
and Barthelmess must go up--becomes a comic scene; the
unlikeliness of the gun's action becomes another, accidental
episode of the alternating comic-dramatic conflict between
Grant and Arthur.   She didn't mean to, but she might as
well have meant to.

Hawks makes something of little moments that should not be anything: a shot of Miss Arthur, alone and lost, in the general uproar at the end; Grant pushing past her in the morning and prodding her, "Get a good sleep?" "No!"; Grant playfully fending off a desperate Mitchell ("Go away! Go away!") as he finally separates the latter's double-headed coin from him and picks it up off the floor. Compared to ANGELS, most movies seem to be written, talked out, and played in monotone. With other actors and other movies, listening to dialogue and watching it staged can become a chore. Talk and movement by the actors in ANGELS has the beauty of something sculpted or choreographed, molded to fit the comic-dramatic contours of a situation.

After Grant finishes telling Arthur how he and his ex-girl (Hayworth) broke up because she couldn't take the pressure of his dangerous occupation (flying), she asks what finally happened to her. "I heard she married another flier," he answers wonderingly, his hand lightly cupping the top of a whiskey glass, his wry expression reflecting his awareness of the answer's resemblance to the half-comic punchline to a story. At the beginning of the movie, Arthur can't take the apparent lack of feeling of Grant and the other fliers after Beery's death, and she leaves the table to go out. Grant instantly rises and cuts across the room to go after her. Near the end, after Mitchell's death, Grant leaves the bar (and Mitchell's belongings) and goes off by himself. Arthur begins to go after him, but stops, unsure of herself until Kilian reassures her. Hawks may not have blocked every step of his actors, but he makes their movements and their hesitations count as much as the dialogue, and they reinforce it and give it a context, a world in which to exist.

The ending--maybe the greatest scene in Hawks' movies--is a terrific example of what Hawks calls "three-cushion dialogue"--"because you hit it over here and over here and go over here to get the meaning." It's terrific because the words aren't even spoken. Grant flips Mitchell's coin--"Heads you stay, tails you go"--for Miss Arthur and races off to his waiting plane after the coin comes up, naturally, heads. He leaves the coin with her. She absently turns it over and sees the heads on both sides. Her face lights up. She runs out and waves as his plane takes off. He would never ask a woman to do anything, no.

Notes

1. ONLY ANGELS HAVE WINGS didn't quite finish this plot
   off either.   But a proposed remake entitled "Count
   Three and Pray" might have if it had been filmed.
   There's a note in a treatment for it (slightly updated
   to 1949) which expresses some concern "about how
   this can be converted into an all girl story." One
   suggestion "revolves around the Ruman character who
   has a daughter formerly in the WASPS who operates
   the airport." I don't think they were kidding. ("After
   all, the change of sex worked in HIS GIRL FRIDAY,"
   might have been overheard at one of the story con-
   ferences. )

2. Peter John Dyer, "Sling the Lamps Low," Focus on
   Howard Hawks (Prentice-Hall, 1972; from Sight and
   Sound, Summer 1962, p. 86).

3. "The North Pole Papers," interview by Mark Frank,
   Photon, Number 22, pp. 21-22.

4. The Portable Henry James (The Viking Press, 1956),
   p. 649.

# CEILING ZERO

CEILING ZERO is a real manic-depressive of a movie, alternately great fun and a drag, looking for a while as though it might be Hawks' best film, then turning soft and mushy. It's like a collaborative effort between Hawks and his more sober, strait-laced critics--an action movie congested by themes and morals. It's the kind of movie Robin Wood might write for Hawks--some fun, but rife with points about irresponsibility, the team, maturation, and self-sacrifice. It's a cross between the Hollywood action movie and the "well-made" Broadway play, and the two don't mix here. The trouble is not that it has a conscience, but that it displays its conscience as if it considered that its finest feature.

James Cagney's Dizzy Davis was potentially a great Hawks hero, but the small-minded script by Frank Wead, from his play, proves to be not so interested in its hero as in underlining his flaws and reprimanding him. After some clumsy prefatory passages, Cagney's small whirlwind of an entrace promises great things and, for a while, makes good on its promises. As June Travis' inexperienced pilot Tommy (accent on "inexperienced") puts it, Dizzy is "sort of goofy and tough and sweet all at the same time." He's even more than that: he's romantically self-destructive, reckless, cocky, selfish, loyal to his friends, and selfless, though perhaps not all at the same time, and not all to the same degree. Dizzy is an almost ideal hero--independent, high-spirited, courageous, but doomed by his recklessness to burn himself out. Cagney as Dizzy seems a perfect actor for Hawks, energetic, smooth, able to switch moods effortlessly. He is successively little-boy prankster, smooth operator, stout comrade, and daring flyer, and he makes overall sense of these disparate elements of his character.

The script, however, doesn't let its hero burn himself out; it considerately clears the way for him, preparing us for his entrance and again, later, for his premature exit. The movie is fine when it leaves him alone and leaves its

criticism of him implicit or secondary to the man himself--
the middle third is the best Cagney film I've seen--but when
Dizzy's boss, Jake Lee (Pat O'Brien), tells him, "You've got
to learn to play by the rules," you know the fun is over. [1]
The script didn't really have to come right out and say it
either; at the beginning it shows Dizzy's flashiness and infec-
tiousness to be anachronistic and out of place in an era of
tame commercial aviation.  None of his friends from stunt
flying and pioneering days behaves like Dizzy:  Jake is now
the responsible manager of an airline; Texas Clark (Stu Erwin) is married and harried; and Mike (Garry Owen), left
feeble-minded after a crash, is reduced to polishing doors.

The early scene in which the just-arrived Dizzy approaches Mike and greets him with a too-quick "the only one
crazier than me," before he realizes what has happened to
his old friend, effectively captures Dizzy, his environment,
and his relation to it, that of the ex-insider outsider.  As
long as Dizzy refuses to accept his foreordained extinction,
the script maintains a balance between his casual brashness
and its effect on the dull formality of the "modern" airport.
But when he succumbs to self-pity and becomes no different
from the chorus demanding that he reform and conform, the
movie droops, becoming lachrymose, almost maudlin.  Only
the ending retains a little of the dash-tempered-by-a-sense-
of-mortality of the earlier parts of the story.  The actual
ending, coming after all the sob stuff with Cagney and O'Bri-
en, with Cagney sacrificing his unwanted life to do a last
little bit of pioneering (this time with a new type of wing
de-icer), is unexpectedly moving and fulfilling.  It's nonsense, but with flair, self-justification or self-glorification
rather than self-pity.  It helps to reinforce the movie's
shaky case for being "realistic" and "honest" rather than
simply conformist or nostalgic.  It's a grand way for the
earlier Dizzy Davis to go.

CEILING ZERO should have been more of a one-man
show; that is, more like TWENTIETH CENTURY and HIS
GIRL FRIDAY.  The point of the movie is that it isn't, which
is a valid point; however, though a single character may
carry a whole movie, a single point can't carry even half
of one.  Dizzy tells Tommy that the thrill of flying is that
"When you're up there, you're on your own.  It's strictly
a one-man show."  The script is too insistent that Dizzy is
wrong; that now, on the ground or in the air, flying is a
team effort.  At its best Dizzy's response is a sarcastic,
"Are you meaning to infer, sir, that I am not a cog in the

wheel?" The script cheats us of a genuinely romantic hero,
killing him off dramatically some time before it kills him
off physically. From the beginning, the weight of the script
is on the other side, and the only way to balance it is to let
Dizzy be himself, which he is, wonderfully, for a while,
whether he's singing, "I Can't Give You Anything But Love,
Honey Baby, " over the radio before his grand entrance, or
shedding mock-tears while on the make for Tommy, or haras-
sing poor Texas about his wife and mother-in-law. For a
while, his antics have an added, devil-may-care charm because of their contrast with everyone else's stodginess.

The turning point is the death of Texas. Dizzy has
sent him up on a flight in his place by faking heart trouble
so that he could date Tommy. His sense of responsibility
for Texas is at first lost in the action, converted into the
furious activity at headquarters that precedes the crash of
Texas' plane. It's the high point of the movie, the sole sequence in which both the romantic and the egocentric sides of
Dizzy are implicitly present and in which they mix, and Otis
Ferguson caught its sense of excitement:

> There is an intricate art by which the line of feel-
> ing is kept uppermost and rising in the midst of a
> staccato din of commands, interjections, screams,
> speakers, plane-motors, tickers, sometimes as
> many as five or six voices going all the time, so
> that the crash of Erwin, coming in too low in the
> fog and blowing up on the wires, careening across
> the field on fire and smashing into the glass win-
> dows of the hangar, is a terrific bit of action. [2]

Everyone immediately begins to lay into Dizzy, and the movie
parades his guilt and sense of responsibility as if it were
trying to expiate its own guilt at letting him run around loose
earlier generating some excitement. Isabel Jewell as Texas'
wife, sobbing pitifully before Dizzy, is reproach enough, but
she comes right out and tells him, "You're no good!" Twice.
The film ends there.

Up to that point, Hawks keeps the film moving, but
the visual/verbal razzle-dazzle is a little self-conscious at
times. Everyone is running around noisily, more, it seems,
for effect and show than for good reason. O'Brien's staccato
snapping off of orders sounds more like an excited telegraph
than a pressured airport executive. And the speeding up of
the action causes as much congestion as excitement. The six

co-plots are spliced together so crazily that the camera
seems to be recording a day in the life of an ant hill in
fast motion rather than a hectic day at the airport.   Wead's
screenplay is a little too tidy and clever at times:   three of
the co-plots converge calculatedly when Mike is told that
Texas is flying in ceiling zero weather and he warns Dizzy
that he, Dizzy, is getting "too old" to fly.   Mike adds that
he slammed into a wall on a night like this.   The scene,
however, as played against the background of fog outside the
window and dominated by Mike's almost supernatural presence, is downright eerie.


## Notes

1.   That same year (1936) O'Brien played the head of anoth-
      er commercial airline in another Frank Wead-scripted
      movie, CHINA CLIPPER, which had lots of aviation
      history but no drama.   It was the past to CEILING
      ZERO's present, with O'Brien pioneering trans-pacific
      flights, etc.

2.   The Film Criticism of Otis Ferguson (Philadelphia,
      1971), p. 115.

# The CROWD ROARS

The year 1932 was Hawks' best. He made one excellent film, SCARFACE (actually made in 1930, but not released until 1932), and two good minor ones, TIGER SHARK and The CROWD ROARS. Of his two Cagney films, CEILING ZERO is more exciting but less even than The CROWD ROARS. CEILING ZERO promises more, but The CROWD ROARS winds up delivering almost as much. Dizzy Davis is a great character, but CEILING ZERO, in effect, kills him off midway and goes on without him. Joe Greer may not be as memorable a character, but he's still around at the end of The CROWD ROARS. Cagney doesn't dominate The CROWD ROARS as he does the first half of CEILING ZERO. It's a little, four-character drama, as TIGER SHARK is a little, three-character drama.

By "little," I mean that the two films finally seem undeveloped, fragmented, static but pointed, and in the case of The CROWD ROARS it's not surprising that it leaves one feeling that something is missing. On the two occasions I've seen it a fifteen-minute segment was missing, the reunion of the brothers, Joe and Eddie Greer (Cagney and Eric Linden, respectively). The official running time is 85 minutes, but I clocked both prints (one on television, one at the Los Angeles County Museum of Art) at about 71 minutes. The gap makes the finale, in which the brothers race to victory at the Indianapolis 500 in the same car, seem sillier than it probably would be if a few clues were given as to how they got together again after about a year of separation and bitter feelings on both sides.

The Cagney character bears some relation to the egomaniacs of SCARFACE, TWENTIETH CENTURY, HIS GIRL FRIDAY, and of course CEILING ZERO, but here the film isn't all with him at any time. And the other characters aren't all monsters either, as they are in SCARFACE, or pawns, as they are in TWENTIETH CENTURY and HIS GIRL FRIDAY, or walking moral lessons, as they are in CEILING

ZERO. The script is fairer with the people around the central figure. Linden is just a kid who's crazy about racing. Ann Dvorak is crazy about Cagney. ("I don't know if he needs me. I need him.") To spite Cagney Joan Blondell calculatedly sets out after Linden, then falls for him.

Everything would work out fine--no triangles or romantic complications here--except that Cagney lives by a double standard: it's all right if he lives with Dvorak, but he doesn't want his younger brother getting mixed up with women, especially with man-hating mantraps like Blondell. (Linden: "Did you see me drive?" Blondell: "No. That's a thrill I'm saving up.") He knows something about sex, but not much about love. He can estrange Dvorak to set a good example for Linden, and can take Blondell for what she admits she is at the beginning of the film and not buy her for what she says she is later. He's at once unsympathetic because of the way he treats Dvorak and sympathetic because Dvorak for some reason loves him. But she doesn't go around saying, "There's something noble and good and fine in him." She can't say why she loves him and doesn't try to. When Blondell warns her that Cagney is coming to her apartment drunk and mad, her first concern is that he's going to be racing that day. Blondell wonderingly observes, "You think a lot of him."

The movie expresses quite a bit of emotion, but deftly avoids sentimentality. After sexual stalking turns to love, Blondell begins to cry and tells Dvorak, through her tears, "I've never been so happy!"[1] When Cagney sends Dvorak away, Hawks unobtrusively punctuates the scene with a travel shot, from Dvorak's point-of-view in her departing cab, of Cagney greeting his brother, the cause of their separation. The shot suggests, rather than displays, Dvorak's feelings. The script doesn't take sides, condemning or forgetting one character while concentrating on another. Cagney's recklessness on the track causes his friend Frank McHugh's death, but the movie doesn't dwell on Cagney's subsequent descent into obscurity, as CEILING ZERO dwells on the slow extinction of Dizzy Davis after the latter indirectly causes a fellow pilot's death. It merely suggests, via racing bills, that he's not the top draw he once was, then picks him up again when Dvorak finds him at the Indy 500.

The first step of his rehabilitation has already been taken--he has given up drinking. The second step--his reunion with Dvorak--is reticent, and affecting in its reticence.

Inside her hotel room, they both keep their hands in their pockets at first. Cagney is simply unhappy with himself and unwilling or unable to share his unhappiness with her. She's afraid to scare him away by showing how much she still cares for him. But the scene ends with him crying on her shoulder.

The final steps to the restoration of his self-esteem are just not there. The too-happy ending, as it is, and would be even with the missing footage included before it, is the usual, juvenile, action-picture ending which tidily resolves all problems and conflicts. It doesn't fit this movie, which is generally quite grown-up in its attitudes toward love, sex, family, and friendship. Without the intervening steps, the ending is ludicrous; it seems like an afterthought, spliced in from another movie (like RED LINE 7000, which also ends with the women happily, sappily watching their men). It's not helped by the fake suspense of the climactic race either, with the announcer crying, "Greer leads by inches, but watch that tire! The tire's going to go any second!"

The concluding sequence, in which the Greers have their ambulance race another racer's ambulance to the hospital--the tire did go--is fun and a sly comment on Dvorak's characterization of racing as "a lot of people hoping for wrecks and roaring for blood." It's a comic-defiant answer to death and race-track crashes like McHugh's, in which he burns and the other drivers quit the race rather than smell the burning flesh as they drive past the wreck on each lap.

Blondell, Dvorak, and Linden are good, and Joe Greer is one of Cagney's best early-Thirties roles--almost as good as his crybaby con man in BLONDE CRAZY (1931), which may be the best of all from that era. His early scenes with Dvorak and Blondell are modeled on the grapefruit scene with Mae Clarke in PUBLIC ENEMY. When he wants to talk to Dvorak alone, he pulls Blondell up off the couch and propels her out of the room before him. He proceeds to give Dvorak the brush-off, and she slaps him. She's shocked at her action and afraid of his reaction. He just dismisses it with a little wave of his hand--but the wave also dismisses her, as if her slap sealed the end of the affair, to his satisfaction. It's a stunning moment, in what it reveals about Cagney and in its abruptness. He walks away, but she tries to keep him there. As he opens the door and steps out, she tries to hold it open or to follow him, but he pulls it shut behind him. The last shot is of his hand on the doorknob.

As Greer, Cagney has just the right proportions of super-
ciliousness, hypocrisy, and toughness.

     The difference between The CROWD ROARS and its
remake, INDIANAPOLIS SPEEDWAY (Warner Brothers, 1939),
is probably more a matter of James Cagney and Pat O'Brien
than Howard Hawks and Lloyd Bacon.     (Hawks is given screen
credit for the story of the remake. )   The story is pretty
much the same, except that:   1) stricter 1939 censorship
makes Joe and Lee occupy separate apartments;[2] 2) Joe's
disgrace is carefully if economically rubbed in--Spud's wife
accuses Joe to his face, "You killed my Spud!" in an unwise
borrowing from CEILING ZERO, and O'Brien looks guilty as
hell; later, a boy accuses Joe of not being his brother Eddie,
the Greer who's currently champion; 3) Eddie is an inventor,
for no good dramatic reason; and 4) a driver in the climactic
race conveniently burns up in his car to provide Joe with a
reminder of Spud.   The film also gives us a hint as to what
was in the footage excised from the original:   Lee talks Joe
into replacing the crippled Eddie in the race, Joe talks Eddie
into letting him take over, and Eddie takes the mechanic's
place rather than wait out the race on the sidelines.   Nothing
you couldn't have guessed, but it's nice to know.

     The few obvious changes don't explain why the remake
is almost totally unmemorable.   It's not particuarly bad, but
it's as if all the life had been drained out of the story--part
of which had seemed pretty good--through a small, undetect-
able hole.   It's smoother than the original, which is to say
duller, with no flavor or bite.   Cagney, Dvorak, Blondell,
and Linden give you moments, and in Cagney's case more
than moments, to remember.   O'Brien, Gale Page (Lee),
Ann Sheridan (Frankie, the Blondell role), and John Payne
(Eddie) give you nothing (though Sheridan's retort to Payne's
naive, "You having one?"--"Why not?   It's my liquor"--qual-
ifies as a little something, I guess).   If Cagney had re-done
his Joe Greer role, we might have seen once and for all
time how much better a director Hawks is than Bacon.   But
since O'Brien subbed for him we can only see how much better an actor Cagney was in the Thirties than O'Brien.   (I
like the slower, mellower O'Brien of the Fifties, in things
like The LAST HURRAH.   He just didn't belong at Warners. )

     The differences between The CROWD ROARS and
INDIANAPOLIS SPEEDWAY are touches and details--like
Dvorak's cab leaving Joe and Eddie, or Cagney bending down

into the frame to pick up a couple of dirty bananas--and most
of the details are in Cagney's performance.   O'Brien doesn't
brush off Page with a little, contemptuous wave of the hand--
if he did, it might not mean the same thing as it did with
Cagney, anyway.   O'Brien isn't either a sympathetic or an
unsympathetic character; he just isn't a character at all.
He's just vain and spiteful, like an angry child, and his
spitefulness is irrelevant to the story.   He was evidently
trying for something more substantial than spite, like Cagney's hypocritical arrogance.   His mechanical, staccato
delivery is almost comical at times.   It's as if he knew that
Cagney did it before and did it too well and he resented being asked (or paid) to follow in Cagney's footsteps.   The difference between a relatively good movie and a bad one can
be just one key role well cast or miscast, or just a few
touches here and there that indicate that someone was awake
on the set.

## Notes

1.   Hawks' grandmother inspired the scene:  "Whenever she
     was happy she started to cry.   She'd say I'm so
     happy! and start to cry. "  ("Hawks Talks, " Film
     Comment, May-June 1974, p.  44. )

2.   This makes rather comically unconvincing the explanation
     of how brother Eddie winds up in Lee's apartment
     before Joe gets there:  "Since Joe wasn't in his room
     I thought I'd come here. "

RED LINE 7000

RED LINE 7000 is Hawks' worst movie.   At least, I
hope it is (I haven't seen most of his earliest films).   It
may be recognized as a Hawks movie only in the sense of
what ONLY ANGELS HAVE WINGS might have been if everything that could conceivably have gone wrong with it had gone
wrong.   It's ONLY ANGELS HAVE WINGS without indirection
of emotion, dramatic distancing, acting, humor, or suspense.
(In the ideal course for aspiring directors, the two films
would be shown back to back. )   It's what RED RIVER threatens to become when Joanne Dru steps in.   To its credit it
does show a concern for people and a willingness to probe
(if that's the right phrase) their emotional recesses.   But
the way it shows it!   Everyone in the movie is severely
wounded emotionally and goes around bleeding all over everyone else.   Everyone is Vulnerable.   It's a real bloodbath.
Hawks, as usual, gives his actors plenty of time, so that if
there had been something worthwhile in the material or the
actors that could have been brought out, it would have
emerged.   In this case, however, his generosity only gives
the actors enough rope to hang themselves.

All the characters are emotionally screwed-up and
let you know exactly how.   But they Come to Terms with
Themselves and Others.   And that's all they do.   This is the
kind of audience-losing problem film that Hawks says he
knows better than to try.   The people in RED LINE 7000 are
conceived only as problems, and watching them solved is as
involving as watching rats go through a maze.   The characters wander unmemorably in and out of scenes, and it's all
you can do to keep the names, faces, and problems straight.
Someone mentions "Dan McCall," and you ask yourself, "Now
which one was he?"; that is, if you're not already preoccupied
with the question of who the person is who is doing the talking.   Then someone else rattles off the names of twelve
characters you've forgotten were even in the movie--"Mike"
and "Holly" and "Ned" and "Lindy"--and you're really lost.
The characters are so unindividualized--it's their problems

that are particularized--that when two of them are together,
you have to give your memory a hard jog to recall when and
where they met, or if they met before, what their problems
were, and how their problems relate to each other.

The script alternates between scenes of two people
(one male and one female) aggravating each other's emotional
problems because they're in love and scenes of one person
telling another (in male-male, male-female, female-female
combinations) why he/she should/shouldn't be so upset about
the difficulties between him/her and his/her girl friend/boy
friend.  I think the matches were Mike/Gaby, Ned/Julie,
and Dan/Holly, but they might as well have been Ned/Holly,
Dan/Mike, and Julie/Gaby for all the difference it makes.
(Pat and Lindy were just referees.)  A supremely foolish
shot at the end shows the three happy girls (Gaby, Julie, and
Holly) beaming as they watch their boys on the race track.
Everyone's straightened out, but the more interesting film
would have begun with everyone straightened out and ended
with everyone screwed-up.  At least then those damn girls
wouldn't be grinning idiotically at the end.

Robin Wood's analysis of RED LINE 7000, in his book
on Hawks, is one of the best examples I know of a not-inac-
curate, thorough explication of a film which is, however, almost entirely irrelevant.  It might have been written directly
from a reading of the script for all the idea it gives you of
the experience of seeing the movie.  Wood thinks it may be
"the most underestimated film of the sixties," but he can't
quite make up his mind what's so special about it:

> Indeed, the economy throughout the film is such
> that one feels Hawks was trying to see how much
> he could leave out--or, alternatively, how much he
> could pack in; seldom in a film can so much ground
> have been covered in so short a time.

He believes that "Hawks's statement that he lost interest in it
is belied by every shot," but gives you no idea at all what
those revealing shots are.  The perfection of the film is for
him a given, and he goes on from there, only once expressing dissatisfaction, with an actor who "lacks the necessary
authority for the part...."  You have to assume that the
other actors have the necessary authority for their parts because Wood never discusses acting otherwise.  Nor does he
give any samples of the flavor of the dialogue.  (Sample:
Gaby: "The racing car is to me like some kind of great

animal," a kind of line ridiculed in ONLY ANGELS HAVE
WINGS--Jeff: "Reminded you of a great, big beautiful bird,
didn't it?" Bonnie: "No. It was like a human being....")

     Wood does, however, unwittingly provide a few clues
as to what the movie is like:

> Further, the Wildcat Jones of Holly MacGregor's
> song carries a strong suggestion of self-parody
> (intensified by the bizarre accompaniment of what
> has been described as 'a quartet of female dwarfs').

Wood provides no context for his reference to self-parody,
but the movie does at times ring so artificial and unbelievable
that it seems Hawks must be parodying himself, racing pictures, or something. Blaring juke-box music magically
stops just as a woman walks up to a man and the two begin
a conversation. (Loud music and its insulation of listeners
from the outside world is either a motif or a running gag in
the movie, depending on how you take the movie.) A tele-
phone rings right on cue as someone finishes a sentence.
Lightning announces a girl's entrance into a hospital room.
Inside of a minute six cars crack up in a big stock-car race.
James Caan (as Mike, or was it Ned?) apologizes to the
racer he tried to kill on the track, asks him to hit him, gets
hit, says, "That's what I came for," and leaves. RED LINE
7000 may someday be resurrected as one of Hawks' classic
comedies.

     Wood delineates the character relationships as if
everything about them and the rest of the movie were hunky-
dory. He buys Holly's "perverse and obstructive superstition"
that she's a jinx to race-car drivers who fall for her, then
makes the jump with her from that shaky premise for a
character to her realization (considerately verbalized for her
by Lindy) that her conception of herself as a jinx gives her
"a feeling of her own importance...." At the end she is
"cured" of her sickness because she has "progressed" through
a relationship with a "healthy" partner. What Wood doesn't
tell you is that all the relationships are realized, defined,
and developed in the dialogue, and that the movie is all on
paper; Milton Krasner might just as well not have brought
along his camera. If you haven't seen the film Wood's
analysis sounds reasonable except at the critical points,
where he reveals that even on paper (where almost any movie
can be made to sound good) it's a bad movie:

> By following through the uncontrollable impulses
> arising from his neuroses [translation:  Mike tries
> to kill Dan during a race], Mike is forced into an
> awareness he could not otherwise have achieved.
> This is the focal point of the film, resolving in
> one instant two of the three relationship problems.

If only life were that simple.   Wood writes as if instant resolutions to character conflicts were a good thing in a "work
of art" (which Wood calls this movie).   I agree with Wood
that ONLY ANGELS HAVE WINGS is some kind of a work of
art, but the art certainly doesn't lie in its resolutions.   It
lies in Hawks use of actors and visual detail to indicate conflict and resolution.   When Wood cites visual detail, it's a
meaningless literary symbol/cliché:

> The resolution of the Mike/Gaby relationship is
> set in the pouring rain--there is release and puri-
> fication.

In the context of the film, it's mostly just water.   In order
for a metaphor to work, it has to grow out of something, not
just fall on one of a set of interchangeable characters.   Wood
keeps talking about "intensity" in connection with RED LINE
7000, but that's about the last word to be connected with
Mike, Julie, Lindy, Ned, Gaby, Dan, and Pat.   (Well, maybe
"economy" is the last word--it's 110 minutes long. )

## A GIRL IN EVERY PORT

Hawks' A GIRL IN EVERY PORT is a wonderfully improbable little comedy-drama. It switches midway from genial, hyperbolic comedy to muted drama; from an exhilarating, thoroughly juvenile story of two sailors who love to fight to a precise study of a three-cornered relationship (two sailors and a girl). It changes, but not enough to split the movie into two irreconcilable halves. It doesn't disown its beginnings. It's the same story, told from two different angles. The film is so precisely designed, developed, and controlled that if you didn't know that Hawks later mastered the sound film, you might resent the fact that sound arrived just as he had mastered silent-film technique.

An unobservant critic might complain that A GIRL IN EVERY PORT depends too heavily on coincidence, inevitability, and exaggeration, as if the makers of the movie were unaware of the very source of its vitality. One of the titles suggests the quality of Hawks' visual hyperbole: "Loading in Marseilles--Where a toothache reduces the menace to France by one-half." The first half of the film is deceptive in that it doesn't ask to be taken at all seriously; the second half makes some demands. The first half is perhaps the most unabashedly adolescent passage in all of Hawks' work, unqualified as it is by any considerations of maturity, sobriety, or responsibility. The second half qualifies the first, but it doesn't dismiss it as foolish or unrealistically carefree. The first half joyously, boisterously defies restricting laws of probability, geography, and averages. Sailor Spike (Victor McLaglen) travels from Holland to Rio to Panama and invariably finds that another sailor has gotten to his girls first and left his mark--an anchor within a heart--on them. During his travels, he keeps running into another sailor, Bill (Robert Armstrong), without realizing that this is his rival.

Hawks builds one incident on another, within scenes and from scene to scene, for comic effect. Spike first returns to a Dutch girl, after a hiatus of several years, and

breaks into a big, silly grin as she steps out onto her front
porch. The grin fades as a little boy follows her out. A
second and third child wander out. Instead of presenting the
whole family at once and getting one lone laugh, Hawks skillfully milks the gag. Spike bows out. Later, after Spike has
discovered that Bill is his rival, and the two have joined
forces, plucky little Bill still wants to fight, but Spike is
warming up to a girl at a barroom table. Again and again,
Bill methodically places a chip of wood on his shoulder, dares
someone to knock it off, knocks it off himself when his offer
is refused, then calls on Spike to help him. Spike, irritated
at the constant interruptions, finally obliges Bill himself and
flattens him, then returns to the girl. (This is called "punctuating the gag.")

The tone begins to change when they visit the apartment of another of the girls in Spike's little black book.
They find a boy sailing a boat in a bucket of water. Bill
thinks he sees a resemblance between the boy and Spike, and
Spike refers to the book to check the date of his last visit.
He counts out the years on his fingers to see if the total
matches the boy's declared age. Bill immediately says it
does. But when Spike asks about a picture of a sailor lying
on a dresser, the boy explains that it's his father and that
he was drowned. A close shot of Spike leaves Bill in the
frame, but out of focus behind him: the boy's story has a
stronger effect on Spike.

The light-heartedness of the first half of the movie,
once checked, is never really regained, though the roisterers
are reunited at the end. Spike becomes enamored of tempt-
ress "Mademoiselle Godiva" (Louise Brooks), a carnival high-
diver whom Bill knew under another name many years earlier
at Coney Island. Bill doesn't tell Spike of their old affair,
but he also rejects her and the possibility of reviving it.
He refuses either to put an end to Spike's romance or to
develop the three-way relationship into a full-fledged triangle.
Thus the film rejects both tragedy and melodrama and freezes
the relationship, the better to examine it. The situation in
which the three find themselves isn't an excuse for emotional
fireworks. Bill is not even disgusted with the girl's action;
he's just uneasy with her. The film continues its modest
essay on the nature of friendship and romance and--new ele-
ments--the exploitation of friendship and romance.

Mlle. Godiva is content as long as Spike's money holds
out (and as long as she doesn't have to marry him). Spike is

blissfully oblivious of her mercenary nature.   And Bill is
afraid to enlighten Spike and thus wreck him.   The situation
is temporarily stable since Bill is not just another sucker to
be taken in by the girl.   He shares an innocent complicity in
the deception, but he stands by Spike and keeps the girl at
arm's length.

The tang, the brittle quality, of this section of the
film is due in part to the difficulty Bill has in keeping Mademoiselle at arm's length.   Louise Brooks does not raise
stereotyped visions of unfaithful women, and though she
doesn't have quite the devastating insolence of Marlene Dietrich in THE DEVIL IS A WOMAN, she has style, and her
cold-souled predator is a striking creation.   When she
presses herself against Bill as they sit awaiting Spike's return, or when she plays with her bracelets (which conceal
the anchor-in-heart mark) and Bill's shoulder, behind Spike's
back, you begin to appreciate his powers of resistance.
Spike is polishing her shoe, as the Edward G. Robinson
character in SCARLET STREET polishes contemptuous Joan
Bennett's toenails, in a similar situation.

The rupture finally, inevitably, comes when Spike finds
Bill's insignia on the girl and nearly kills him.   But his exhilaration at vengeance accomplished turns to concern when
Bill fails to get up off the floor.   Spike comes to his aid.
The bond between them is strengthened, and "the characters,"
according to Robin Wood, "remain arrested at an immature
stage of development."

The likability of A GIRL IN EVERY PORT is due in
large part to Victor McLaglen's near-irrepressibly good-natured brute and to Robert Armstrong's compulsive little
scrapper.

# TIGER SHARK

TIGER SHARK is a simple, effective drama that very neatly skirts pathos and melodrama. These latter routes would have been easier, but the movie stays honest almost until the end. There really isn't much to it, but what there is is good. It's direct and simple to the point of skimpiness, but you appreciate the documentary footage on tuna boats and tuna fishing even after you begin to suspect that much of it is there because there wasn't enough story for a feature.

The story is about two men, best friends, Mike Mascarenhas, Portuguese captain of a tuna boat, and Pipes, a crew member, who love the same woman, Quita, daughter of another fisherman who is killed by a shark. She marries Mike, but loves Pipes. Resemblance to the basic, steamy, eternal-triangle tale ends there. Tempers don't flare, and passions are quelled or put off until the following day. By way of negatively suggesting what the movie is like, two sudden lovers' clinches ring loud, false, but isolated notes in the narrative. It's almost as if, with these two momentary lapses, Hawks wanted to show you he knew what he wasn't doing--without them one might not realize that this project could have turned out very badly.

Positively describing what it's like is more difficult without moving pictures of Zita Johann (one of the few "Hawksian women" who is not over-rated) and her long, flat face and blunt delivery of lines, or of Edward G. Robinson's good-natured pushiness and Richard Arlen's ruggedness and retiring manner. Although the triangle in TIGER SHARK bears striking resemblances to the triangle in A GIRL IN EVERY PORT, the two are very different films, and Hawks is not to be accused of "already repeating himself" so much as to be admired for finding at least two ways of expressing one part of himself. McLaglen=Robinson, Brooks=Johann, and Armstrong=Arlen, mutatis mutandis; but the changes make all the difference in the world. The main change from film to film, aside from questions of tone and structure, is

that the girl isn't after the guy's dough and that she lets him
know she doesn't love him before she agrees to marry him.
Another change is that the other guy can't resist the girl
(in part perhaps because she is honest, unlike the girl in the
first film).    These aren't just small twists; they alter the
mood and direction of the story.

In both movies the men are best of friends, and in
both the one doesn't know there's anything between the other
and the girl.    But it's Zita Johann's performance and character that are most responsible for the special quality of
TIGER SHARK.    Quita is the one who shapes the drama, who
formulates the rules of the game, by trying to make Mike,
the man who saved her life yet a man who repels her physically, happy.    (SYMPHONIE PASTORALE is a variation on
this theme.)    But she weakens as she finds it impossible to
live only for someone else, at least when she finds so tanta-
lizingly close, in the person of Pipes, the possibility of living for herself.    The impossibility of the situation is borne
out by the ending, which summarily disposes of Mike and
simultaneously of the question in the viewer's mind:    how
will they write themselves out of this corner?    But at least
the movie ends before it goes very far wrong.

Hawks and writer Wells Root play fair with the three
protagonists.    There's a good balance between self-interest
and selflessness in all three.    Each one likes the other two
too much.    There's no scheming, sinister deception, or
slinking around.    Pipes tries to avoid hurting Mike by flee-
ing Quita and him.    Chance keeps him in the game--a fishing
accident even puts him in Quita's personal care.    She later
puts it to him:    Okay, so Mike saved you and he saved me
once.    That was then; now is now.    There's no morbid
dwelling on suffering and, on the other hand, no easy release
from prickly situations (until the end).

Hawks and Root play against the potential pathos of
Robinson's unloved, unlovable character.    He isn't laughing-
on-the-outside, crying-on-the-inside; he is happy.    He considers himself such a splendid specimen of manhood that he
holds his ugliness immaterial.    He even jokes about it to
barbers and beauticians:    "Make me look pretty.    I dare you
to."    Hawks avoids melodramatic effects.    Mountains don't
move when a man and a woman (Pipes and Quita) look at
each other across an empty room, as they do when Phillips
Holmes discovers Constance Cummings in The CRIMINAL
CODE.    There's little, if any, music, to kill fragile scenes.

There's even the surprised-lovers scene without the embarrassment of a surprise:  Hawks first indicates Mike's entrance with an extended close shot of the lovers' faces, underlining the inevitability rather than the surprise.  It has to happen; it's only a question, rather unimportant, of when.

The story generally doesn't proceed by violent movements, but by delicate nuances or impressions, subtle, indefinable matters of tones of voice, looks, and gestures-- Pipes' moment of uneasy hesitation when Mike asks him to dance with his bride at their wedding celebration; Pipes and Quita, in separate close shots, on either side of Mike, looking at each other as Mike chatters away happily, unaware that she has just told Pipes she loves him.  Narrative points are muted and given different degrees of emphasis--as Mike and Pipes sing at one bunk, the camera is on two other fishermen, one silently admiring pictures of the other's girl. At their first meeting, Quita keeps calling Mike on his tall stories, but Zita Johann's smile as she says "You're lying about that too" qualifies her directness with warmth and naturalness.  Basically, she's a sad character, but she brightens up believably when Mike is around, before she falls in love with Pipes.  (Her initial amusement at the latter's name is a good way of beginning the relationship, on a light note, with no gloomy omens. )  Neither her sadness nor her happiness seem phony.  Hawks has her bridge the gap between her initial uneasiness at Mike's proposal and her final glad "Yes" with a neutral tone and line ("Got a light?").  It's like the deliberate shifting of a gear.

There is a little ambitious talk about some powerful forces--"them" or "they"--at work behind the little drama, the forces of fate that take Quita's father and Mike's hand, but "them" seems to boil down to a couple of alert sharks and those damn coiled harpoon lines that clumsy fishermen (like Mike, "The best fisherman in the whole Pacific Ocean") keep stepping into and following out to sea.  Both sorts of lines can be safely ignored.

## BARBARY COAST

BARBARY COAST is the kind of tame, docile movie
I associate with Samuel Goldwyn and a clean, well-lighted,
easy-to-follow-if-you-care-to type of moviemaking, for those
who want everything spelled out and immaculate, but not too
exciting. There isn't a moment of real excitement in it,
though there is a little manufactured excitement near the end.
It progresses dully from situation A to B to C, without
pausing or looking around to see if there might not be some
other, better way. It has a perfunctory, set-bound look
which is particularly unsuited to something about gold and
grime in San Francisco around 1850. At the beginning of
each scene, you get the feeling that the actors must have
stood in their places for about ten minutes before the camera
started to roll and were quite relieved to move finally and
to get the scene out of the way. The stars always look as
though they are posing for 8 x 10 glossies, and the lighting
and staging seem calculated only to fix the best pose.

Miriam Hopkins and Edward G. Robinson assume their
roles of the cynical golddigger and the gambling czar, respectively, as if they were simply suits of clothes to be put
on. Miss Hopkins begins by admitting flatly that she's mercenary, but the script doesn't add much about her after that.
Mr. Robinson gets off to an even better start, telling Miss
Hopkins, "I hope you like San Francisco. I own it." But
the script leaves him pretty much alone after that too. Miss
Hopkins decides she would like a share in his San Francisco
and teams up with Robinson as his hostess at the roulette
wheel. When she tells him that the arrangement is strictly
for money and not love, he gets mad.

She goes for a ride and meets prospector Joel McCrea,
who fans a little air into the plot. His prospector is given
to sudden literary and historical allusions, and McCrea makes
them without underlining their fanciness or oddness. He
tells her he wants to make it home past the "harpies" of
San Francisco casinos with all his gold. She doesn't let on

that she's one of the harpies, but he winds up in Robinson's
place and finds it out for himself, losing his gold to her in
the process.  Someone tells Robinson that Miss Hopkins met
another man on her ride, and he gets mad again, not realizing that he has hired the man.  Meanwhile, McCrea cleans
the place out, first literally, then figuratively, the latter with
the girl's help.

Here the plot begins to get sillier and more amusing.
The movie still looks the same--dull, but the characters
start talking faster and more excitedly.  This torrent of
words is, to say the least, without any kind of solid founda-
tion, but part of the amusement lies in the discrepancy between their extravagance and the movie's basic flimsiness.
Miss Hopkins gives up everything to McCrea, via the roulette
wheel, except herself.  Robinson finds out and sets out after
him.  McCrea slips back into Miss Hopkins' room and tries
to convince her that there's something pure and untainted in
everyone, including and especially her.  She protests volubly,
but he overrides her objections and spirits her away by row-
boat, forgetting his money outside her window--the movie's
idea of a romantic touch.

Robinson follows them with his men in another row-
boat, through the fog.  At first it appears that he will kill
one or both of them (three possible tragic endings right
there), but she promises Robinson that if he lets McCrea go,
she'll stay with him and try to love him (another possible
tragic ending).  As Robinson and Miss Hopkins walk away
after seeing McCrea safely onto a ship, however, Robinson
has a change of heart and tells her to go back to McCrea.
And none too soon for his redemption:  a vigilante party
rushes up and drags him away, apparently to hang him (the
only possible tragic ending left).

The ending is winning by virtue of its very arbitrariness and contrivance.  All of a sudden everyone becomes
just too noble and self-sacrificing and finds it in his (or her)
power to change everyone else's life.  All concerned get a
chance to roll the dice of Fate and give the story at least
one false ending.  The actual ending simply depends on who
gets the last roll.  The difference between the rest of the
movie and its final scenes is that the writers stuck to a few
tired clichés for most of the film's length and then threw in
every one they could think of for the ending.  The overcrowd-
ing is amusing.

## COME AND GET IT

Howard Hawks, William Wyler, and Richard Rosson
all worked on COME AND GET IT (1936), but it's a Classics
Illustrated Samuel Goldwyn film as surely as BARBARY
COAST, which Hawks directed for Goldwyn the year before.
Even poor Edna Ferber seems left behind in the dull, unre-
lieved progression of the plot, such as it is, even if it is
partly hers. (I refuse to read the book just to determine
the extent of her responsibility.) The movie has the Goldwyn
gloss and hollowness. The plot points all plug in mechanically, as if the movie were a switchboard--you just wish
they'd get the wires crossed once or twice. Even on its
own plot-oriented grounds the film is a failure: it's less
one, coordinated plot than seven characters with seven little,
occasionally intersecting plots of their own. It doesn't have
the sense of continuity that an epic needs, from scene to
scene and from character to character. It's not even what
you could call "big," as Hawks' later epics, RED RIVER
and LAND OF THE PHARAOHS, most emphatically are. How
can it be if the parts don't add up? The plot points are all
there--and that's all there is--but they don't make much overall sense. They seem to be lifted randomly from different
plots.

Edward Arnold's lumber king's pursuit of Frances
Farmer is appealingly perverse, if a trifle monotonous--she's
the daughter of the woman who loved him and whom he re-
jected for money and position. But, emotionally and dramatically, it has next to nothing to do with her own mercenary
exploitation of his attraction to her. Arnold's son Joel
McCrea's love for Miss Farmer seems an arbitrary afterthought that enables the movie to end happily. The Farmer-
McCrea love match serves primarily as a formal correction
of Arnold's loveless marriage--dramatically it's only vaguely
related to Arnold's unseemly lust for her (pure, reasonable
love vs. an impure, unreasonable love). And Arnold's daughter's (Andrea Leeds') marrying for love rather than money
is simply redundant. Walter Brennan's Swede is there just

to patch the various stories together.  His kindness in marrying the betrayed mother is a narrative non sequitur.  Perhaps the story got confused in the transition from book to
film.

Miss Farmer's mercenariness is at first surprising;
one would expect her to be the reverse of her gambling-hall
mother (also played by Miss Farmer), that is, a sweet young
thing finally soured.  But the plot quickly assimilates the
accidental element of surprise, and she instead reenacts her
mother's discovery of love and romance--from sour to sweet
again.  (But McCrea doesn't betray her, as Arnold betrayed
the mother.)  Her scheming isn't even revenge for what
Arnold did to her mother--she apparently doesn't know anything about the relationship.  It's just a flavorless, unreso-
nant story element.  Near the end the script tacitly acknowl-
edges its inability to resolve the patchwork plot:  Arnold
tries to goad son McCrea into a fight when he, Arnold, finds
him in an embrace with Miss Farmer.  But the scene plays
with an odd dullness, as if the director (evidently Wyler)
were oblivious of its tinge of craziness.  With the help of
Miss Farmer, who calls him an "old man," and of his wife,
who tells him he "can't have everything," Arnold achieves a
sudden self-realization that's supposed to serve as a denoue-
ment, but it's very unsatisfying because it just sweeps away
most of the rubbishy plot.

The story is generally predictable, right down to the
daughter's singing of "Aura Lee" for Arnold--the mother
sang it for him too.  Only here does the girl inspire in
Arnold guilt for her mother, as well as lust for her own
person, when the intermingling of the two themes might have
been the most interesting narrative approach.  The ends of
scenes are implicit in the beginnings.  When Miss Farmer
purposefully delays her arrival at her father's house, to
make Arnold's anticipation keener, and Arnold starts to go
out for her, we know they'll meet at the door.  When McCrea
goes to Miss Farmer to break up her relationship with his
father, we know they'll further their own relationship.  They
do it, however, through the charming metaphor of getting
stuck together pulling taffy.

The best sequence--in fact just about the only good
sequence, though a wild saloon mélée with trays is also
fun--is the logging montage, credited to Rosson.  Robin
Wood, however, finds it "clearly Hawks," which may be true
since it resembles the documentary tuna footage in TIGER

SHARK. But Rosson also worked on that film, so maybe both sequences are his. (Many and delightful are the problems of auteurship!) The mountains and avalanches of logs are far more impressive than the lumbering story itself.

Brennan got the Oscar, but the best performance is Miss Farmer's, uneven as it is. [1] Even when she's overdoing the tough-broad bit, as the mother, at the beginning, she's striking. When she drops it, she's almost heartbreaking. And I think she would be even if I didn't know that her own story (Hawks: "And then she fell in love with a guy [Clifford Odets] who ran away from her") paralleled her character's. Her unexpectedly deep, no-nonsense voice undercuts her pert, glossy look and complements the life in her eyes. As the daughter, she pitches her voice a little higher and is consequently duller; however, as in EXCLUSIVE (1937), in which she makes her plot-bound character a fairly complex combination of independence, acquisitiveness, frustration, sweetness, and brains, she's a live spot in a dead movie.

Arnold is badly miscast as a semi-human, as a misguided hero rather than an iron-willed villain, which is what he was best as. He unintentionally undercuts his own character's jolliness and exuberance, which is always threatening to turn into a simple, more believable sneer. He also gets the most unfortunate line: "What's she doing in a place like this?" and a dumb smart answer to Miss Farmer's "You think that kind of money grows on trees?": "Mine did."

Brennan is just too cute as the Swede. The crude sentimentality of his role probably got him his Oscar. McCrea, the bright spot in BARBARY COAST, is wasted here.

### Note

1.  "I never devoted greater effort to any motion picture than COME AND GET IT.... Howard Hawks was one of the finest and most sensitive directors in the business, and there was nothing routine or cut-and-dried in his approach. He gave every scene a minute examination, both psychological and visual, and under his direction I was secure and full of anticipation."--Frances Farmer, Will There Really Be a Morning?

# HATARI!

HATARI! is a bad dream for anyone who likes Howard Hawks. Robin Wood understates the problem when he says that "it isn't the film one would send anyone to to convince him of Hawks's greatness...." Auteurist Stuart Byron, never one to be outdone by Wood in making dangerous claims, has declared that, "Even John Simon, forced to see HATARI! ten times, would understand its greatness." I would not wish HATARI! on anyone even twice, and if Simon were forced to see it ten times, he might even take back his charitable classification of Hawks as a "competent technician." HATARI! is in fact the first film one would choose in making a case against Hawks: it looks and sounds at times like a typical Hawks film, it was obviously a major production, and, except for the animal-catching sequences, it is a hack job.

It's a clumsy, empty movie, indifferently, and in some cases badly, acted. Both Hawks and star John Wayne just go through the motions of making a movie; the animal footage is obviously all that Hawks was interested in. The actors and story were just the commercial wrapping. Wood does his damnedest to find meaning in the juxtaposition of animals and actors, then does his usual about-face, concluding: "All of which explains why HATARI! is such a pleasing and enjoyable film," when it's clear that he wasn't even attempting any such explanation. Actually, Pauline Kael's "a terrible bore" is closer to the truth and a sight more succinct, though the animal stuff isn't boring.

What makes HATARI! so disconcerting is that it cheapens and trivializes what is usually of prime importance to Hawks--the interrelationships of the actors. The lines and situations one finds in Hawks' best movies are here too, but they weren't worked out with the actors. It's as if just any mediocre action movie had been (poorly) dubbed into Hawksian language. You can almost see other actors in earlier Hawks movies saying and doing the same things better while you're watching these performers. They don't talk

113

like actors in a Hawks film so much as like people who have
seen too many of his films.  It isn't enough for Hawks' actors to look as if they're having a good time together, as
they appear to be here; Hawks and his writers have to make
some narrative sense of their camaraderie.  Otherwise, all
you get is a vague impression of "an informal party, of
long duration, " in Wood's phrasing.  (He adds, hopefully,
"at which one is never bored..., " but the party drags on
for over two and a half hours.)  Not far into the "story, "
you begin to become impatient with the actors and just wish
they would shut up and go out and hunt some more wilde-
beests.  Hawks should have stuck to the scoreboard of game
and used that as the script.  As it is the film looks more
like an expensive home movie than a documentary or an
action film.

Wood and other critics have noted that it's seeing
the actors and the animals in the same shot that creates a
lot of the excitement of the hunting expeditions.  This excitement, however, doesn't have much to do with the story, or
with the characters the actors are playing.  The actors in
the story and the actors on the hunt just happen to be the
same ones, but they might as well not be.  For the hunting
scenes, John Wayne doesn't have to act; he simply has to
be there.  Unfortunately, he's just there throughout the movie.  The script is so flimsy that it doesn't give him any
characterization to work at, so it isn't surprising that he
doesn't know what to do with the lines it does give him.
("Give us a hand with the wildebeest" is one, and it's hard
to imagine what anyone could have done with it.)

Actors' actions and lines are over-emphasized, and
unimportant incidents are dragged out.  Red Buttons, who
obviously thinks he's the life of this party, gives the worst
performance.  He's like someone trying to amuse his friends
with his antics, and Hawks was apparently too kind to tell
him that he just wasn't amusing.  Elsa Martinelli begins the
movie as though she's merely going to be another woman
tagging along behind the men, but she evidently worked so
well with the animals that she was allowed to take over the
movie.  In lieu of credible actor-actor relationships, actor-
animal relationships are most welcome.  The international
cast mixes about as well as the names of their characters:
Dallas, Chips, Pockets, Brandy, Indian, Sean, and Kurt.
Michèle Girardon as name number four is striking as what
Hawks called the "big, lusty kid ... who kind of lumbered
around, " but as one side of a quadrangle, she has the most

artificial role of all.   (Buttons, Hardy Kruger, and Gérard
Blain are the other three sides.)   At its very worst, the
dull, mechanical script has her impersonally tend the badly
injured Kruger and Blain after their jeep overturns, then
solicitously care for Buttons after he takes a little fall off
a fence.   The humor of such irony never leaves the script.

Henry Mancini's music, too playful during the playful
animal sequences, gives the hunt scenes an added charge.
Obvious back projection interferes with the sweep of their
movement, and the plot never seems more artificial than
when it interrupts a hunt; but when a charging rhino almost
gores a camera strapped to the side of a truck or a lashed-
down rhino stirs as Wayne steps past him, you can at least
understand why Hawks wanted to undertake the project.

# PART IV

# OTHER GENRES

The BIG SLEEP


## Part One, or Plot, Wit, Feeling, and Violence

The plot of a good mystery movie (like The THIN
MAN or AFTER THE THIN MAN) can be incidental to the
fun, but there's so much plot and so much verbal rehashing
of it in The BIG SLEEP that to dismiss it is to just about
dismiss the movie (which is, in effect, what critics like
Pauline Kael and Robin Wood do).  If you're only concerned
with who killed whom or, rather, if you think the movie is
concerned only with who killed whom, the script's preoccupa-
tion with names and places and motivations may seem simply
entertainingly silly.  But the atmosphere of menace and
dread in The BIG SLEEP is more than a question of fog,
rain, and Max Steiner's enthralling score.  It originates in
the plot and in the dialogue that deals with the plot.  It
derives from our not knowing who the murderers are, who's
allied with whom, who's dangerous, friendly, or just neutral,
or why particular people are in a particular place at a particular time.  It's the whodunit carried to its logical extreme
--every name and every situation is a mystery, and the idea
is not to solve each mystery as it comes along but to build
one upon the other into a tangle of suspicion and uncertainty.
The script never resolves itself into a plain search for a
murderer.  There are always several pieces missing from
the puzzle, even after the movie's over.  These loose ends
are mostly an accident of transition from book to film.  Certain matters explicit in the novel could only be hinted at in
the film.

Every change of setting, every re-grouping of characters and re-shuffling of names, produces a new configura-
tion of the plot of The BIG SLEEP.  Most movie mysteries
are episodic, a series of varyingly amusing or illuminating
encounters between the detective and the suspects and leads,
with little to connect them but the question, whodunit?  In
The BIG SLEEP, the scenes between Marlowe and Mars and
Canino and Joe Brody don't simplify the mystery; they

complicate and enlarge it (or, in some cases, over-compli-
cate it).  The focus widens rather than narrows.  New people (Canino, Jones, Mrs. Mars) are introduced, and old
faces (Vivian, Mars, Canino) and names (Regan, Taylor,
Geiger) re-introduced in new combinations.  The movie di-
vides into halves, into two separate but interrelated mysteries.
The first half is concerned with Geiger and Brody; the second
with Mars and Regan.

       You don't always have to know exactly what's going
on to get this effect of shifting alliances.  The script in fact
attempts ingeniously to override objections of obscurity and
over-complexity by absorbing accidental confusion of the plot
into intentional mystification.  It fails occasionally and it's
underhanded, but clever.  In the movie's context of sudden
death, guns, shiny-sinister black cars, mist, and the omi-
nously swelling background music, the shadowy relationships
--the alliances and re-alliances--take on an air of menace
and terror. [1]  Marlowe is the only stable element until Vivian throws in her lot with him near the end.  The others are
question marks, often little more than names to be juggled
in the dialogue as elements of the mystery, and their names
are a large part of the surface of the film:  Sian Regan,
Carmen, Geiger, Joe Brody, Eddie Mars, Canino, Owen
Taylor, Agnes, Carol Lundgren.  The dizzyingly fast pace
of action and dialogue allows Hawks to retain most of the
convolutions of the book's plot, but the names fly by so
quickly at times that the effect of the lightning speed begins
to verge on parody, and the movie does have a tendency to
reduce its secondary characters to names.

       But it's the pace which makes the movie superior to
the book, which, good as it is, hasn't the cohesiveness or
beauty of design of Chandler's best novels, like Farewell,
My Lovely or The Lady in the Lake.  The book sprawls and
sometimes seems to have no design at all.  It's held together
only by the character of Marlowe and by the wit of the writing.  It takes the long way 'round to arrive at somewhat the
same conclusion as the movie, a conclusion suggested in
chapter 25:  "[Harry Jones' story] had the austere simplicity
of fiction rather than the tangled woof of fact."  The book's
discursiveness blunts the intended effect of bewildering complexity; the movie's incoherence--when complexity lapses into
confusion, and the movie becomes more bewildering than
intended--similarly blunts the effect.

       But the movie's streamlining of the plot actually gives

more point to the Chandler material by not allowing it to
stagnate.   The movie, complicated as it is, always seems to
be going in one direction; the book sometimes seems to be
going in several at once.   Hawks and the writers managed
to accommodate part at least of almost every episode of the
200-page book, except for about 25 pages' worth in the middle and 25 pages' worth near the end, and throw in some
new scenes and dialogue to boot.   Gone is a lot of meticulous
description, pointed but expendable, not necessary for the
overall effect of the movie, and a lot of inessential dialogue. [2]
What's left is almost pure plot, with comic/romantic inter-
ludes, usually no more than moments, with Marlowe and
Vivian.   The way the film moves keeps the viewer on edge,
in suspense.   The book takes time out for explanation and
elaboration.

    The superabundance of plot doesn't allow much time
for diversion--there's much wit and some feeling, but all
on the run.   In fact, the wit and feeling are often in part
generated by the pace.   Many of the best lines are in the
book:  one about Peter Pan, another about Marlowe's business
and the pay.   (The movie adds one when Carmen asks Marlowe if Mars is cuter than he:  "Nobody is.")   They gain
by Bogart's deadpan delivery and by his studied indifference
to the reaction to them.   And they're usually tossed off
effortlessly in the middle of rapid-fire exchanges or over
someone's shoulder.   They're funnier for seeming incidental
to the action.   Only when whole scenes depend on the witti-
cisms does the movie get into trouble, as in an extended,
inconsistent, too-blatant metaphor about horse racing that
sounds as though it's from one of the two-bit imitations of
The BIG SLEEP, like HARPER or MARLOWE. [3]

    The movie's witty physical details are a suitable sub-
stitute for Chandler's evocative descriptive stunners (e. g.,
"She tried to jack the smile back up on her face").   Those
little moments, like Marlowe's encouraging Vivian to scratch
her leg, or her trouble with the doorknob and his disclaimer,
or his swinging his cigarette hand just under a hood's nose,
aren't in the book.   In book and movie, Joe Brody, fishing
for an alibi, tells Marlowe, "I was right here.   Agnes was
with me.   Okay, Agnes?"   Chandler doesn't state her reaction.   In the movie she offers a dry, "Ha!" and disdainfully
jerks her head away.   Chandler's pungent, idiosyncratic descriptions ("I stood watching the roll of wrapped coins dance
in Canino's hand") couldn't be duplicated on film--the roll
of coins is present but it doesn't dance--but Hawks, the

Bogart, Bacall and Bob Steele in The BIG SLEEP.


actors, the cameraman, and the art director give you plenty
to watch.   There's a wealth of atmosphere in the look and
sound of John Ridgely, Bob Steele, Elisha Cook, Jr., Louis
Jean Heydt, and Tom Rafferty as hoods--the movie was almost "made" in the casting.   There's too much to watch,
in fact, what with the dialogue overflowing with names which
you try to attach to faces before the associations fade in
your memory.

        "Wit" isn't exactly the term I would use to describe
one of the movie's recurring motifs.   In the book, Carmen's
obsession with Marlowe, Regan, Taylor, etc., is seen as
aberration, an aberration which leads to murder in one case
and attempted murder in another.   In the movie she seems
merely eccentric, spoiled-cute, and most of the other women
in the movie are replicas of the movie Carmen.   This isn't

Chandler's idea.   It sounds more like one of Mickey Spillane's.
It's someone else's fantasy--Furthman's, Faulkner's, Hawks',
or (Miss) Brackett's.   It cheapens the movie, which otherwise plays fair with its characters.   The hat-check and cigarette girls aren't in the book.   Dorothy Malone's part is
expanded from the book, in which she's "just interested" in
Marlowe.   And the "fresh-faced kid" who drives Marlowe to
Brody's becomes a lady cabbie in the movie!   The unlikeliness of this manifestation is comically redeeming. [4]

Robin Wood claims to have read the Chandler original,
but it's difficult to believe in light of his reference to "Marlowe's slick and crude sensibility" and his assumption that
Vivian was "the killer" in the book.   (In the book it's Carmen who kills Regan. )[5]   Wood has evidently read about
Chandler rather than read him.   Reputations are admittedly
sometimes difficult to pierce.   Even Chandler sometimes
forgot what exactly it was that he had written:

> I ... found [The Big Sleep] both much better and
> much worse than I had expected--or than I had
> remembered.   I have been so belabored with tags
> like tough, hard-boiled, etc., that it was almost a
> shock to discover occasional signs of almost nor-
> mal sensitivity in the writing. [6]

There is, in fact, as much feeling in the book as in the
movie.   It's more Marlowe's world that's "tough" than it is
Marlowe, though I wouldn't characterize him as "soft" either,
as Pauline Kael does.   She, like Wood, seems to have read
about, more than read, Chandler.   She takes Chandler's
word on himself and Marlowe--his description of him as a
knight--and Chandler himself sometimes sentimentalized his
hero in talking about him (and in writing the later novel,
The Long Goodbye, which Kael obviously has read).   Marlowe
simply attempts to soften his world up a bit, to find the
elusive positive in all the negative:  Mrs. Mars ("I never
saw her again"), Harry Jones ("There was something I liked
about him").   He tries to undo damage done to others like
Carmen and Vivian and risks his life in the worst places,
for what he's not that sure.

The movie regains the feeling lost by the shallower
characterization of Marlowe with his attachment to Vivian.
It expands her part to make it a more conventional romantic
mystery.   She's quietly dropped into extra scenes with Marlowe and into the sequence at Joe Brody's, and she takes

over Mrs. Mars' role.   But this isn't just another dumb
movie romance.   The demands of the plot and the slick dialogue keep it light and engaging.   Feeling seeps in, but no
one drowns in it. [7]

        The roles are ideal for Bogart and Bacall.   Bogart
doesn't have to get tough or idealistic and reveal his limited
range, and Bacall, who's mainly a voice in her two Hawks'
films, gets to use its ironically sensuous formality on the
slick Chandler-Faulkner-Furthman-Hawks dialogue.   There's
emotion, but we sense it more than see it expressed.   Their
mutual attraction is the more believable for the lack of in-
sistence on it.   They don't have to go out of their way to
prove they love each other.   It's enough that Bogart says,
"I guess I'm in love with you, " and keeps on driving the
car.   There's no time or need to have a scene by the side
of the road, or for big, soggy close-ups.   There's really
no guessing involved.   It's probably Bogart's best performance, the one film in which he's everything he's supposed to
be.   He and Chandler's dialogue should have gotten together
more often.   They didn't, so this is the Bogart film.

        The most affecting scene is the famous one in which
Marlowe finds that he has just witnessed the murder of
small-time grifter Harry Jones ("Nothing's funny") and that
Jones didn't sell out his girl.   There's nothing mushy about
it--the movie even improves on the book by adding an intro-
ductory scene in which Jones stands by while two thugs give
Marlowe a going-over in an alley, and then explains to Marlowe that common sense dictated he stay out of it.   This
leaves no opening for undue sentiment for Jones, while it
compounds Marlowe's sense of complicity and frustration at
overhearing Jones' death and doing nothing to help.   Elisha
Cook, Jr., who gave the best performance in that other
classic private-eye movie, The MALTESE FALCON, has the
most memorable scene in The BIG SLEEP, as Jones.

        A note on Violence:   somewhere Hawks picked up a
very simple, effective trick for making death-by-gunshot
felt.   (Fritz Lang uses it, too, in MINISTRY OF FEAR. )
Ten thousand characters have been shot in movies, and
probably no more than one per cent of those shootings are
other than vital statistics.   The other guys are just dead,
and you take the script's word for it.   In The BIG SLEEP,
when Lundgren shoots Joe Brody, the nasty hole in the door
says that a bullet went through it; and if it went through
solid wood, it could probably penetrate flesh.   Hawks uses a

table similarly in TO HAVE AND HAVE NOT. And a dotted-
line of bullet holes in Geiger's front door makes you think
that Eddie Mars must have been sawed in half as he stepped
out. It's the perfect solution to the problem of how to sug-
gest the physical effects of violence without dwelling on them.
The loose coins that Canino drops into his hand after slugging
Marlowe--they were the roll before--are also very suggestive.


## Part Two, or The LONG GOODBYE as Answer
## to The BIG SLEEP, and Connections

The passages in Part One on plot constitute, I think,
a Nice Try on my part, but, after seeing The BIG SLEEP
again twice since writing them, I'm less convinced that the
plot is that important, one way or the other. I may have
been overreacting against those who dismiss it outright. Although the plot elements never really add up, however, the
movie does have unbeatable mystery elements: the ceremo-
niously laid out corpse (Geiger), the two cars driven away
(by Owen Taylor and Joe Brody, respectively?) from Geiger's
after the shooting, the car dredged out of the bay with a
body (Taylor) in it, the drugged girl (Carmen), the tail on
Marlowe (Jones), the concealed camera, the code book, the
car-drop. My point is that they don't have to add up, though
I now think so for somewhat different reasons.

Comparison with the Robert Altman-Leigh Brackett
The LONG GOODBYE is helpful. This film of an inferior
and untypical Chandler-Marlowe novel (as William S. Pechter
has noted) is evidently intended as a sort of anti-nostalgic
corrective for current nostalgia for the real and reel past.
The use of "Hooray for Hollywood" to frame the film at least
appears to be ironic. What blurs the film's intentions is its
uncanny resemblance to typical movie mysteries. Pauline
Kael tries to put some distance between it and them, at her
most desperate saying that you can't take "venerable pulp
author" Brackett's credit literally because the dialogue was
obviously improvised. But the shock device whereby the detective's friend turns out to be the murderer goes back at
least to SLIGHTLY HONORABLE (1940) and has also been
used in The CRIME AGAINST JOE (1956) and HARPER (1966).
Kael thinks the logic of this resolution of the friendship between Marlowe and Terry Lennox "is probably too brutally
sound for Bogart-lovers to stomach," but it's just a hoary
old bit of push-button cynicism. And the use of the device
is not more, but less, organic this time. The attempt to

base the whole movie on this irony is a total fizzle because
the movie assumes rather than establishes the Marlowe-Len-
nox friendship.  The person Marlowe is so sappily trying to
help simply seems to be a different person from the one
who, at the end, admits killing his wife and duping Marlowe.
There's no connection and hence no shock.

The movie's stock weirdos--Henry Gibson's petulant
sanitarium head, Mark Rydell's sadistic villain, Sterling
Hayden's has-been writer--aren't answers to the freaks who
populate Hollywood thrillers; they are the freaks.  As for
Elliott Gould's Marlowe, he doesn't seem to me to be an
imitation of Bogart or an answer to Bogart so much as a
muffed comment on Bogart.  I don't think it's possible to
define his Marlowe as a "fool," as a "character seen quite
affectionately" (as Pechter sees him), as a "wryly forlorn
knight" (as Kael sees him), or as anything; the movie is too
badly confused as to what it and its protagonist are about.
The script never decides if he's a slightly seedy hero, an
avenging hero, a sap, or a third-rate night-club comic.

The movie has real problems.  One difference between
The LONG GOODBYE and The BIG SLEEP is that each scene
in the latter makes its own sense even if the plot doesn't.
Most scenes in The LONG GOODBYE don't make sense since
Altman and Brackett don't know what attitude to take toward
their characters, and you can't have a scene without characters.  They apparently take Hayden's writer more seriously than they take Marlowe.  The scenes between Hayden and
Nina van Pallandt are dead serious, but they're the worst-
written ones in the movie, sounding at times like an unintentional send-up of soap opera.  In one of those "crowning
visual effects" (which are "like ribbons tying up the whole
history of movies") that Miss Kael finds teeming in Altman's
movies, Gould's reflection in a big glass window is dwarfed
by the figures of Hayden and van Pallandt behind it.  Is this
supposed to symbolize Marlowe's irrelevance to the "real"
world?  Or is it just a "nice shot"?  It's better as a pretty
shot than as symbolism since Hayden and van Pallandt are
the last people in the movie qualified to represent cold, hard
reality.  (Well, maybe the comic hoods and the impressionist-
guard are the last.)  The characters are functioning at different, unsynchronized distances from writer, director, and
thus audience.

I now think that it's the foreground relationships between the characters more than the background suspense that

make The BIG SLEEP the best private-eye movie (with all
due apologies to MALTESE FALCON, SAINT IN NEW YORK,
and MR. DYNAMITE).  There aren't any relationships in
The LONG GOODBYE because there aren't any characters.
(I shouldn't be absolute:  Marlowe relates fairly believably
to his cat and to the writer's dog. )  We not only have to
take Marlowe's friendship with Lennox on faith; we have to
take Marlowe on faith.  Hawks defines his characters by
their immediate, physical relationships, not by vague resemblances to or differences from characters in other movies.
Bogart's Marlowe is not just a detective interrogating an odd
assortment of "characters. "  He makes definite, moral-per-
sonal contact with each person.  The BIG SLEEP has an
actor-to-actor believability, even memorability, in the connections it makes between its characters.  It doesn't pretend
to present whole persons (as The LONG GOODBYE does), just
their surfaces, which may be deceptive or accurate, all there
is to them or just a fraction of themselves.  The connections
it makes are precise, idiosyncratic but not incredible, and
fresh.  Marlowe creates a strong rapport, tension, or alternating rapport/tension (as with Vivian) with everyone he
meets.

     The connections are usually made with words, but also
with actions, movements, and looks.  Marlowe and Mars
challenge each other, talking fast and cautiously.  Canino's
words practically jump on Jones', daring him to give wrong
answers.  His insolent, joking tone is ironically menacing.
Jones' directness undercuts Marlowe's glibness; after Jones'
death, Marlowe makes brief, un-underlined references to
him in his recappings of recent events--"He was a nice little guy.  I liked him"--and goes right on recapping.  Marlowe's open contemptuousness fails to pierce Agnes' hard,
businesslike manner, and that failure is an implicit comment
on her.  His "Your kind always does" just hangs in the air
unchallenged after he leaves her in her car.  Marlowe keeps
tripping up Joe Brody or getting him to trip himself up as
he spins out stories and alibis.  Marlowe's aggressive skep-
ticism aggravates Brody's jittery, forced amiability.  Marlowe will pause for a moment to kiss Vivian, then add summarily, 'Now that's settled, " and get back to business.

     There's a lot of talk in the movie, but it's made by
very particularized characters.  The movie doesn't die when
these people are talking.  The varied rhythms of delivery,
the tone, the volume, the words themselves keep it alive even
through name-dropping speeches like Marlowe's "You see the

The BIG SLEEP:  Bogart, Bacall, Louis Jean Heydt and
Sonia Darren.


dead man was Owen Taylor, Sternwood's chauffeur.  He went
up to Geiger's place 'cause he was sweet on Carmen.  He
didn't like the kind of games Geiger was playing. "  The movie exists on small, vivid connections between its people, its
actors, like Marlowe and Lundgren, Marlowe and Ohls, Joe
and Agnes.  These connections add up, not quite to a vision
of the world, but to something like a pungent impression of
it.


Part Three, or The Further Adventures of The BIG SLEEP

     How many times do you have to see a film to really
see it?  I've seen The BIG SLEEP now at least seven times
and I thought I knew its scenes by heart.  So it was more
than a gentle surprise for me when, in the middle of my
most recent viewing, I suddenly realized I was watching a
scene that was new to me.  I thought at first that I was
dreaming or that this was just an unimportant scene I didn't

happen to remember.   However, it went on and on and finally changed to another scene I didn't recall ever seeing before.
Then it went back to The BIG SLEEP.   The Little Sleep (as
I am going to call it) begins just after Lundgren's arrest and
ends just before Marlowe, in his office, calls Eddie Mars.
It is two scenes long and it replaces at least two, discontin-
uous scenes in the authorized version:   the one with Marlowe
and Vivian in the cafe (which includes the horse race dialogue) and the one in which Carmen visits Marlowe's office.
The cafe scene belongs where it is; the one with Carmen
occurs later in the regular version.   The Little Sleep covers
some of the same story ground that the cafe scene does.   In
the first scene--which originates in the book--Ohls informs
the D. A. and Cronjager of the homicide squad that Marlowe
has caught a killer (Lundgren) and that there are a couple of
other dead bodies (Geiger and Taylor) in the vicinity, and
rubs in the fact that Cronjager should have known all this
already.   In the second scene, in a hallway, Marlowe and
Ohls seem to agree that the Geiger case is closed.

No explanation was attached to the (16mm) print for
this curious phenomenon.

## Notes

1.   "There is a fantastic quality about all this excitement due
     to the apparent lack of integration between crimes, the
     sudden appearances of bizarre underworld figures and
     their more sudden startling disappearances into the
     murky environment. "--Manny Farber, The New Re-
     public (Sept. 23, 1946), 351.

2.   Excised also are most references to and sections of the
     story dealing with the nude photo of Carmen and
     Geiger's porno-book rental business.   These deletions
     are responsible, as much as the transformation of
     Vivian from minor character into costar, for the un-
     resolved confusion of the movie.   (Before I read the
     book, I thought the photo was, as blackmail material,
     valuable only as evidence of Carmen's presence at the
     scene of a murder. )   Gone too are scenes between
     Marlowe and:   the D. A. , Captain Gregory of the Miss-
     ing Persons Bureau, Carmen, and Vivian.

3.   RED RIVER is cleverer with a similar sexual metaphor.
     After they first meet, John Ireland tells Montgomery

Clift, "Only two things better than a good gun--a good Swiss watch and a woman.... Ever had a good Swiss watch?"

4.  Evidently it's not that unlikely, at least in movies--UP IN MABEL'S ROOM (1944) also has a female cab driver.

5.  Wood praises Hawks' "indifference to plot," but the in-difference seems more like Wood's.

6.  Dorothy Gardiner and Kathrine Sorley Walker, eds., Raymond Chandler Speaking (Boston, 1962), p. 212.

7.  Except Wood, who claims that the book "offers no equiva-lent for the tenderness, so simply expressed, between Bogart and the girl in the bookshop..." (italics mine).

SCARFACE

## Scarface

Few traces of Armitage Trail's book, fortunately, remain in the movie SCARFACE. Only some of the names are the same. The book at times pretends to be a valuable social document: given his sordid slum environment, Tony Camonte (né Guarino) had to become either a gangster or a crooked cop; gangs pay off Chicago cops, judges, and the D. A. But the writing is so poor that considerations of truth or factuality are irrelevant. The book is a primer on how not to write a book. Descriptions of physical characteristics are primitive: eyes are always glittering or blazing; mouths are cruel or ugly; teeth are always gritted; and faces are always turning white, green, or purple. Thumbnail descriptions of characters ("Schemer Bruno, wily leader of the strong North Side gang") are repeated again and again, as if the reader couldn't be trusted to remember anything from one page to the next. Trail's book is generally just bad, but its low points are something else again, and are worth recording:

> Did he know Vyvyan Lovejoy? Did Romeo know Juliet?

> It wasn't a nice thought to know that your own brother had sworn publicly to hunt you to the death. God!

> Thus another decent home spawned another gangster, as inevitably as an oyster creates a pearl.

> Knowing the tremendous value of a surprise attack, Tony decided to pull one.

> His black eyes, now blazing with anger, were shifty and set far too close together.

... he knew that the remains of the Spingola gang
were actively and murderously on his trail.   It was
a nerve-wracking week.

Facing a pistol is one thing; facing red hot iron
against one's bare flesh and other unknown tortures
is another.


## SCARFACE

"Scarface" Tony Camonte (Paul Muni) is the first of
Hawks' great, unstoppable monsters, forerunner of Oscar
Jaffe (John Barrymore, TWENTIETH CENTURY), Dizzy
Davis (James Cagney, CEILING ZERO), and Walter Burns
(Cary Grant, HIS GIRL FRIDAY).   (Ben Hecht, incidentally
or not, had a hand in all but CEILING ZERO. )   SCARFACE
is the best of the lot, in part because Tony Camonte doesn't
have to drag a "play" along with him.   He doesn't have anyone to answer to or listen to (until the end).   He's on his
own and he's allowed to burn himself out.   Tyrants like Tony
and Walter Burns don't fit into ordinary conceptions of the
well-made play or scenario since they're both hero and villain.   There's no "story," just an accelerating series of
events touched off by the central character.   There are no
points of social or moral reference (as is the case with
TWENTIETH CENTURY and HIS GIRL FRIDAY) or there
are implicit points which are made explicit by the end (as is
the case with SCARFACE--the points in CEILING ZERO
should have been implicit).

Arthur Penn's 1958 Western about Billy the Kid, The
LEFT-HANDED GUN, is almost a remake of SCARFACE
(1932). [1]   Tony Camonte and Paul Newman's Billy are both
aggressive, brutish, childlike--and likable when not violent.
They act without thinking, without considering the possible
consequences of their actions.   As all that Tony knows is
what he wants, so Billy cries defiantly, "I do what I want!"
Each has slow-witted companions--Tony, the comically inef-
ficient Angelo (Vince Barnett); Billy, Tom (James Best) and
Charlie (James Congdon)--who echo and qualify them.   Hawks'
and Penn's films are not so much about the protagonists'
acquiring moral awareness as about their acquiring a feeble
sense of their lack of awareness.   But this half-knowledge
is enough to kill them.   And in each case it's the rejection
by the woman he loves that finally brings the hero-villain
face to face with his isolation:   in The LEFT-HANDED GUN,

SCARFACE:  Edwin Maxwell (seated), Paul Muni and George Raft.

Saval's wife Celsa (Lita Milan) rejects Billy when he approaches her before Saval; in SCARFACE, Tony's sister Cesca (Ann Dvorak) turns on him when he kills Guino Rinaldo (George Raft), his bodyguard and her husband.

As Cesca dies, Tony realizes, "I've got nobody." At the end of The LEFT-HANDED GUN, Billy sums up his life, "I lost Tom ... I lost Charlie ... can't read ... got myself all killed." (Billy earlier pretended that he could read. Tony goes to a play, "Rain," and leaves Angelo behind to find out how it ends when he has to go murder someone. Art is as baffling as life to Tony and Billy.) The LEFT-HANDED GUN focuses on the consequences of the hero's actions. SCARFACE focuses on the actions themselves. The dead bodies of Billy's friends keep coming back to haunt and accuse him. The excitement of SCARFACE, the best

gangster movie before Penn's BONNIE AND CLYDE, is that
Tony seems to be getting away scot-free with murder until
the very end.

Chicago is a combination playground-shooting gallery
for Tony Camonte. Soon after the film begins you get the
message that this is going to be a gangster film about gangsters, rather than a gangster film about social outcasts,
products of bad environments, or bad boys who still love
their mothers or perform good deeds. The gangsters get
their way here, in a frightening world that's always night.
All of the action seems to take place in a subterranean
nightmare world where there's only enough light to see faces
and movements. Like vampires, these gangsters come to
life only at night; they're always in shadow.

Tony becomes king of this underworld realm because
the idea of his own death or the death of someone who means
something to him never occurs to him. The movie is so
good that you hope he never gets the idea. In this city of
gangsters and molls, Tony's actions aren't circumscribed by
social convention or etiquette. Oscar Jaffe, Dizzy Davis,
and even Walter Burns are tainted by civilization; Tony can
do anything he wants. And the Hecht-Miller-Mahin-Burnett
script is quite imaginative when it comes to thinking up
things for him to want to do. Muni's Tony is a sort of
good-natured slob whose apelike amble and stunted speech
are interrupted by abrupt fits of violence. [2]

Tony's alarming directness is sketched in casual,
sometimes almost comic terms. When he sees his sister
dancing with some other guy, he immediately pushes his way
across the crowded dance floor to knock him down and drag
her out of the club. (His army of bodyguards, typically,
instantly swarms around him as he gets up; the impression
given of a vast body moving as one is a contrast to Tony's
isolation at the end.) Campaigning for customers for Johnny Lovo's booze, Tony enters a saloon, steps behind the
bar, twists the owner's arm behind his back, and propels
him into the back-room office, all in one, long, continuous
movement. When Tony wants to look at a new weapon, the
Tommy gun, while he and his men are under siege by enemy
forces in a cafe, he has Guino pick off one gunman in a passing car and run out and bring back a sample. The whizzing
bullets and breaking glass are just comic counterpoint to
this demonstration of Tony's single-mindedness. To signify
a change of leadership Tony throws a spittoon through the

office window bearing the name of the gang czar he just
killed.    Later, after his new boss, Lovo (Osgood Perkins),
tries to have him eliminated--Tony keeps stirring up the
North Side gang--Tony, bare-fisted, smashes the window to
Lovo's office bearing the words "John Lovo. "

The script is in perfect sync with this power-mad
homicidal maniac.    It doesn't take off on its own--it goes
where he goes.    When Tony fails to kill one gangster, Mee-
han, who winds up in a hospital, the script detours with
Tony to the hospital to finish the job.    This breathtaking
sequence is over in maybe less than a minute--the error of
fate which let someone in Tony's way live is promptly recti-
fied.    Since the script, daringly, gives you no one to care
about except Tony (and perhaps Angelo), it has to get its
moral-physical shock effects through the audacity of Tony's
acts rather than their consequences for others.    Everyone
else is either an obstacle or an accomplice.    His sister is
sex-crazy the way he's violence-crazy, only she isn't as
lovable.    (And even he isn't as likable an illiterate brute as
Victor McLaglen in A GIRL IN EVERY PORT.    No one is. )
He has an open field until he finds out, too late, that he
can't do without his sister.

Hawks sometimes takes longer than he needs to on a
scene, and there are some awkwardnesses in the staging of
this generally excitingly staged film; and the dialogue occasionally veers off from the wittily idiosyncratic (girl, when
duty calls Guino away: "This is worse than being in love
with a grasshopper") into the mundane (Tony's poor mother:
"Once I have a son, I have a daughter").    The conception of
the central figure, however, is solid, and Hawks and Muni
take it all the way to its logical end in madness and hysteria.
The exhilaration of making a whole wall-rack of pool cues
dance with a burst of Tommy gun fire becomes the claustrophobic horror, at the end, of a roomful of tear gas.    In an
imaginary city where there are no rules or laws, Tony
Camonte makes his own rules, but a joker in the script, his
sister ("All I want is the same as you"), kills him, and
without breaking his rules.    Their incipient incestuous relationship is briefly consummated, in violence, at the end,
when Cesca, deliriously happy, joins him in defending his
steel-shuttered barricade against a police siege, in one of the
screen's most perversely romantic scenes.    But their double
strength vanishes when a stray bullet hits her.    (If only he
had been a bit quicker closing those shutters. )    To take
strength in another is in a sense to admit weakness in oneself,

Ann Dvorak and Paul Muni at the end of SCARFACE.


and Tony panics as Cesca dies.    She sees his fear and mut-
ters something about Guino's not being afraid.    Tony is
proven human after all, but in a bizarre, circuitous manner,
on his own terms, with no cheating by the script, no moralizing, no compromising.

        Karen Morley as Poppy and Ann Dvorak as Cesca are
two of Hawks' more memorable women.    You couldn't forget
them if you tried.    They're what you might expect to find
growing in a place that never sees sunlight.    Miss Morley
has a double-edged role as Tony's girl friend, making him
at once laughable and more likable, as she feeds him
straight lines and he responds with unwitting gag lines:    Poppy (as she surveys his apartment):    "Kinda gaudy, isn't it?"

Tony: "Ain't it, though?" She's apparently intrigued by his
combination of brute strength and little-boy naiveté; she
can admire him and patronize him at the same time. At
the beginning he's Lovo's right-hand man and she's Lovo's
mistress. When they first meet in Lovo's apartment, he's
nothing to her and she lets him know it, with an ill-conceal-
ed disregard--"Unh huh," is her response to his introduction
of himself--that's supposed to be withering. But he isn't
far enough along on the evolutionary scale to know that he
should wither or get mad. It's obviously the beginning of a
beautiful relationship. It reaches a peak which prefigures
the consummation of Tony's relationship with Cesca at the
end--and echoes Tony's crazy grin as he Tommy guns the
pool cues--when Tony announces that he has killed Lovo,
and she's <u>delighted</u>. (This moment also prefigures the scene
in Ford's The SEARCHERS when the girl tries to stop the
fight over her, then gives up and furtively exults in it.)
The women's casual acceptance of the violence around them
becomes a gleeful embrace of it. Tony, Poppy, and Cesca
were meant for each other.

Vince Barnett's Angelo is a sort of understudy to Tony
Camonte--dumb, violent, single-minded, but unambitious; a re-
verse-Keaton who can't cope with such elementary objects as
a phone or a gun; a sort of inept Scarface, Jr. He's Tony's
secretary, but he doesn't know how to answer a phone or to
take down somebody's name. When he gets mad at the person at the other end of the line, he pulls out a gun and
threatens to shoot the receiver. (His incidentally violent
directness prefigures the purposefully violent directness of
Lee Marvin's blasting of the intercom in POINT BLANK.)
He can't keep even one thing clearly in his mind so he's
entirely helpless when pressed by three concerns: when the
parade of gangsters opens up on Tony and his men in the
cafe, Angelo is on the phone, and he stays on it through the
entire battle, only vaguely aware of a lot of noise and of
scalding water spouting out over him through a bullet-punc-
tured coffee urn.

It's not necessarily that his loyalty to Tony knows no
bounds. He's such a simple creature that he subsists exclusively on loyalty. Even when he's dying, he answers the
phone. Shot by the police, he staggers into Tony's stronghold behind him, shuts the steel door, and totters over to
the ringing phone to answer it. Tony doesn't even notice his
death because he's dying too, a little more slowly, and he's
not much more observant than Angelo.

It isn't difficult to see why censors demanded an apology for the movie at the beginning of it and within the film itself (in the form of policemen and newspapermen condemning all this lawlessness).  It's a potentially dangerous movie because it operates in a self-contained world and lets in no purifying air from the outside.  Fortunately, the pompous official admonitions are like intermissions unrelated to the movie.  They actually make it more exciting by making it seem verboten.  (The fact that the Howard Hughes interests prohibit public screenings of it, and thus necessitate private, clandestine viewing, also contributes to its allure.)

The esthetic affectations around the edges of the film-- the Cook's Tour "The World is Yours" sign that the camera pans up to from Tony's body at the end and the proliferation of crosses as signs of death, which as much as say, "Artist at work"--are more intrusive than the irrelevant, added scenes, civilizing at least if not actually disruptive.  Along about the time a woman turns and reveals gown straps that form an "x," you begin to think it's a game--spot the "x"'s--rather than a movie.  The "x" motif almost wrecks the scene in which Tony discovers Guino with his sister.  There's an "x" on the door (for what non-symbolic reason I have no idea); Guino opens it, and, like magic, there's another one behind him in the light and shadow of the background.  Robin Wood, in what's otherwise a fairly commendable job on SCARFACE, attempts to find a meaning and an "emotional charge" in the crosses to qualify the ferocity of the film's violence.  He can't quite accept that the ferocity is the film, and that the crosses were just a bad idea.  The only qualification is built-in--the balance between Tony's success and the short-livedness of it.  The gangster's glamour is offset only by its evanescence.

## Notes

1.  I don't know how Penn feels about SCARFACE, but Hawks, I'm sure, wouldn't care to be associated with The LEFT-HANDED GUN.  In a question-and-answer session once, he remarked, "... you get somebody who's going to make a Western about a psycho or a left-handed gun or something like that, then it's no good, it doesn't live up to what people want in a Western."-- Focus on Howard Hawks, p. 25.  Perhaps he thought he was being plagiarized.

2.   Muni played a similar "subhuman creature" in the 1946
     ANGEL ON MY SHOULDER.   He must have undertaken
     the role in order to repent publicly of SCARFACE.
     His ex-con Eddie Kagle's particularly unconvincing
     conversion to God and good is accomplished by Anne
     Baxter, a group of nice little boys, a prospective home
     and family, and a few well-chosen words from the
     Bible.   It's SCARFACE with saccharin.

The THING

## "Who Goes There?"

John W. Campbell, Jr.'s story "Who Goes There?",
the basis of The THING, mixes fantastically convoluted plotting with juvenile description and dialogue.  It's alternately
ingenious and silly.  It bears more resemblance to INVASION
OF THE BODY SNATCHERS than to The THING in its story
of a monster "from a world with a bluer sun" that multiplies
itself by imitating the forms of the dogs, cows, and humans
it attacks, then uses its "original bulk" to attack the next
animal.  It duplicates its victims so perfectly that no one
can tell who is a "monster" and who is not.

The ground rules of the creature's powers keep changing until there are so many possible plot combinations and
permutations that it seems the humans may as well give up.
It can change shape, read minds, project its thoughts, and,
apparently, somehow strain itself through the tiniest cracks.
The monster's powers are so awesome that the ending, in
which the humans too easily and cleanly defeat it, is very
dissatisfying in its smug sense of finality and its attempted
justification of the whole human race by this one triumph
over alien forces.  Suspense doesn't build in one straight
line, but out in all directions, and is thus dissipated.  The
story, which is really a glorified guessing game, is mostly
in the dialogue, in technical, scientific explanations of the
monster.  It's intermittently fascinating, but finally too
tricky for its own good.

The non-technical dialogue is childish and given to
over-statement.  ("Blair's blasted potential life developed a
hell of a lot of potential and walked out on us.")  Description
of action and character is stilted:

It roared a challenge to the white silence of Ant-
arctica.

> An air of crushing menace entered into every
> man's body...

It's pure plot and only shows it whenever it attempts to prove
otherwise.

> Lederer's script is almost an original screen story.
Water drips from the ice-caked Thing as it unthaws, and The
Thing attacks the huskies.    But all the other details are
original with the movie, which is markedly better than the
story.


## The THING

> Two comments by critics on Hawks movies "fix" the
look and feel of The THING:

> His best films ... have the swallowed-up intricacy
> of a good soft-shoe dance... (Manny Farber, 1957)

> There is an intricate art by which the line of feel-
> ing is kept uppermost and rising in the midst of a
> staccato din of commands, interjections, screams,
> speakers, plane-motors, tickers, sometimes as
> many as five or six voices going all the time...
> (Otis Ferguson, on CEILING ZERO, 1936)

The THING is one of Hawks' most superficial films and also
just about one of his best.    It's a pleasure to watch and listen to it.    I've seen it more often--nine times at least--than
probably any other Hawks movie.    Late at night, on TV, it's
one of the best, scariest horror movies; any time of day, in
a theatre, with an audience, it's one of the best, most exciting science-fiction movies.    It's always a little disappointing in that it's finally "about" nothing at all; when it ends,
it ends, and that's that.    But it's better than HIS GIRL FRI-
DAY at not letting you catch on to its hollowness until it's
over.    While it's in motion it's a thing of beauty, preferable
to any number of movies that are "about" the most pressing,
important matters but that "are" really nothing.    The THING
is a sort of essence of Hawks--it's strong on setting, atmosphere, ensemble playing, but it's not grounded in a central,
informing performance or performances.    It doesn't have a
Dizzy Davis or a Walter Burns (though it's a better, more
even movie than CEILING ZERO).

The THING: James Young, Kenneth Tobey, Douglas Spencer and Robert Nichols.

More than any other Hawks film (except perhaps AIR FORCE), The THING is a team effort, but the teamwork is not expressive of some theme like The Subordination of the Individual Will to the Needs of Society that one might discover if one took the film just one, tantalizing step further. There are good, but hardly dominating, performances by Kenneth Tobey, Margaret Sheridan, Douglas Spencer, James Young, Dewey Martin, Eduard Franz, John Dierkes, Paul Frees, and William Self. The actors are less characters than voices commingled and orchestrated. Just enough information is offered about each person to keep him busy until the movie is over (though the reporter, Spencer, and the head scientist, Robert Cornthwaite, run down a little early). Only when one or two actors have the stage to themselves for too long do you begin to notice their one-dimensionality. Hawks and

Christian Nyby use the actors to create a primary effect of
solidarity threatened:  the movie consists essentially of
strong co-senses of camaraderie and menace.  (Robert Altman's McCABE AND MRS. MILLER is a similar, and I think
less successful, two-mood piece.)  The film is in the inter-
play between the actors, in the rhythm of sound and movement, the pace, and the documentary-like treatment of The
Thing (James Arness).  As the secondary characters in The
BIG SLEEP are sometimes reduced to names, so the characters in The THING are often just voices.  Hawks doesn't
even give you time--and more to the point, doesn't need to
give you time--to figure out who's saying what.

Hawks uses overlapping dialogue for suspense and
shock effects as well as for comic purposes, and words fairly dance in the film.  Although the delivery occasionally
lapses into the self-conscious staccato of parts of CEILING
ZERO, lines are generally spoken, and actions performed,
sotto voce.  Particular actions are de-emphasized, becoming
part of a general flow of movement, and particular lines are
caught up in an almost mellifluous, unending stream of words.
From one part of a room comes, "We're getting nowhere";
then, from another, "We're consistent."  From behind a just-
closed door:  "What do you mean, 'A gun's no good'?"  The
movie has a convincing sound as well as look, though a few
of the more hysterical lines interrupt its documentary feel.

The script employs technical jargon both to build suspense and to puncture it by self-conscious kidding of it:  out
of a drily read technical report, Tobey picks the key, impressive phrase, "20,000 tons!", and lets the reader continue.
After listening apparently attentively to another report, he
admits that it left him way behind.  The dialogue has a documentary-like precision.  Doctors Cornthwaite and Frees
describe the path left by a mysterious aircraft when it hit
the arctic ice:

> Cornthwaite:  The bottle shape apparently was
> caused by the aircraft first making contact with the
> earth out there at the neck of the bottle, sliding
> toward us and forming that larger area as it came
> to rest.

> Frees:  With the engine or engines generating e-
> nough heat to melt that path through the crust, then
> sink beneath the surface.

Hawks keeps the movie moving by avoiding aural monotony, giving a key line to each actor in a scene, alternating the modes of speaking--excited, hushed, angry, bantering, dry, scared, edgy, portentous, etc.; and by punctuating lines with other lines, with silence, with noise--like the sudden appearances of The Thing--or with music.   Conversations don't stagily start and stop; they're picked up in progress; they interrupt each other; they overlap; they're crammed into the spaces before The Thing's attacks, when the flow of words and actions accelerates markedly.   Scenes and sequences pivot on dialogue--an exchange of comments on the roundness of the mystery aircraft is interrupted by a cry ("Dr. Carrington!") which acts as a transitional device.   A group discussion becomes a whispered conversation between Tobey and Martin on the advisability of halving the length of the shifts the men take guarding the ice-bound Thing.

The THING is more in the (at the time established) tradition of horror movies than in the (soon to be established) tradition of s-f movies.   (It rivals BRIDE OF FRANKEN-STEIN as the best monster movie.)   It helped to establish the tradition of horror movies disguised as s-f movies--e. g., INVADERS FROM MARS, INVASION OF THE BODY SNATCH-ERS, FIEND WITHOUT A FACE.   Thematically, it's tangentially related to INVADERS and INVASION in its suggestion of the advantages of eliminating inhibiting emotions from humans.   The Thing's emotionlessness is the s-f equivalent of the Stoicism of ONLY ANGELS HAVE WINGS, or perhaps betters it since The Thing can't--and not simply doesn't want to--express emotion.

Structurally, the movie is related to H. P. Love-craft's Cthulhu stories, which are, in effect, documentary science-fantasies.   The stories are less narratives than piecings together of information--from photographs, documents, dreams, hieroglyphs, chants, newspaper articles, books, letters, and recordings--that chart whole races of "elder Gods" and various other beings existing in this and other dimensions.   Lovecraft's stories are essentially mythic horror-mysteries; The THING is more a techno-biological horror-mystery.   What makes the creature tick?   Later, what will make him stop ticking?   The scientist-Air Force officer-sleuths employ Geiger counters, microscopes, stethoscopes, moviolas, thermometers, sound detectors, and other hardware.

The details of its physical and biological make-up

make The Thing one of the few really frightening movie monsters. [1] There are some wild references to the possibility of its conquering the world--it has great reproductive capacity--but the real horror lies in its digestive and reproductive systems themselves, not in the consequences for the world if it lives. Its hand moves even after it's severed from its body and it ingests the dogs' blood on it. It also drops seeds. With a stethoscope, scientists hear the crying of the fertilized sprouts, which sounds "like the wail of a newborn child that's hungry." Sprouts nearer the blood supply grow faster. The Thing itself replaces the severed limb. It drains the blood of the men and dogs it kills, hanging the men upside down on meat hooks and slashing their throats. (I remember a horror comic of the Fifties which graphically depicted such a scene on its cover; in the movie this incident is, fortunately, related only in dialogue, though rumor has it that it was filmed.)

The THING employs the Val Lewton theory of suggestive horror-details more successfully than any of the Lewton shockers, which are, in comparison, docile and sweet. The dialogue-related details, like a classic radio horror show, stimulate the imagination--which may be why radio wizard Orson Welles' name is sometimes connected with the movie. [2] And, though Dimitri Tiomkin's electronic score punches the shock scenes home too hard, it's generally as evocative as the dialogue.

The film reinforces its suggestion with impressive visual details: soldiers and scientists fanning out to determine the size and shape of the aircraft they've found embedded in arctic ice come to form an almost perfect circle--i.e., "flying saucer." For punctuation--in this case an exclamation point--the camera pans slowly to the left across the circle of men. It's one of the great moments in s-f movies. When someone slams a heavy door on The Thing's hand, it shears out a chunk of wood in pulling its hand free. Drenched in kerosene and set afire, it cuts a swath of flame across a mattress with a swipe of its arm. Later, a blow from that arm sends a talkative scientist (Cornthwaite) somersaulting across a corridor into an unconscious heap. The scientists and Air Force men first see The Thing as a vaguely defined, human-like shape in a block of ice; then as an impression left in the thawed ice; later as a shadowy figure fighting huskies in driving snow; as a huge form silhouetted in a doorway; and as a giant thrashing about violently as he burns or melts. He's never shown in a good, bright light,

but, in the cozy, claustrophobic atmosphere of the arctic
outpost, the brute physical presence of The Thing makes itself felt like a chilly blast of air in a cheerful, firelit living
room.

The THING has always posed a problem for auteurists.
Christian Nyby gets the credit for directing, but everyone
seems to agree that Hawks must have directed it.    Since he's
not sure, Andrew Sarris has to list it nineteen lines down
on its year (1951).    (If he ever does become sure, it will
probably zoom up to, say, fourth on the year, between The
PROWLER and that little glory of the cinema, The STEEL
HELMET. )  Hawks has responded differently to different
questioners when confronted, usually saying that he came in
to help Nyby whenever Nyby asked him to.    When Kenneth
Tobey, who should know--he was in it and was also good in

Who directed The THING?   A dialogue rehearsal for the film:
(counter-clockwise) Arthur Siteman (standing), Douglas Spencer, James Young, Kenneth Tobey, Dewey Martin, William
Self, dialogue coach Larry Sherwood, Christian Nyby and
Howard Hawks.

I WAS A MALE WAR BRIDE--was asked, "Who really directed The THING?", he replied:

> Howard Hawks.  Technically, of course, Chris Ny-
> by directed it and is given screen credit for it....
> He was new at directing, and Mr. Hawks main-
> tained a kind of overseeage on the picture....
> Howard has a wonderful ear....  He'd listen to a
> scene during a rehearsal and, if it didn't sound
> normal or if it sounded a little stilted, he'd say,
> "Let's do that again...."[3]

This sort of problem can make the auteur theory seem like
a mystery game, and I think it's just what the more closed-
minded auteurists deserve.  While everyone else sits back
and enjoys the movie, they have to worry over whether particular details are Hawksian, Nybian, a little of each, or
Wellesian.  (And how much credit goes to Charles Lederer
and Ben Hecht??)  It looks and sounds like a Hawks film,
and that's good enough for me.  Hawks should have given
The BIG SKY to Nyby and kept The THING for himself and
saved everyone a lot of concern.

### Notes

1.  In the first draft screenplay of The THING, the monster
    had "multiple eyes" and ten "stringy looking fingers"
    to each hand and a "bulbous head" with no ears.  In
    the film he looks more human, and thus I think more
    frightening, like an undomesticated version of the
    Frankenstein monster.  There were also a few im-
    pressive touches in that first draft that don't appear
    in the final version of the film:  1) The people in the
    underground passage hear, over the intercom, thing-
    plants "mewing" in the greenhouse; 2) The radioactive
    Thing burns its way out of the iron greenhouse wall;
    and 3) The Thing nearly decapitates Dr. Carrington
    with its spiked hand.

2.  Hawks, in fact, recruited at least three of his actors--
    Young, Cornthwaite, and Sally Creighton--from radio.

3.  "The North Pole Papers," interview by Mark Frank,
    Photon, Number 22, p. 21.

## GENTLEMEN PREFER BLONDES

The opening number, "We're Just Two Little Girls from Little Rock," with Marilyn Monroe and Jane Russell in super-vivid red, dancing before a super-vivid purple backdrop, is Philistine vulgarity at its most exhilarating. The girls, the clashing colors, and the movement are so good to look at that it's a shame the movie has to follow. After it begins, there's Marilyn Monroe on the one hand, and, on the other, there's Jane Russell. What Miss Monroe plays is less a character than an arsenal of affectations named Lorelei Lee. GENTLEMEN PREFER BLONDES is just a showcase for her, and she responds with an amazing variety of squirms, squiggles, and whinnies. It's as if Hawks just told her to go out into each scene and do something irresistibly dumb and cute. Her frisking about doesn't really amount to a full-fledged performance since the plot and Miss Russell keep interrupting her, and she attacks each scene a little differently (somewhat as Groucho Marx did in MONKEY BUSINESS, 1931), with no rhyme or reason, and with a slightly different voice and persona for each. She doesn't seem quite human, just the essence of the adorable dumb blonde.

The effects I like best are her eyebrows crashing together like waves to underscore some pointless point and her squeal of "Oh, Piggy!" drifting across a crowded dance floor. Her presence in MONKEY BUSINESS (1952) and GENTLEMEN PREFER BLONDES is about all those two Fox-Hawks films have to recommend them. Her type of aggressive, brainless, painless sexuality is apotheosized in the "Diamonds Are a Girl's Best Friend" number, which is stunning in its controlled garishness and drive. The movie as a whole has a formless, ugly garishness to it, but in the opener and in this number the grotesqueness is excitingly stylized.

The big joke in, or on, GENTLEMEN PREFER BLONDES is that Jane Russell is supposed to be the sincere

148

one of the two showgirls, and she never spoke a line in a movie as if she meant it.   She can't seem to talk without sneering, as if she despised each word she spoke or hated her job.   Marilyn Monroe seems less affected as a put-on than Miss Russell does straight.   The latter's impersonation of Miss Monroe at the end is neither funny nor accurate (how could it be when she can't even be herself?), and her big number, "Ain't There Anyone Here for Love?", with a gymful of musclebound Olympic athletes ignoring her as they do choreographed calisthenics, qualifies as a perversion of sex, acting, musicals, and the Olympics.

The rest of the movie is disposable comic-romantic plot with Charles Coburn, Elliott Reid, Tommy Noonan, and Taylor Holmes.   The boy George Winslow's foghorn voice is funny, whether coming from Miss Monroe to baffle Coburn or just coming from Winslow himself as the dirty-young-man counterpart to Coburn.   ("You have a great deal of animal magnetism," he flatters Miss Monroe.)   The movie borrows or adapts an idea from Erich von Stroheim when Miss Monroe sees Coburn's head as a shimmering diamond.   (In The MERRY WIDOW, as Roy D'Arcy eyes Mae Murray's necklace and bracelets, they light up like neon lights.)

# LAND OF THE PHARAOHS

LAND OF THE PHARAOHS begins like INTOLERANCE, but ends up just another EGYPTIAN, although it's never quite as dull and obtuse as the latter, one of the worst of the "epics." It begins big and gets bigger and bigger, temporarily at least suspending or putting off questions of ultimate objectives and direction, which is perhaps the best way for an epic to go, disregarding the viewer's inevitable attendant doubts about size for size's sake. If it had continued along the same lines to the end, it could have been impressive simply as an engineering feat, like the pyramids, going on and on and not stopping, but it runs into Joan Collins and disintegrates almost instantly.

For its first forty minutes it's a technical marvel, concentrating on Khufu and his limitless greed and the construction of the pyramid that will be his monument. There's no sense of purpose to the movie even then: with near-absolute power, Khufu gets what he wants, and what he wants happens to be, fortunately, everything. The magnitude of his greed matches the magnitude of the production, and as long as no questions are asked, LAND OF THE PHARAOHS is a true epic. Hawks alternates passages of planning and displays of Khufu's ruthless single-mindedness with sequences of the actual building of the tomb, and you may not have any idea of where the thing is going (the authors probably didn't have any idea either), but you know it's surely going somewhere with all that equipment.

Big as the production is, Hawks seems to be in control. Just about the only memorable line, or fact, in the movie is one about the enormity of the Pharaoh's project, which requires some three million 5,000-pound blocks. (There are a few memorable, anachronistic phrases, along the lines of "You said a mouthful, Princess," but the fastidiously colorless dialogue rarely even ventures beyond the superfluous adjective in something like "Bring the snake in a strong basket.") Hawks seems to know what he's doing with all those blocks, as he fashions sequences of thousands of Egyptians singing off to work like dwarfs or chiseling away at endless vistas of rock, but once he gets indoors with Miss Collins, Dewey Martin, and Luisa Boni, he reveals the pointlessness of the script.

Various esthetic excuses might be made for Miss Collins' ruthlessness, but the essential difference between hers and Jack Hawkins' is that he has all of Egypt behind his lust for wealth and she has only Sydney Chaplin behind hers. It's the difference between legendary tyranny and petty court intrigue. At times Hawks appears to be burlesquing standard historical-religious epics, with Miss Collins' Princess Nellifer pacing back and forth fretfully or tossing her head defiantly after she has been slapped, but the end result is so like those other epics as to be indistinguishable.

There are good performances by Hawkins, who gives added force to the opening sequences, as Khufu, and by James Robertson Justice, in the familiar role of the wise old man of the people.

Hawks and James Robertson Justice on the set of LAND OF THE PHARAOHS.

The CRIMINAL CODE

Hawks appears to have been one of the major directors most intimidated initially by the advent of sound. (Hitchcock was dumbstruck too at first when saddled with a bad, talky play--see The SKIN GAME.) The difference between the silent A GIRL IN EVERY PORT and the sound The DAWN PATROL and The CRIMINAL CODE could justly be described in terms like "fall" and "disintegration" if we didn't know now that the setback was only temporary, a way-point between the assurance of Hawks' silent technique as manifested in A GIRL IN EVERY PORT and the technical assurance of his later sound films like HIS GIRL FRIDAY. His handling of actors and dialogue, for which he was to become renowned, is, in The CRIMINAL CODE, generally inept.

All of the movie's creakiness can't be blamed on Martin Flavin, who wrote the play. Hawks dutifully brings out and heightens the play's artificiality and lack of imagination, without retaining much hint of the possible validity of its bleak view of prison life (and, in turn, its view of life). Every move the actors make, every word they say, seems wrong, false. By simply reading a play, you don't always get a complete picture of what's right and wrong with it. But when you see and hear actors in a production or film adaptation of it, you instantly sense faults in diction, character relationships, basic assumptions. Hawks doesn't seem to have corrected any of the faults; instead, his staging underlines them.

When State's Attorney Martin Brady brings up the titular code, Hawks has Walter Huston shove a copy of it into screen center and pause significantly. When convict Robert Graham, deadened by six years' work in the prison jute mill, first sees Mary Brady, warden Brady's attractive daughter, he goes through six stages of Spiritual Awakening--Phillips Holmes carefully marking all transitions as he glances up--as they stand at opposite ends of the warden's office. Brady's answer to every statement of fact, exclamation, or even a declaration of love by his daughter is a

noncommital "Yeah. " In fact, the movie finally doesn't have
much to do with prisons or chance or the injustice of life--
which was the intended center of the play. It's simply one
hundred ways for Brady to interject, "Yeah. " The high
point of this accidental comedy classic is perhaps Graham's
conclusion of an impassioned speech with a "No!" and Brady's
infallible rejoinder, "Yeah. "

The movie exposes the play as a mass of words, none
worth remembering (and some, like Brady's "That's the way
things break. You have to play the cards the way they fall"
eminently worth forgetting), and without characters. Chance
is behind everything, and most of the breaks the characters
get are bad. The play very neatly works to an unhappy ending: Galloway, a convict who kills a squealer, isn't caught,
and Graham, who, with provocation, kills the brutal yard
captain, Gleason, is. But it's as contrived as the movie's
happy ending, in which Galloway kills Gleason and is shot,
and Graham is led in from solitary by Brady to his waiting
daughter--and out of Sordidness emerges Bliss (or so the
scene plays).

Huston is rather admirable as Brady, giving Flavin's
stock lines and stage mannerisms a kind of futile conviction.
He's trapped, but he doesn't seem to know it. (His emphatic
delivery of his do-your-duty-as-a-citizen lines in a similar
role in William Wellman's The STAR WITNESS that same
year--1931--is just grotesque. )

Boris Karloff as Galloway is the movie's one bright
spot. His appearance is so cadaverous that he doesn't even
have to move to scare anyone. All he has to do is say to
Gleason, "Come in and get him, " when Gleason demands that
Graham come out of his cell bunk. His slow, considered
pivot to the side of the narrow steps as he meets Gleason
going the other way is more intimidating than any overtly
threatening gesture could be. A simple "Tea, madam?" is
as good as a snarl coming from him. Hawks' one feat of
staging is Galloway's murder of Runch (Clark Marshall), the
squealer. Karloff slips into the warden's office unnoticed
by Marshall and stands, unmoving, framed huge in the foreground, while Marshall, small, opposite him on the right in
the background, peers out the window. When Marshall finally
turns to face him, Karloff produces a knife from his sleeve,
and all the force of Karloff's massive figure is behind that
simple movement.

Most of the other actors are embarrassments.

PART V

WAR DRAMAS

# TO HAVE AND HAVE NOT

TO HAVE AND HAVE NOT is supposed to be "the prototypical Hawks film," and there was a time when I thought so myself; now, it strikes me as less Hawks than Furthman and Faulkner (just as CASABLANCA is probably less Curtiz than Epstein, Epstein, and Koch). That is, its virtues seem to me to lie in the dialogue and in Bogart's and, to a lesser extent, Bacall's and Walter Brennan's delivery of same. Hemingway, at one end, and Hawks, at the other, don't seem to me to have much to do with its success as a light, witty entertainment. Hawks won his bet with Hemingway and made a good movie using the title (and not much else) of Hemingway's "worst" book, but the movie makes as little use of Hawks as it does Hemingway.

The book is not good. Without its idiosyncratic description and dialogue, there would probably be nothing; even with it, there is very little. But it has some strong passages, mostly those with Marie, Harry Morgan's wife and widow. It also has some witty dialogue ("I wish I was a man," his wife said. "You'd go a long way with that build," the green-visored man said into his beer. ), none of which turns up in the movie; but it's disembodied dialogue, with no sense of the people behind it or the setting. Some of Harry's exchanges with the rummy make it to the movie ("I want you rum-brave. I don't want you useless. "), but the relationship between the two is decidedly less sentimental in the book. (At one point in the book, Harry considers killing him so he won't talk. ) That doesn't mean that it's better, though, since Hemingway's treatment of Harry is as condescending, in a cold, sterile way, as Hawks' is of Eddie. In the book, Harry lets Johnson, his client, get clean away without paying, then kills the next person who could double-cross him. Hemingway doesn't give you much to go on to decide if Harry's ruthless, foolish, or near-insane, and less to decide if you care.

To Have and Have Not is like 13 Writing Exercises

for Ernest Hemingway, and the movie has a rambling (time
out for sixteen "numbers"), slapped-together feel too.  Hawks
admits that the political intrigue didn't interest him and he
occasionally has his characters wittily echo his detachment.
At one point, Marcel Dalio (representing the plot) bursts in
on Bogart and Bacall, who are just getting to know each
other in Bogart's hotel room, and Bogart politely requests,
"No--later, Frenchy," and pushes him right back out.  But
Hawks also has other problems.  At times the movie resembles Dramatic Arts II (Romantic Overkill) for Bacall; at
others, Character Acting 33 (Tics and Shudders), with Brennan fantastic, but too showy, as Eddie.  The main problem
is that TO HAVE AND HAVE NOT as a film is simply clumsy.

It's dull, when it's not painful, to look at.  It looks
cheap, as though it were done quickly, like a Raoul Walsh
Warner's.  A scene is just two or three actors with a lot
of dead space around them.  There's no atmosphere, or
method in the staging, and, since there's very little music,
you can't help but notice the deadliness of the pace.  Scenes
are sometimes shot with the camera obviously in the wrong
place:  Hawks has to cut intrusively to a shot of one Vichy
henchman for a Bogart gag.  The cut, whose over-emphasis
pretty much kills the gag (which concerned the man's customary inconspicuousness), could have been avoided if both
actors had been in the same shot.  He has the camera dwell
on Brennan's three-ring circus of jerky, spasmodic entrances
and exits.  (Brennan certainly does give you more to look at
than Hawks does. )  And there are ungainly close shots of
Bacall grinning at Bogart and Bogart smiling patronizingly
at Brennan, as if Hawks didn't know what to do with the camera.

Fortunately though, the film has the sharpest dialogue
outside of the first half of THEY DRIVE BY NIGHT, which
also needed all the help it could get from its writers.  Everyone but Hemingway probably deserves a little credit for the
ripostes, but, in the absence of first-hand testimony, I give
most of it to William Faulkner and Jules Furthman for the
following examples:

Bacall:  Give her my love.

Bogart:  I'd give 'er my own if she had _that_ on.

Bogart hesitates as he carries Dolores Moran,  out cold:

> Bacall: What are you trying to do, guess her weight?

Dalio explains that wounded Free Frenchman Walter Molnar is on the premises:

> Bogart: Why didn't you put him on the center table, in the goldfish bowl, and be done with it?

Another fast exchange:

> Bacall: Was you ever bit by a dead bee...?

> Brennan: I feel like I was talking to myself.

Bacall returns the bottle Bogart returned to her.

> Bogart: It's getting to be quite a problem, isn't it?

The consistency of wit carries the entire film, with help from the actors. (Anyone who thinks Bogart and Bacall made this and The BIG SLEEP all by themselves should see DARK PASSAGE and KEY LARGO, in which they got little or no help from script and director.)[1]

Humphrey Bogart seems himself here and in his other Hawks film, The BIG SLEEP, rather than that other guy, Bogart the Actor, sweating and straining in John Huston films like KEY LARGO, TREASURE OF THE SIERRA MADRE, and The AFRICAN QUEEN. Pauline Kael accuses audiences of the time of rejecting TREASURE out of a sentimental wish to see their old, familiar hero doing his old, familiar thing. But I think a sentimentality of another sort is at work on Miss Kael's part, in her wholehearted acceptance of a hollow, uncertain performance as a terrifying culmination of Bogart's previous roles. Audiences at the time may not have been seeing what they wanted to see, but Kael saw what she wanted to.

I like the real Bogart here better than the Actor. He just seems phony whenever he tries to get tough or intense or cute--he gets tough with the Vichyites only once here, in a scene paralleling one with Clift and Paul Fix in RED RIVER. He was better the less he tried, or the less it looked as though he were trying. He had a natural sincerity that he perceptibly betrayed whenever he put on the

Bogart and Bacall in TO HAVE AND HAVE NOT.

heavy stuff.  (Even in CASABLANCA he's not believable when
he suddenly begins to disintegrate under the influence of
Ingrid Bergman's reappearance. )  He obviously didn't have to
pretend that he liked Lauren Bacall.

        Bacall is also better passive; she seems silly when
she turns on the vulnerability or sensuousness.  Thanks to
her, it's hard to tell if some of her lines in the slinkiest
scenes are dumb, mock-dumb, or ultra-sophisticated, or if
she's supposed to be sensuous, mock-sensuous, insolent, or
all three at once.  She's best when bantering or mocking her
competition, Miss Moran, by batting her eyelids goofily at
Bogart.  Hawks goes all out with the camera and lighting
effects to cover for her deficiencies, but she still attacks
her big lines as if they would bite her unless she bit them
first.  (James Agee thought that all everyone else on the

film was trying to do was to "set this arrogant neophyte off to the best possible advantage, to cover up her weaknesses-- or turn them into assets--and to toss campstools under her whenever she wobbles.") Andy Williams apparently dubbed her singing; someone might have dubbed some of her dialogue too. (And did she do her own singing in The BIG SLEEP?)

Hoagy Carmichael, emanating quiet assurance at the piano and flirting with his female adorers, is about all the movie has in the way of atmosphere or mood. Hawks sticks Molnar and Dalio with most of the plot. Walter Sande as Johnson and Dan Seymour as the head Vichy villain are good. Brennan's Eddie is around rather too obviously to prove that Harry is really a nice guy, but his ulterior purpose proves secondary to a more superficial one: to give Bogart and Bacall another partner off whom they can bounce their word-play--the dead bee routine, his unreliable-memory routine, etc.

## Note

1.  KEY LARGO may be as good as TO HAVE AND HAVE NOT, but not because of Bogart and Bacall.

# AIR FORCE

War movies are almost invariably helpless when they
try to justify themselves. Straight anti-war movies come
equipped with a built-in justification--the cold realities of
death, brutality, and men killing men--which they can either
coast on or make vivid and specific. In-between movies like
The DAWN PATROL and SERGEANT YORK--war dramas masquerading as anti-war dramas or vice versa--try to have it
both ways. They're not so much meaningless as about mean-
inglessness, while they're also hero-worshiping and action-
oriented, and their dual purposes cancel each other out.
Straight war movies like AIR FORCE at best have an unac-
knowledged pointlessness and at worst make crude points
illustrating What America Means to Me. They're pointless
unless seen as the simplest kind of action movie or as propaganda.

AIR FORCE does pretty well as an action picture,
when the script is concerned with the business at hand,
whether it's a frantic attempt to save a plane from snipers
or to rescue a kid parachuting out of a disabled plane from
an enemy jet. The structure and plotting have a mechanical
beauty, in the delegation, rather heavily emphasized, of a
specific job to each member of a bomber crew, and in the
slow building-up of their frustration at taking off and landing
and taking off again, from one base after another, without
doing much but protecting their investment. They're told
horror stories of how the U.S. bombers and jets at Hickam
Field, Pearl Harbor, were sabotaged and left sitting on the
ground December 7, 1941. They're forced to leave Marines
at Wake Island behind, virtually unprotected from enemy attack. The crew chief (Harry Carey) is informed that his
son, a pilot, died at Manila and "didn't even get into the
air." There's a sense of fulfillment when they finally take
to the air and lead the attack on the Japanese fleet. It's
like a horror or science-fiction movie (like The THING) with
the monster saved, very sensibly, for the payoff. The movie
is action-filled, but it saves the primary action for last.

162

The plot, however, leaves the movie's wartime mor-
ality unaccounted for.   Robin Wood sees the crew of the
Mary-Ann as

> ... an ideal democracy in microcosm:  the atmos-
> phere is one of voluntary service, of discipline
> freely accepted; a perfect balance is achieved be-
> tween individual fulfilment and the responsibility of
> each member to the whole.   The crew <u>enact</u> the
> values they are fighting for.

This gives the efficient, mechanical plot a lot more credit
than it deserves.   The process whereby the misfit Winocki
(John Garfield) and the "independent" fighter-pilot Rader
(James Brown) are absorbed into the B-17's team is a basic,
indispensable, war-movie cliché, though here it isn't the
whole film as it is in, say, CORVETTE K-225, in which
James Brown plays the misfit.   (CORVETTE K-225 and AIR
FORCE also share another cliché, the dog-mascot; in fact,
I think they share the very same dog.)   What Wood says of
AIR FORCE could be said of every third war movie, or of
quite a few at least.   There's an acute sense of disproportion
between the fact of a half-dozen men working well together
and the history of the United States.   According to Wood,
the movie displays "the triumph of individualism placed at
the service of something beyond itself...."   But individualism
can't be expressed through stock characters, and the script's
expression of "something beyond" individualism generally
runs along the lines of "You're going to play them 'The Star-
Spangled Banner' with two-ton bombs."

The film is left without a justification of its protagonists' violence except violence--i.e., revenge, an eye for an
eye.   A Japanese jet machine-guns a boy (a <u>boy</u>!) as he
parachutes to the ground, and Winocki shoots down the pilot
after he emerges from the downed plane.   The Americans
are fighting against the Japanese and their "dirty treachery,"
but it's less clear what they're fighting <u>for</u> (and it's not for
a well-run ship).   There's no qualification of Winocki's
vehemence--his outburst was and still is pure propaganda;
there are no overtones of madness to his act of revenge as
there are to those of the heroes of Fritz Lang's revenge
sagas, which are closely analogous to war pictures, morally
and dramatically.   There's no second-guessing or self-exam-
ination in AIR FORCE.   The anarchic SCARFACE is a more
moral film.

The movie presents its heroes as themselves, as members of a team, and as the spirit of democracy, and it fails on the first and third counts. Even so, it's superior on all counts to John Ford's highly overrated THEY WERE EXPENDABLE (scripted by Frank Wead, who's closely associated with both Ford and Hawks), the usual cross-reference for AIR FORCE, and, even at only 135 minutes, one of the longest movies ever made. The message you carry home from it is that a lot of people died for General Mac-Arthur, and very slowly. At least that's what you get from the images--syrupy, lingering close-ups of noble or admiring faces; long takes which dwell on insignificant actions as if to lend them significance; shots of veterans smiling benignly and paternally at new men. At the beginning Robert Montgomery confronts John Wayne, "For yourself? Or the team?" By the end, Wayne is for the team, as Garfield is in AIR FORCE, some time after the latter's superior explains how manning a bomber is like playing football. And the Ford film looks amateurish, with awkward cutaways for close-ups of the most trivial lines or the wannest comic relief. It's simply an unprofessional job.

AIR FORCE is at least an exciting, professional work, with pace, suspense, and a fine look (thanks to James Wong Howe) and sound to it. Hawks' two main jobs were to keep it moving and to establish the suspense situations cleanly and clearly. The dialogue is generally functional and unobtrusive, though dotted with phrases like "Blast 'em off the earth!" and "sneakin' little Nips". The dialogue, more than anything else, is responsible for the feeling of unity and cooperation among the Mary-Ann's crew; that is, the mere sound, not the content of the dialogue is responsible. The actors and their voices are in harmony, as practiced for their jobs as the men they portray are for theirs. John Ridgely (pilot), John Garfield (aerial gunner), George Tobias (assistant crew chief), Harry Carey (crew chief), Gig Young (co-pilot), Arthur Kennedy (bombardier), Ward Wood (radio operator), Charles Drake (navigator), and James Brown (replacement pilot when Ridgely dies), with what James Agee calls their "diverse and authentic speech," work and talk together like a team, at least when they're not making overt references to teamwork.

Occasionally, the dialogue is better than functional. The chaff between the fighter pilot (Brown) and the bomber pilots touches on both professional rivalry and differences between individual and group effort in air war. The death

of the captain (Ridgely) is at once moving and corny.   He
imagines on his death-bed the ship preparing for takeoff,
and his men go through the takeoff procedure with him.   The
sequence at first seems simply a blatant restatement of the
movie's main theme of teamwork,  but the dialogue's imagery
culminates in a stunning image of death when the captain sets
the course:   "Due east--into the sunrise. "   The one word,
"sunrise, " makes the sequence and gives the film its one
fine moment.

The DAWN PATROL

You can see the beginnings of ONLY ANGELS HAVE
WINGS in Hawks' The DAWN PATROL, but that doesn't make
it any more interesting than it would be if you couldn't.
It's still a dull, plodding film, Hawks' first all-talking picture.   It's an antique of interest only to those who (like me)
love some of Hawks' later films and want to see everything
he did, to find out where those later films came from.
Hawks once cited The DAWN PATROL as one of his three
personal favorites (along with SCARFACE and TWENTIETH
CENTURY).   He later changed his mind (to SCARFACE,
HATARI!, and I WAS A MALE WAR BRIDE).   Maybe he saw
it again in the interval between those judgments.   It's stolid
and stammering and faintly hypocritical:  in the dialogue it
says that war isn't fun, it's hell and death, then it goes out
and has a lot of fun cracking up planes and doing stunts with
pilots flying on wings.

There are no characters, and there isn't any story.
That's the point:  in war, one man is the same as another--
you either go out to battle prepared to die or you send men
out prepared to see them die.   I would have said that it's
the stiff acting and artificial speech patterns of Richard
Barthelmess, Neil Hamilton, William Janney, and Gardner
James that muffle the point, but the Edmund Goulding remake
(1938) is better acted, at least by Basil Rathbone, and it is
mediocre too.   The point is valid; it's just made unimagina-
tively in both versions.   Hamilton, commander of a World
War I Royal Flying Corps squadron, almost cracks under the
strain of his job of "executioner."   When he's promoted else-
where, Barthelmess takes his place and, in turn, begins to
crack.   Rather than send Douglas Fairbanks, Jr. out on a
suicide mission, Barthelmess goes himself, and Fairbanks
takes over command.   "Inevitability" and "fatalism" become
"predictability" when each new mission leader responds to
his new commander's despised orders with a snarl and a
"Right!"   New fliers walk in with a smile, not knowing What
We Know.   They soon find out.   The film's single point is

made most concisely and unforcedly by the ending, which
cuts off the third squadron commander of the film, Fairbanks,
in the middle of his orders for another dawn patrol.

The spectacular stunts carry more cinematic weight
than the stilted war-is-hell sentiments, and the film is probably "fondly remembered" by the public more for them than
for its patterns of "inevitability." The script's pseudo-Stoical attitude toward war is further compromised by the commander's reaction, unqualified by the script, to the news
that a pilot died honorably in battle: a hearty, "I'm glad,"
which is no reply to any sort of statement that someone has
just died. For a movie that's supposed to be so "sensitive"
to the pressures of men in war, The DAWN PATROL can be
awfully insensitive and unthinking.

There are scattered pleasures: the atmosphere, at
headquarters, of camaraderie in the face of death, with the
pilot whose best friend was shot down brooding silently in
the background while the other fliers sing about "The Next
Man to Die" in the foreground. (Hawks, however, cuts to
the brooder once too often, and the latter's silence begins
to seem a little loud); the staging of the scene where Fairbanks flaps his arms around, imitating the silly high spirits
of the captured German flier ("How do I get rid of the
blighter?"); the scene, moving and embarrassing at the same
time, in which, as Barthelmess leaves the now-drunk Fairbanks behind to take his place on the suicide run, Fairbanks
sleepily mumbles that he's not mad at him any more for
sending his brother out to die. (It's this kind of scene that
blossoms into ONLY ANGELS HAVE WINGS.) But the announcement of the changeover from Brand to Courtney is done
better by Rathbone in the remake, with the latter directing
his savage glee right at Errol Flynn: "Do you know who
will replace me? Do you?"

# SERGEANT YORK

I hadn't seen SERGEANT YORK before I started this book.  The two or three times I had tried, I gave up before slogging very far along into it.   I have certain vague priorities for seeing movies.   There aren't any that I absolutely refuse to see.   There are a select few that I haven't seen--An AUTUMN AFTERNOON, EQUINOX FLOWER, almost any Ozu, La CHIENNE, The MARRIAGE CIRCLE--that I want to see as soon as possible.   There are many others that I actively want to see but can, I suppose, wait for--COUNSEL-LOR-AT-LAW, The SAINT STRIKES BACK, BLACK MOON. There are those I can see any time, no big hurry.   Lastly, there are certain types of films I find I can do very well without--silent drama, most dubbed movies, war movies, and a genre I would call the Hollywood monstrosity.   SER-GEANT YORK makes the latter two categories; others that I haven't seen that I would put in that last category include PRIDE OF THE YANKEES, MRS. MINIVER, The BEST YEARS OF OUR LIVES (I got through half of that once), The GOOD EARTH and GIGI.   They have no single common de-nominator, but this type of movie is generally long, heavily honored, very respectable, dull-sounding.

SERGEANT YORK might in some ways be considered well-made, but not in any way I would entertain.   It's one of the most artificial, unspontaneous movies I've seen.   Holly-wood is never more Hollywood than when it knocks itself out trying to be something else.   In this case it tries to be Appalachia and France, World War I.   I can't say with any certainty that it betrays Appalachia and France, but it's faithful as hell to Hollywood.   Having skimmed the source material, I realize that Alvin York and his friends and rela-tives didn't give the film makers much to go on, but that doesn't excuse their lack of imagination.   The questions and conflicts are there, but they're poorly posed and stated. The movie flickers to life occasionally when Gary Cooper as York is simply talking, stating his case or expressing self-doubt in the same hesitant way York did.   But it fails completely in its attempts to organize and dramatize York's experiences.

The two key movements of the film are York's conversion from rowdy to religious man and then from pacifist to soldier. No writer would ever willingly begin with such difficult premises, but Hawks' scriptwriters were stuck with them because they were both well-known facts and virtually the only facts known about Alvin York. They constituted a challenge at best, a real handicap at worst. Writers Finkel, Chandlee, Koch, and Huston took them as a handicap. They make no more sense of the inherent contradictions than anyone could from just reading or hearing about York. They don't fill in the gaps in the story with anything that illuminates it or, conversely, that indicates due respect for insoluble mysteries. They take the secondary facts about York-- influences like his mother, his pastor, his girl; his willingness to work and his skill with a rifle--and pretend that they're the answers, when they at best narrow the gaps. SERGEANT YORK amounts to a rather sneaky glorification of hard work (and a good aim). There's scant sense of a man behind the exploits.

Hawks for his part doesn't help matters by playing up the primary facts as if they were the fifth book of the Gospel, in a movie that looks not so much directed as engraved or etched. The big scenes are mounted on Max Steiner's music and treated as if they were the logical culmination of something rather than non sequiturs, which is what they really are. The movie is just a glossy, souped-up restaging of highlights from Alvin York's life rather than an attempt to reconcile those highlights with each other and with the man himself. In highlight number one, lightning re-forges Alvin's rifle (while he's carrying it) into junk, in a scene imitated by The GHOST OF FRANKENSTEIN the following year. Alvin takes the incident as the sign from God for which he has been waiting and heads for the meeting house. Inside, the congregation flocks around him as if it had been formed for the express purpose of seeing Alvin converted (a rather literal rendering of "the ninety and nine") and had witnessed the miracle. His mother (the creepy Margaret Wycherley) greets him with amazed "Praise the Lord" looks, looking more as if she were the one struck by lightning.

A very shoddy transition scene has Alvin teaching Sunday School and reading, "Thou shalt not kill," as a rider storms into town on Steiner's music to announce the entry

of the United States into World War I.  Thus the script skips
intermediate scenes and gives the impression that Alvin got
religion just in time to become a conscientious objector.  He
talks himself out of resisting the draft when he realizes that
that would lead to violence on his part for sure.  His com-
manding officers give him a week or so to wrestle with his
conscience before they promote their sharpshooter to corporal,
and Alvin goes up into the hills of Tennessee to wrestle.
He doesn't wrestle alone, however--the omnipotent Max
Steiner is apparently secreted, with an orchestra or two and
a pipe organ, behind the rocks Alvin leans against, and what
might have been a quiet scene of one man confronting himself
becomes a ringing justification of war.  The Biblical verse
that Alvin reads--"Render unto Caesar the things that are
Caesar's, and unto God the things that are God's"--reverbe-
rates like an echo on wings of Steiner, and every question
Alvin or anyone else might have had about anything seems
to be answered by that one sentence.  It's lip service to
solitude and introspection, and you wonder how York could
even think with all that racket.

The war sequences are particularly disappointing for
their presentation of an authentic heroic exploit as comedy.
The shots of German troops surrendering to York and filing
out of the trenches, or appearing in a body all along the
crest of a hill, are imaginative, too far-fetched to be dismissed as the usual war-movie heroics, and grounded firmly
in our realization that it really happened.  But the comic
reinforcement of these scenes, with Cooper, George Tobias,
and comic German and American officers chagrined and
astounded, respectively, by the feat, seems ill-advised pad-
ding, paltry invention supporting the main fact.  The scene
in which York draws the German soldiers from cover by
using his turkey call is evidently accurate, but art should be
a little more selective, and no one in his right mind would
have selected such an incident out of York's battle experiences and depicted it on the screen without some kind of
qualification.  It's a moral as well as an esthetic blunder
and irresistibly summons up the parallel between humans and
game in RULES OF THE GAME.  It forfeits the film's last
claims to sensitivity to its subject, the conflict between the
state and religion.  And, ironically for a Hawks film, and
a Hawks film of war, the presence of death is hardly felt,
directly or indirectly, through physical means or through
the attitudes of the characters.

The sequence of the awarding of medals to York and

of the parades can be taken as irony or as due recognition of merit, but the concluding image of York and Gracie running up to the farm established for York by the state of Tennessee can only be taken as endorsement of York's participation in the war effort.   He did what his country wanted, and his country got him what he wanted.   The York who said, "What we did over there ... ain't for buying and selling," isn't quite the same York who accepts the state's gift without any qualms, or if it is, the script doesn't acknowledge the inconsistency.   The ending of SERGEANT YORK presents the usual argument for war--some must die so that others may live in freedom--not as an argument but as undoubtedly the answer.   The ending goes against the tentativenss of York's moral positions.

SERGEANT YORK is just the sort of arid, phony movie that ONLY ANGELS HAVE WINGS sounds.   Hawks' complicity in the artificiality extends to the direction of the comedy scenes, which all play as if they had been over-starched.   Steiner's music is everywhere, unleashed by the worst scenes, underlining actions and even thoughts in all scenes, smothering and killing everything it touches.   Cooper's performance is very uneven, too cute at times, touchingly reticent at others, more often just buried under the music and lighting.   Walter Brennan is just a pair of eyebrows as Pastor Rosier Pile.   Joan Leslie as Gracie, who would be a knockout at Sunset and Vine now, is an anachronism in the Valley of the Three Forks of the Wolf half a century ago.

Max Steiner plays most of the other roles.

## The ROAD TO GLORY

The ROAD TO GLORY is the dullest of Hawks' war
movies, none of which is that thrilling.  It begins and ends
with the senselessness of slaughter in battle.  Like The
DAWN PATROL, it's cyclical.  At the end, Fredric March
becomes captain of the French regiment when Warner Baxter
dies heroically (and senselessly) under his own artillery barrage.  The film concludes with March's address to the regiment, the same address Baxter makes at the beginning.
Single-mindedness and sincerity of purpose seem intended to
substitute for imaginative development.  The calculated senselessness of the climax says somewhat the same thing as the
ending of Jean Renoir's World War I film, GRAND ILLUSION,
but without any of the latter film's subtlety, naturalness, or
delicate sense of irony.  Things don't happen so much as
fall into place.  When Lionel Barrymore, as Baxter's father,
shows up as a replacement, you known that the picture won't
end until he gets killed, just as The DAWN PATROL dragged
in Douglas Fairbanks' brother only in order to kill him and
compound the senselessness.

Hawks has a dull ear here.  An occasional surprise
line (Gregory Ratoff's "Would the sum of five francs be
exorbitant?") breaks up the monotony of the dialogue, and
there are oases of humor (March "establishing a mood" for
June Lang with the piano), but a movie that has arrived at
its conclusion at the beginning has nowhere to go.  Miss
Lang's prayer to let the soldiers live is more moving than
any of the script's contrivances, saying simply and directly
what the film tries to say in its tortuous way.

There's self-sacrifice--March giving up Miss Lang
for Baxter's sake--and noble sentiments--Barrymore's offer
to the blind Baxter to "be his eyes."  But a movie with no
life isn't one to make points about death.  March and Miss
Lang are good, but the other actors are as lifeless as the
film.

172

APPENDICES

## AUTEURS AND AUTEURISTS

I am indebted to the auteur theory of filmmaking and the auteurists primarily for giving Howard Hawks the recognition he deserves. In fact, Hawks is the key Hollywood auteur:

> The test case for the auteur theory is provided by the work of Howard Hawks. Why Hawks, rather than, say, Frank Borzage or King Vidor? Firstly, Hawks is a director who has worked for years within the Hollywood system.... Secondly, Hawks has worked in almost every genre.... Yet all of [Hawks'] films ... exhibit the same thematic preoccupations, the same recurring motifs and incidents, the same visual style and tempo. [1]

> Certainly one has only to consider the development of the greatest American artist--I mean Howard Hawks--to see how relative this idea of classicism is. [2]

> Hawks holds a special place as a rallying cry of auteurism because, of all those directors considered really great by auteurists, he is the most "commercial".... Truffaut and the original French auteurists sometimes termed themselves 'Hitchcocko-Hawksians,' and as Joseph McBride has pointed out, when auteurism first hit the United States a critic could always get a laugh by defining these strange creatures as the people who liked Howard Hawks. Moreover, it is through Hawks that most people 'come to' auteurism; it is usually while watching a Hawks film that one 'sees the light' ... one day (I think it was during 1935's CEILING ZERO, but it might have been 1939's ONLY ANGELS HAVE WINGS), it all suddenly hit me: at once I understood even the films I had seen--and dismissed--

175

days before.  I was hooked on a certain philosophy
of cinema and for good. [3]

Byron's testimony for Hawks is for me the most interesting,
first, because it identifies an acceptance of Hawks' work with
an acceptance of the auteur theory and, secondly, because he
dates his illuminated state from a viewing of one or the
other of the two films for which I originally began writing
this book.  The chapters on CEILING ZERO and ONLY AN-
GELS HAVE WINGS were to have been the center of my book
on Hawks.  Unfortunately, CEILING ZERO proved less in-
spiring for me when I saw it again during the actual writing.
I ended up writing mainly for one film--ONLY ANGELS HAVE
WINGS.

If Hawks is the key auteur, ONLY ANGELS HAVE
WINGS is the key auteur work; if any movie could convince
me that the auteur theory was The Answer, it would be that
one.  I have to add that it doesn't convince me of anything
of the kind; it just gives me a privileged glimpse into the
inner workings of auteurism--an hour or two as an auteurist,
as it were.  Unlike Byron's, my conversion is never per-
manent.  ONLY ANGELS HAVE WINGS works beautifully
every time I see it, but it doesn't work for 2, 000 other
auteur movies or even for all of Hawks' other movies.  They
remain dismissed.  The basic banality and tawdriness are
there each time in ANGELS and in those hypothetical 2, 000
other "commercial" jobs, but only in the case of this one
Hawks movie do the clichés--the coward who proves himself,
the stoic hero--seem more or less irrelevant to the fine
work of Hawks, his writer Jules Furthman, and the actors.

The classical cinema was more functional than the
modern cinema.  It knew its audience and their
expectations, but it often provided something extra.
This something extra is the concern of the auteur
theory. [4]

Sarris' statement goes to the heart of what I believe is implicit in the auteur theory--at least in the American version
of the original Bazin-Truffaut-Godard-& co. politique des
auteurs.  Explicitly, the theory posits that the director is
responsible directly or indirectly for everything in the film,
which assumption or question I find of relative unimportance--
relative, that is, to the question of the quality of the film.
Questions of authorship can be amusing (if authorship isn't
simply assumed), as Robin Wood demonstrated in a recent

inquiry into the origins of TO HAVE AND HAVE NOT, but they
also distract from, at least as much as they contribute to,
the main concern of the critic:  to determine if and why a
film is good or bad or partly good and partly bad.   Who
came up with the image of the dancing pool cues in SCAR-
FACE--Hawks or Hecht or the prop man--is less important
an issue to me than the fact that the image is there in the
film.   Of course, if one assumes that Hawks did, there's
no problem.   I assume that he at least recognized its potential power and realized it as best he could.

What is most intriguing and annoying about the auteur
theory is the implicit idea that a director can add "something extra" to almost anything in a script, that he can virtually "rewrite" anything with his camera and his actors,
that what the scriptwriters give him is just raw material,
meaningless without his contribution.   I find it intriguing in
part because I think it's true in part.   Stanley Kauffmann,
for instance, showed how Max Ophuls made something--a
visually dazzling, if not great, film--out of nothing, a bad
novel and script, in LOLA MONTES.   John Ford performs
a similar feat with a basically dull screenplay and several
different, vivid uses of actors (Henry Fonda, Victor Mature,
Walter Brennan) and scenery in MY DARLING CLEMENTINE.
James Dean and Nicholas Ray make the script's heavy-hand-
ed melodramatics in REBEL WITHOUT A CAUSE exciting to
watch.   Orson Welles' direction and Russell Metty's camerawork make TOUCH OF EVIL electrifying entertainment despite an outlandish script (by Welles)--in fact, it's the very
outlandishness that's electrifying.

Such wonder-working, however, is rare, or occasional
at best.   Directors do not usually do very good work when
they're at odds with or handicapped by a script.   Auteurists
wildly overestimate the power of a director to transform dull
or shoddy material into good cinema.   Even the best can't
always perform miracles.   Ernst Lubitsch only half-redeems
"Wilde's silly melodramatics" (to quote Sarris) with his ele-
gant visual elision in LADY WINDERMERE'S FAN--you can
still hear the palpitating heart of its melodramatic plot when
Lubitsch can't distract attention with a witty visual point.
And he redeems even less (a few scenes) of The STUDENT
PRINCE.   Color, movement, and excitement surround the
dull principals of Renoir's FRENCH CANCAN, but they're
still dull.   Hitchcock's MARNIE, like the Selznick-Dieterle
epic PORTRAIT OF JENNIE, is crammed with camera movement, music, talk, and ideas, but the plot is still a silly

mess, and the cramming makes the movie just watchable, interestingly bad.

A case could be made for my being an auteurist, or at least a semi-auteurist, based simply on the fact that all but three (Ozu, Satyajit Ray, Kurosawa) of my favorite directors (Renoir, Hawks, Ozu, Keaton, Welles, Ray, Sternberg, Kurosawa, Buñuel, Ford, Hitchcock, Capra) are certified auteurs. [5] I wouldn't mind being labeled an auteurist (too much) if that didn't imply a blind acceptance of a few dozen other directors in Sarris' upper and upper-middle ranges (in The American Cinema) who were apparently selected as auteurs out of sheer perversity.  My objections to the basic theory of directorial authorship aren't as strong-- the theory is so ill-defined and vast that it's almost objection-proof--as my objections to particular applications of it; that is, to some of those arbitrary designations of directors as auteurs and to the means used by critics to justify the work of auteur directors.

My antipathy to Wood's approach to Hawks is demonstrated in the chapters on MONKEY BUSINESS and RED LINE 7000, but my favorite unlikely justification of a Hawks picture is Stuart Byron's of RED LINE 7000:

> The race cars in RED LINE 7000 constantly circle the same track--and as Hawks shoots it, the empty oval inside becomes a symbol of the godless nothingness outside. [6]

If you buy that, you'll buy anything (i.e., you're a hard-core auteurist).  Peter Wollen is not without his charm either:

> Hawks first attracted attention because he was regarded naively as an action director.  Later, the thematic content which I have outlined was detected and revealed.  Beyond the stylemes, semantemes were found to exist; the films were anchored in an objective stratum of meaning, a plerematic stratum....  Thus the stylistic expressiveness of Hawks's films was shown to be not purely contingent, but grounded in significance. [7]

Wollen makes film scholarship sound like a treasure hunt or an archaeological dig and Hawks sound like the bone in BRINGING UP BABY.  (Most auteurists belong in Sarris' category, "Strained Seriousness."  Sarris himself fluctuates between "Strained Seriousness" and "Lightly Likable.")

Many of Sarris' Far Side of Paradise (the second-best category) and Expressive Esoterica (third-best) directors seem to me barely capable of preserving the strengths of their scripts, and so are hardly likely to add anything "extra" to one. I am thinking of action directors who are often lumped with Hawks, like Anthony Mann, Raoul Walsh, Sam Fuller, Don Siegel, and Budd Boetticher, and also of directors like Cecil B. DeMille, Andre de Toth, Allan Dwan, Otto Preminger, Tay Garnett, Frank Tashlin, Robert Siodmak, and Edgar G. Ulmer. [8] When Borden Chase was asked why he didn't want to see the dailies on an Anthony Mann picture that he wrote, he replied:

> I know exactly how they're going to be. They're going to be exactly the way I wrote them, word for word, every shot.... Mann ... is supposed to add $75,000 worth to my writing. He hasn't added 10¢ to my writing. [9]

The words and shots in Mann westerns are so conventionally conceived that they seem almost stamped in. It wouldn't be so bad if the scripts were worth shooting straight or if Mann didn't emphasize Chase's dull moralizing: in BEND OF THE RIVER, Jay C. Flippen observes of Arthur Kennedy, "His kind never change." In an underlining close shot, James Stewart--Stewart is also "that kind," but Flippen doesn't know it--adds, "I sure hope you're wrong." Emphasizing the script's simplistic moral scheme hardly constitutes adding something extra. Sarris sometimes tries to separate a film's dialogue (if it's lousy) from the auteur's style in order to salvage the film, but when, as in BEND OF THE RIVER, the visuals merely reinforce the lousy dialogue, that's patently impossible. Chase liked Mann because he never tampered with his writing, and might have liked most of the other directors mentioned above too.

Incomprehensibly, André Bazin called the Mann-Sam Rolfe-Harold Jack Bloom The NAKED SPUR "the most beautifully true western of recent years...." He praises Mann's "infallible sureness of touch in bringing together man and nature, that feeling of the open air,"[10] but The NAKED SPUR is less skillful than Hawks' The BIG SKY at convincing you to overlook its stale, moralizing plot, even planted as it is in a rugged Rocky Mountains setting. There's the same sense of waste (of actors, of scenery) as in the Hawks Western. The setting is less inspirational than incidental to the action, however many picturesque rocks, trees, and rivers it covers in its course. It's the very fact of location

shooting rather than any special use Mann makes of it that
gives the movie a little "something extra. "

For David Thomson, every action in The NAKED
SPUR "has not only the spontaneity of vital movement in a
natural environment but serves as definition of every man's
nature. "[11]   But the definitions that the actions provide are
all too simple and clear-cut:  James Stewart doesn't kill a
man when he could have (hero), and Robert Ryan does when
he has the chance (villain).   And Janet Leigh helpfully spells
out this difference in the dialogue.   Mann's only direction
for Stewart must have been "Intense!"  He makes him look
ridiculous, showing him anxiously gritting his teeth in close-
up at the beginning and breaking down in close-up at the
end.   Mann's clumsy overemphasis ruins the only good bits
of acting Stewart gives him.

Auteur directors, according to auteurist critics, are
always adding dimensions to their films with mysterious
camera movements that transform the mundane into the sub-
lime.   Again on Mann, Jean-Luc Godard analyzes a scene
from MAN OF THE WEST:

> As he comes out, Gary Cooper is framed in medi-
> um shot.   He crosses almost the entire field of
> vision to look at the deserted town, and then (rath-
> er than have a reverse angle of the town, followed
> by a shot of Gary Cooper's face as he watches) a
> lateral tracking shot re-frames Cooper as he stands
> motionless, staring at the empty town.   The stroke
> of genius lies in having the track start after Gary
> Cooper moves, because it is this dislocation in
> time which allows a spatial simultaneity:  in one
> fell swoop we have both the mystery of the deserted
> town, and Gary Cooper's sense of unease at the
> mystery. [12]

I read this passage not long after seeing the movie and I
could not even recall the shot to which Godard refers; only
after several re-readings did I finally at least understand
what he was getting at.   But the shot makes about as much
difference to the movie as a grain of sand does to a beach;
nothing, really, could help Reginald Rose's script, with its
monotonous, one-note characters droning on and on, and its
central dramatic question--Is Cooper one of the outlaws?--
posed so dully and answered so laboriously that the answer
hardly matters.   (He finally challenges his outlaw-uncle,

"You've outlived your kind, you've outlived your time, and I'm coming to get you, " and shoots him, after regaining his breath. )

In the same article, Godard suggests that Mann's art consists of rigorously doing nothing:

> Simply compare the famous pan shot which reveals the arrival of the Indians in STAGECOACH with the fix-focus shot in The LAST FRONTIER of the Indians just appearing out of the high grass to surround Victor Mature and his companions. The force of Ford's camera movement arises from its plastic and dynamic beauty. Mann's shot is, one might say, of <u>vegetal</u> beauty. Its force springs precisely from the fact that it owes nothing to any planned aesthetic. [13]

Aesthetics certainly owe nothing to The LAST FRONTIER (script by Philip Yordan and Russell S. Hughes), which consists of juvenile comedy, simplistic characters, and crude dialogue (Mature: "Captain, how can you and the colonel wear the same type of uniform and still be so different?"). Much could be made of the film's use of heights in relation to moral stature, I suppose, but only as a last critical resort. There's just nothing there, which Godard, in his way, admits, [14] but--since Mann is one of his auteurs--sees as a meaningful, willed nothing.

Auteurists are quick to assume the viewer's involvement in auteur films when such assumptions are necessary to their arguments. V. F. Perkins sees the main tension in the Mann-Chase The FAR COUNTRY as

> between our identification with the Stewart character and our awareness of his shortcomings. The FAR COUNTRY is shaped by our desire to see the hero become a more satisfactory identification-figure, not just attractive and accomplished but admirable as well. The film exploits the ambiguity of our reactions to the lone-wolf hero.... We want [him] to be liked and admired by the other sympathetic characters. [15]

This shaping is accomplished through dialogue which interrupts and conveniently explicates the action for us. The script doesn't allow the viewer to think for himself, and Perkins lauds this narrowness of vision:

But because our involvement is shaped to make us
want his choice, we accept from a wide range of
possible attitudes the one proposed by the film. [16]

Examples of shaping, from the film:

> Corinne Calvet:  You help others, right?
> James Stewart:  I take care of me.
> Calvet:  Ben said you don't like people.
> Walter Brennan:  You're wrong, Jeb.  You gotta
> help 'em.
> Stewart:  I don't need other people.
> Calvet:  You've got to help people.

By the time Mann and Chase are through drumming their
solitary point into your head, you wish the "sympathetic characters" would just shut up and go away (Calvet especially:
"I'm not a freckle-face.  I'm a woman!").

Auteurists usually see only what they want to see in
a movie.  (I think Joseph McBride is dead wrong when he
says that auteurism "looks at the film and tries to see it for
what it is. . . . ")  They accept without question the auteur's
intentions, or what they believe are his intentions.  They
don't see anything outside the frame of reference of the director's (real or imagined) objectives.  You have to see the
movies that they write about fully to appreciate the dichotomy
between the pictures they draw of them and the movies themselves.  There are congruities of course, but they are as
nothing compared to the incongruities.  Perkins and Wood,
in particular, sound fairly reasonable, if dull, when they're
extracting moral schemata from their subjects.  Most auteurists just sound like a cross between con artists and idiots, but Wood and Perkins give their arguments a logical-
sounding development that must have taken some time and
practice to arrive at.  However, they usually fail to take
into account in their little schemata matters like the possibility of didacticism and plain lack of imagination, miscast-
ing (Stewart is helpless with Chase's stamped-in, cynical
dialogue for The FAR COUNTRY), clichés (such as the dramatically expendable character, here Ruth Roman, conveniently caught in a crossfire; and in Mann's WINCHESTER '73,
Shelley Winters), possible lack of audience involvement, and
ideas stillborn in the script.  They assume sound scripts,
literate dialogue, impeccable casting, and the viewer's bated
breath when they want to.  But these same assumptions don't
apply to non-auteur films, which don't wear the magic sign,
or whatever it is that protects auteur films.

Perkins spends over two pages on one scene in Otto Preminger's CARMEN JONES and makes it sound like a pretty important scene.  He admits that the story is familiar and sets out to demonstrate how Preminger's direction gives it "a specific and unexpected significance," how his direction of a scene in a jeep with Harry Belafonte and Dorothy Dandridge "transforms what is, in synopsis, a rather familiar situation:  brassy dame makes unsuccessful play for disapproving male."  It sounds good:

> The camera records the beginning of her song from the jeep's bonnet, seeing both the prisoner and her guard within the windscreen's stable frame.  A metal strut at the centre of the windscreen divides the image so as to isolate and confine each character within a separate visual cage.  But Carmen's movements shatter the rigid symmetry of the image. [17]

Before I saw the film, I reread Perkins' argument in order to test it fairly against the film.  But all I saw was that familiar situation--no visual cages or shattering of rigid symmetry, just a jeep and a windscreen.  (Even Chaplin's CARMEN, which is no great shakes, is better than Preminger's.)  Themes of freedom and confinement are evident in the art direction and camerawork of CARMEN JONES, but the movie is just as dead as if they weren't.  Symmetry is nice, but it doesn't make a movie.  Perkins adds that

> we can assign a specific significance to Preminger's treatment only because it brings out possibilities latent in the story and dialogue.

I can only assume that there were no possibilities latent in the story, the dialogue, and the acting out of the story because Otto Preminger, of all directors, would have spotted any possibilities in a story, his story sense is so keen--he chose this story, didn't he? [18]  (Apparently the more familiar a story, the more latent possibilities there are supposed to be in it.)  Why Perkins would go to such lengths to make a case for such an indefensibly conventional scene and film I don't know.  He's ingenious, though, and if I had any lousy movies I wanted instant cases for, I'd go to him.

Sarris talks a good "visual revolution" when he's discussing Preminger's movies, but his analyses of Preminger's visual style usually boil down to one or two vague, baffling

sentences which do not relate to his dismissal of the rest of
the movie:

> As his camera sweeps across the ecclesiastical
> canvas represented by Rome, New England, Geor-
> gia, and Vienna, Preminger's meaning comes
> through more strongly in his feeling for architec-
> ture than in his feeling for drama.  It is significant
> that the opening credit sequence depicting Father
> Stephen Fermoyle ascending an endless series of
> steps lingers in the mind long after the same char-
> acter's final speech has been completely forgotten. [19]

You don't even have to see the movie (The CARDINAL) not
to know what he's talking about, as you do with Perkins,
who makes some kind of sense until you see the movie.
What significance the above images carry in the context of
the movie Sarris leaves you to guess.

> To watch his camera prowling around a girl's
> school, an unoccupied house, a pervert's lair, a
> lackluster pub, from room to room, up- and down-
> stairs, in and out of doors, with the sustained
> frenzy of a director concerned with integral space
> is to realize the majesty of mise-en-scène.  There
> is one sequence when Olivier walks up the steps to
> the school with a fixed focus on the revolving
> police light in the foreground.  Preminger virtually
> tosses the effect away, and this is only one of
> many such casual coups that make his movies so
> hard to evaluate. [20]

But Sarris doesn't even try with BUNNY LAKE IS MISSING.
One is left with the impression of a meaninglessly busy
camera and a stock focus shot that any director would have
thrown away.  (That is, I assume that it's stock, that it's
the camera that's focussed on the light.  It's a neat trick if
Olivier's eyes are fixed on the light as he walks up the
steps. )  The critic's task is to render the mystical (i. e. ,
art) understandable, not vice versa.  Sarris has a habit of
leaving out vital links between points in his reviews that
makes the most mundane film sound mystically inspired.
Sarris admits that Preminger's films begin as trash, but he
can't explain how they conclude transformed.

He dismisses the dialogue ("flowery silent film titles
verbalized") in Fuller's SHOCK CORRIDOR, then goes on to

say that "Fuller's camera style is fluid enough to lend at
least visual conviction to his rhetorical characters. " What
the one aspect of the movie has to do with the other he
doesn't explain.   Admittedly, the characters rant on and on,
but the camera doesn't make them look any better or sound
any more eloquent.   Fuller hasn't even the technical compe-
tence auteurists supposedly require of auteurs--in UNDER-
WORLD, USA he laughably over-poses his actors, over-sha-
dows his scenes, and over-angles his camera for Drama.
He's inept at action sequences--the crooked mayor's suicide
attempt in UNDERWORLD, USA is an hilarious botch, and
his scripts seem primarily intended to embarrass the actors.

Fuller borrows a framing idea from Keaton in FORTY
GUNS, and there's a parody of sorts of the horse-race metaphor from The BIG SLEEP in SHOCK CORRIDOR.   The ending of Fuller's The NAKED KISS is like a warped version of
the climactic scene from a Capra movie.   But Fuller is so
inept, his intentions so murky and confused, that it's uncertain if he's plagiarizing, deifying, or putting down his fellow
auteurs.   His films are a parody of the auteur theory.   Alternately perverse and sappy--sometimes simultaneously,
which is some kind of achievement--his movies, like FORTY
GUNS, finally collapse into mush.   (Barry Sullivan:   "You
gotta be big to forgive, " a thought worthy of an Anthony
Mann Western. )

It takes Angie Dickinson, Nat King Cole, and 90 minutes to convince Gene Barry to accept his part-Chinese son
in Fuller's CHINA GATE, a sensationalistic political soap
opera whose anti-Communist and anti-racist co-themes are
apparently supposed to have something to do with each other,
but really don't.   Fuller, an emotional elephant (in George
Eliot's phrase), is a one-man demolition crew, detonating
explosive lines (Dickinson:   "I'm a little of everything and
a lot of nothing"), situations (part-Chinese, anti-Communist
Dickinson pushing part-Chinese, Communist Lee Van Cleef
off a balcony, then dashing off to a cave to blow herself and
a munitions dump up), and characters (a Hungarian legion-
naire who nearly strangles Cole during one enactment of his
recurrent dream of throttling a Communist soldier) as often
as possible in his movies, but to little effect except comic.
Barry and Dickinson's reconciliation interrupts a fantastically
important mission to the China Gate, and Fuller astutely
isolates them in close-up so as to take our minds off the
other members of the team who are standing around awkwardly, but quietly, waiting considerately for the two to

make up.   (Subconsciously, you're expecting one of the others
to call "Time!")

An atrocity like The NAKED KISS is entertaining, but
it's such an ungodly mess that I doubt if any critic will ever
be able to say with reasonable assurance how much of the
entertainment is on the director, how much is at the director's expense.   Fuller is certainly an auteur--who else
would want to claim responsibility for his films?

Sarris has ingenuously suggested that only "outside
interference" prevented Raoul Walsh "from rising to the level of Hawks," as if Hawks' relative independence were the
only differentiation between the two.   I'm willing to concede
that even studio hacks like Walsh (Warners), Michael Curtiz
(Warners), and Dwan (Fox) were occasionally involved in
some pretty good projects (e.g., THEY DRIVE BY NIGHT,
CASABLANCA, FRONTIER MARSHAL).   The idea, though,
that they were inhibited by studio pressure is laughable.
They thrived under it.   They made things fast and cheaply
for their studios, and that's their only apparent virtue. [21]
It's unlikely that they could have operated outside the con-
fines and security of the studio.   Dwan's and Walsh's main
claims to fame are that they've been around forever and
have directed about as many movies as John Ford.   They
were lucky to get some good dialogue or a good actor-star
every fifth picture or so.   Their "style" is exclusively func-
tional--the best angle to shoot the scene fastest.   With
Hawks, the actor, not the budget, dictates angles and shots.

I'm always afraid of underestimating a veteran director like Walsh, but my experience has been that you can't
underestimate him.   Once or twice during THEY DIED WITH
THEIR BOOTS ON I thought a camera movement was trying
to express something rather than simply underlining action,
but I was fooled both times:   it was just making Errol
Flynn's collision with an officer a surprise or making room
for Olivia de Havilland to collapse gracefully.   (Mann's
WINCHESTER '73 has similar pieces of programmed action:
James Stewart and Stephen McNally fall on a floor right in
front of the camera, and, later on, Dan Duryea trips
Charles Drake right into the camera.)   The dialogue in
THEY DRIVE BY NIGHT is terrific (waitress, about a steak:
"It's so tender it'll throw its little arms around you"), but
the movie is still just a Walsh quickie.   Action bits and
even the better lines are over-emphasized, shots never match,
and Walsh obviously didn't take any time to work out the

script physically on the sets. In GENTLEMAN JIM, Walsh
and the script dull and domesticate a good subject--the early
years of boxing--always letting you know when you're supposed to laugh or gasp. The script squeezes the characters
into formula comedy-drama, and Walsh's actors, accordingly,
are unspontaneous as hell.

Hollywood auteur directors are supposed to be expert
storytellers, and some of them are, but how can you tell
with someone like Walsh who rarely got a good, solid story
to tell? A war picture like Walsh's FIGHTER SQUADRON
(script by Seton I. Miller) doesn't even have a story. It's
just scraps from CEILING ZERO (Edmond O'Brien as Dizzy
Davis), AIR FORCE (gunning the parachutist), and DUEL IN
THE SUN (after strafing a train a fighter pilot breaks into
"I Been Workin' on the Railroad"), the latter scrap coming
very close to plagiarism. THEY DIED WITH THEIR BOOTS
ON goes on and on without making much narrative sense--
the villains betray Custer and the Indians and take their own
sweet time doing it--though at stray moments the script
seems to know what it's about, as in a strange scene in
which Errol Flynn scares one villain, Arthur Kennedy, by
opposing money with glory: "Glory you take with you...."
It's a scene with bizarre mystical undercurrents not present
in the rest of the movie. Kennedy's dying "I see what you
meant about glory" and another bad guy's "I think I see why
my son died" (at Little Big Horn) are just meaningless happy-
ending sops. The film is finally just another arbitrary mixture of happiness, unhappiness, comedy, and action.

The principal characters in Anthony Mann's aggres-
sively trashy The FURIES (script by Charles Schnee) alternately love and despise each other, never reaching an ade-
quate compromise. That's the "story." The Mann-Valentine
Davies-Oscar Brodney The GLENN MILLER STORY has no
sense of forward motion either. The script plays on the
viewer's sense that the events depicted "really happened,"
thus relieving itself of the necessity of making narrative
sense of them. It has no life of its own. It exists only as
another formula musical-bio, (hardly) distinguished by a few
motifs that are sometimes called upon to compose whole
scenes because the script is so sketchy. It's just a series
of bands and crowds (and good music), but at least it doesn't
have the usual, grating happy-sad-happy "development" of
most biographical movies, and in that sense it's almost all
"pleasant." The movie's few nice moments aren't original;
they are just echoes of other musical-bios.

The last close shot of the rifle in WINCHESTER '73
(Mann-Chase-Robert L. Richards)--the same gun, different
men!--leaves one with the same feeling of nothing accomplished, of a plot ploughed through, some dull points made,
and time wasted by all.   Mann's THUNDER BAY is basically
propaganda for oil companies--James Stewart:   "Without oil
this country of ours would stop"--but despite its routine
plot, which ties up everything too neatly, and its cut-and-
dried look and enter-speak-exit scenes, Mann allows time
for the actors to act for once, and Stewart gives the only
good performance I've seen him give in a Mann movie.   The
Gil Doud-John Michael Hayes script also provides intermittently good material for Gilbert Roland, Dan Duryea, Joanne
Dru, and Jay C. Flippen.   But there's no real story sense,
just several well-acted scenes, which, however, put it a
notch above most Mann movies.

In what will no doubt be declared a "major reevaluation" of Walsh, William Paul, in the Village Voice (May 23,
June 6, and June 27, 1974), finds several parallels between
him and Ford:

> Ford is generally recognized as the greater artist
> of the two, so much so that Walsh frequently isn't
> recognized at all, but I don't think the matter is
> so clear-cut.

Paul tries to turn the historical parallels between the two
directors into artistic parallels by finding a "distinctive
camera style" in Walsh's work and "direct expressions of
Walsh's vision" in his actors.   This "style," as with Anthony
Mann, amounts to virtually nothing:

> In scenes where conventional Hollywood style of the
> period [1928] would have dictated cross-cutting be-
> tween two characters, Walsh chose to pan back and
> forth between them, thereby making the geographical
> distance between the characters as important as
> the psychological distance.

Paul doesn't say who these characters are or in what way the
distances between them are made important.   Perhaps his
article was poorly edited and he did go on to explain, but it's
hard to imagine how a case for distinctive style in a film
could be based on such an inconsequential affectation.   He
does go on to say:

> In moving the camera between the characters a new
> character is in effect introduced, a narrator whose
> hand is evident as it leads us from one character
> to the other.  The leisurely movements of the
> STRAWBERRY BLONDE opening successfully evoke
> the mood of a bygone era, but in their high degree
> of formal control they also keep leading us to the
> artist behind all this art.

Is our awareness of the camera or of control necessarily an
awareness of an artist?   Can't it merely be awareness of a
busy cameraman or of a labored effect?  (Admittedly, Rouben
Mamoulian, not Raoul Walsh, is the master of the labored
effect. )

> Paul's most amusing, desperate insight is:

> The most typical Walsh shot is a slightly below
> eye-level camera that emphasizes the openness of
> space around his characters, creating the sense of
> a vacuum that his characters must fill by moving
> about as much as possible.

This makes it sound as if the Three Stooges or the Ritz
Brothers would be Walsh's ideal actors.   Voids and vacuums
appear to be "in" in auteurist circles.

> What Walsh puts in front of his camera is more to
> the point than what he does or doesn't do with the camera
> itself.   Paul writes,

> The most intense scene in THEY DIED WITH THEIR
> BOOTS ON is typically not a battle scene but the
> final leave-taking of Custer from his wife....

He evidently picked up "intense" from Wood, and he uses it
equally indiscriminately.   No one could responsibly employ
it in describing a scene--any scene--with Errol Flynn, who
plays Custer.   By your actors shall ye be known.   Walsh
made seven films (of which I've seen five) starring Flynn,
who is not the sort of actor to have around when one wants
some acting done.   Any director who worked that often with
as limited an actor as Flynn does not deserve to be taken
very seriously.   (The high point of GENTLEMAN JIM is the
evidently unintentional in-joke when Alexis Smith remarks of
Flynn as Jim on stage, "Why do people pay good money to
see him as an actor?")

Flynn's brash boyishness is appropriately comical in
the early scenes of THEY DIED WITH THEIR BOOTS ON,
when he's playing the cocky young Custer.   But the boyishness, which is still there, is comically irrelevant to later
scenes with him as Custer the man.   His constipated "hate"
look as he bursts in on evil Arthur Kennedy in the bar is a
pathetic attempt to do something he just can't do--act.   The
most brilliant camera movements in the world couldn't get
around the fact of Flynn in the final leave-taking of Custer
from his wife.   (It's at the end of this scene that Miss de
Havilland collapses, after the camera politely steps back for
her.)   In GENTLEMAN JIM, every scene with Flynn "plays"
the same.   In SILVER RIVER, Flynn's character's cynicism
is that of a peevish child, but this bizarre strain of child-
ishness in him has nothing to do with the movie, only with
Flynn's inexpressiveness.   (Ann Sheridan's childish petulance
is irrelevant too.)

I haven't seen a really fine performance in a Walsh
movie, and I've seen seventeen, though de Havilland is good
in STRAWBERRY BLONDE (which is light enough when it
tries to be light, too heavy when it tries to be heavy), Ida
Lupino and Sheridan are good in THEY DRIVE BY NIGHT,
Clark Gable gives the lightly likable schlock-romantics of
BAND OF ANGELS more authority than they deserve, Ward
Bond's John L. Sullivan in GENTLEMAN JIM is a hearty
caricature, and Bogart is good in HIGH SIERRA (which is
alternately sappy and tough, and good when it's tough).   But,
while Hawks' films at their least usually have stray saving
performances, Walsh's films at their best contain a good
performance or two.   (I'm not forgetting Hawks' RED LINE
7000, which has nothing, but Walsh has more than his share
of RED LINE 7000's--The SHERIFF OF FRACTURED JAW,
A PRIVATE'S AFFAIR, SILVER RIVER, FIGHTER SQUAD-
RON, etc.)   Even Peter Bogdanovich admits that Bogart is
terrible in The ROARING TWENTIES, and Bogart and Raft
are just fair in THEY DRIVE BY NIGHT.   James Cagney is
about the best actor Walsh worked with.   He's fantastic in
his two big scenes--his mother's death, his death--and in
one little scene in which he takes a walk "with mother" in
WHITE HEAT, but Walsh doesn't make much other use of
Cagney's talent in that film, in STRAWBERRY BLONDE, or
in The ROARING TWENTIES.

In The ROARING TWENTIES the script slices him up
into three or four characters--smart, naive, luckless--instead
of developing one, and the picture winds up a combination sob

story-historical drama-gangster movie-character study.   The
least-known Cagney-Walsh film, A LION IS IN THE STREETS,
a forerunner of A FACE IN THE CROWD (the exploitation of
country folk by one of their own), is also the best, although
it has three women in it and no roles for them, and despite
the fact that the Luther Davis script is simply a string of
set-pieces for Cagney to bellow and flail his way through.
But it's the only one of his four Walshes which stays with
him, and Cagney's performance charges the carnival atmosphere of those set-pieces with excitement; his peddler-politi-
cian is a cross between barker and lion tamer as he ha-
rangues his audiences and moves them around into the best
positions (for him).

    Directors like Don Siegel and Robert Siodmak have
some talent for making scenes if not whole movies.   But
calling invisible, talentless directors like Mann, Walsh,
Preminger, de Toth, and Dwan, or distinctively awful directors like Fuller, De Mille, and Tashlin auteurs is the auteurists' own bad joke on their theory. [22]   The theory attempts
to make some sense out of the general senselessness of film
history, but it tries to make more than I think is possible.
And with mistakes like Mann and Walsh it makes less rather
than more sense of that history.   There simply will never be
a reliable guide to most of the movies--those worth seeing
and those not--out of the mass that has been made.   The
chief benefit and the chief drawback of auteurism, in fact if
not theory, is that it has opened up the field of "serious"
film criticism so that virtually every movie ever made can
be discussed "seriously." I more or less agree with Sarris
that

        the listing of films by directors remains the most
        reliable index of quality available to us short of
        the microscopic evaluation of every film ever
        made. [23]

I think it's swell of him to want to save us all the trouble.
But it's still an unreliable index.

    The theory is really helpful only at the very top, in
its location of those few artists and talented professionals
who have created a whole, worthwhile body of work.   Beyond
that it's hit-and-miss, and the good movies are pretty evenly
scattered among "auteurs," "non-auteurs," and sometime
"auteurs." The auteur theory is only for those who want to
take easy, false comfort in the knowledge that they're not

wasting time on "unimportant" movies or missing "important"
ones.  But anything worth doing--seeing movies, writing
about them--is worth wasting some time on.  Auteur critics,
Pauline Kael believes, "devise elaborate theories to justify
soaking up their time. "  They don't have to:

> A scholar who means to build himself a monument
> must spend much of his life in acquiring knowledge
> which for its own sake is not worth having and in
> reading books which do not in themselves deserve
> to be read.... [24]

What auteur critics don't like to admit is that most of the
movies they see aren't worth seeing for themselves, but
only as part of general film history, a director's history,
an actor's history, a genre, or sociology.

## Notes

1.  Peter Wollen, Signs and Meaning in the Cinema (Indiana
    University Press, (1972), pp. 80-81.

2.  Jean-Luc Godard, Godard on Godard, ed. Tom Milne
    (The Viking Press, 1972), p. 29.

3.  Stuart Byron, "Auteurism, Hawks, Hatari! and Me," in
    Favorite Movies, ed. Philip Nobile (Macmillan, 1973),
    pp. 261-262.

4.  Andrew Sarris, The American Cinema (E. P. Dutton &
    Co. , 1968), p. 32.

5.  That is, they're certified by auteurists.  Some auteurists
    would certify the other three too:  Stuart Byron praised
    Ozu and LATE SPRING in the pages of the Village
    Voice, after apologizing to his fellow-auteurists, and
    Robin Wood admires Ray and Ozu.  The lines aren't
    that finely drawn.

6.  Nobile, op. cit. , p. 264.

7.  Wollen, op. cit. , pp. 91-93.

8.  There is not space to go into detail on all these "au-
    teurs, " but the titles I'm basing my (tentative) nega-
    tive judgments on are:

Siegel: The BIG STEAL (fair), RIOT IN CELL
BLOCK 11 (fair, with some good set-pieces), INVA-
SION OF THE BODY SNATCHERS (good plot, bad dia-
logue), The LINE-UP (fair; good set-pieces), HELL
IS FOR HEROES (dud), COOGAN'S BLUFF (fair, with
good--i.e., vivid--violence), TWO MULES FOR SIS-
TER SARA (wretched).

Boetticher: BEHIND LOCKED DOORS, HORIZONS
WEST (dud), MAN FROM THE ALAMO (dud), DECI-
SION AT SUNDOWN (fair; good violence), The TALL
T (some good talk, suspense, but empty, humorless),
BUCHANAN RIDES ALONE (dud; good ending), RIDE
LONESOME (spare, humorless; James Best good),
ARRUZA (for bullfight fans only).

De Mille: The TEN COMMANDMENTS '23 (dud),
THIS DAY AND AGE (incredible), The PLAINSMAN
(dull, but with Jean Arthur), NORTH WEST MOUNTED
POLICE (dud), The TEN COMMANDMENTS '56 (dud).

de Toth: DARK WATERS (a real dud), PITFALL
(fair; Raymond Burr good), CARSON CITY (partly
fresh, partly familiar), HOUSE OF WAX (dud), DAY
OF THE OUTLAW (a real dud).

Dwan: ROBIN HOOD (Fairbanks good, plot dull),
MANHANDLED (dreary sentimentality), The IRON
MASK (see ROBIN HOOD), HUMAN CARGO (vapid
melo, brutal premises), SUEZ (dud), The THREE
MUSKETEERS (at least there are only three Ritz
Brothers), The GORILLA (no thrills; 6-10 laughs),
FRONTIER MARSHAL (Cesar Romero and plot struc-
ture good, Wyatt Earp role dull), LOOK WHO'S
LAUGHING, HERE WE GO AGAIN, UP IN MABEL'S
ROOM (see James Agee), SANDS OF IWO JIMA (good,
as I recall), The RESTLESS BREED (dud), The MOST
DANGEROUS MAN ALIVE (dud).

Garnett: ONE WAY PASSAGE (partly good), CHINA
SEAS (formula but fun), JOY OF LIVING (dud),
SLIGHTLY HONORABLE (dud), MY FAVORITE SPY,
The CROSS OF LORRAINE, The POSTMAN ALWAYS
RINGS TWICE (messy, occasionally fascinating), A
CONNECTICUT YANKEE (unbearable), SEVEN WON-
DERS OF THE WORLD.

Tashlin: WILL SUCCESS SPOIL ROCK HUNTER?
(good, as I recall), ROCK-A-BYE BABY (dud),
GEISHA BOY (dud; funny anthropomorphic rabbit Har-
ry), BACHELOR FLAT (dud), The DISORDERLY OR-
DERLY (dud), The GLASS BOTTOM BOAT (dud), The
PRIVATE NAVY OF SGT. O'FARRELL (dud).

Siodmak:  SON OF DRACULA (dud), PHANTOM
LADY (fair melo with good scenes), COBRA WOMAN
(dud), The SUSPECT, UNCLE HARRY (dull with good
scenes), The KILLERS (good, as I recall), The DARK
MIRROR (some good scenes), The SPIRAL STAIRCASE
(good effects, dumb story).
Ulmer:  The BLACK CAT (dud), BLUEBEARD (dull),
STRANGE ILLUSION (silly), CLUB HAVANA (routine
but compact), MAN FROM PLANET X, DAUGHTER
OF DR. JEKYLL (dud), The AMAZING TRANSPARENT
MAN (dud), BEYOND THE TIME BARRIER (dud).
These are all just opinions of course and shouldn't
be taken as in-depth analyses.  And it will be observed that I haven't seen all the key films of all
these directors.

9.    Jim Kitses, "The Rise and Fall of the American West,"
interview, Film Comment, Winter 1970-71, p. 19.

10.   What is Cinema? Vol. II, ed. Hugh Gray (University of
California Press, 1972), p. 156.

11.   Movie Man (Stein and Day, 1969), p. 93.

12.   Godard on Godard, ed. Jean Narboni and Tom Milne
(Viking Press, 1972), p. 120.

13.   Ibid., p. 119.

14.   Actually, the camera does move upward as the Indians
surround Mature.

15.   Film as Film (Penguin Books, 1972), pp. 149-150.

16.   Ibid., p. 150.

17.   Ibid., p. 80.

18.   There weren't many possibilities in the stories of two
other Preminger movies I saw recently either--
LAURA and WHIRLPOOL.  LAURA is like someone's
oh-so-bright, unresearched idea of high society and
criminal types, with Gene Tierney so conventionally
"glamorous" that the big buildup the script gives her,
and all the hoohah over her, is more vacuous than it
seems at first.  (Hitchcock has a similar problem
with Kim Novak in VERTIGO.)  She makes the fawning

over her and awe for her of the other characters look
ridiculous. And it's very touching that the wife in
WHIRLPOOL can finally come clean and that the husband trusts her despite the evidence, but most of the
movie is taken up by a transparent suspense plot, and
Miss Tierney is again a blank, with dully undistinctive
features and zero presence. The camera is in the
right place once or twice, but those few coups don't
save the script.

19.   Confessions of a Cultist (Simon and Schuster, 1970),
       p. 110.

20.   Ibid. , p. 214.

21.   "See, we had to work so damned fast. You'd be work-
       ing on a picture in June and it had to be in a theatre
       in September. It was pre-sold, and you got money
       from the exhibitors for the production, so you felt
       you really had to bear down on it. "--Raoul Walsh,
       "Can You Ride the Horse?", interview by James
       Childs, Sight and Sound, Winter 72/3, p. 12.

22.   Hawks: "I learned right in the beginning from Jack
       Ford, and I learned what not to do by watching Cecil
       De Mille. "--"Hawks Talks, " interview by Joseph
       McBride and Gerald Peary, Film Comment, May-June
       1974, p. 46.

23.   Sarris, The American Cinema, op. cit. , p. 31.

24.   A. E. Housman--Selected Prose (Cambridge University
       Press, 1961), p. 159.

## HOWARD HAWKS: AN INTERVIEW

by Alex Ameripoor and Don Willis

DW:   I'm taping over BALL OF FIRE.

HH:   I use the tape a great deal.   The next picture we'll have a second unit that'll be working about six months. And a very brilliant man is going to direct it.   Still, every once in a while on a sequence I just sit down and take a tape and I talk as though I were talking to him.   Well, he can go out--and he doesn't have to remember all the things...

AA:   In terms of delivery of dialogue, I think I enjoy your films more than anybody else's.

HH:   Well, the odd thing about it was, when sound came in they asked me what I knew about the stage, and I said, "Nothing."   I'd never been backstage.   "Well then," they said, "you don't know dialogue."   I said, "I know how people talk."   So I wrote a story and I wrote all the dialogue. Dick Barthelmess read it and wanted to do it and wanted me to direct it.   I made The DAWN PATROL, and that was the biggest picture of the year.   Irving Thalberg said, "You son of a bitch.   Everyone'll be trying to do that kind of dialogue that you do and they won't know how to do it."   Because everybody at that time was emoting, you know, really going to it.   That was the first picture of underplaying, just casual things, talking about death and war and everything in the terms that we use.   I found that making pictures with dialogue was a lot easier than making silent pictures.

DW:   But then the next year you did film a play, The CRIMINAL CODE.

HH:   Oh, sure.   But I changed all the dialogue to suit myself.   I shorten a lot of the verbose stuff that writers

do.  I don't <u>change</u> the dialogue.   Just a different delivery.
And also, when the thing calls for it ... I think I was the
first one to use overlapping dialogue.   I used it first in...

DW:  TWENTIETH CENTURY?

HH:  When I worked with Hecht and MacArthur, it
was very easy to do that, because you put a few words in
front of a speech you want to hear and a few words afterwards.   You don't lose a damn thing and you get a feeling
of speed.   Because when we sit here and talk, we all talk
at the same time once in a while.

DW:  There are some great gags in HIS GIRL FRI-
DAY which are just that, with Clarence Kolb and Billy...

HH:  Gilbert.   Well, Gilbert had no trouble doing it.
Kolb said, "You want me to step on somebody else's line?
And they're going to step on mine?"   And I said, "You're
goddamn right they're going to."   It took him about two days
to get used to it.   All his life he'd been playing on the stage
where you don't step on somebody's line.

AA:  And that's where Bogdanovich is learning from
you.

HH:  Oh sure.   Peter sat on the set ... three pictures
he came and sat on the set.   I saw TARGETS and I said,
"You've got a lot of talent making action pictures, but your
dialogue is lousy."   I talked to him about dialogue.   Now he's
pretty good at dialogue.
When we wrote RIO BRAVO, we wanted a gunman who
was a little bit different.   I saw Ricky Nelson on television
and I called his dad.   I said, "I want your boy to do a
picture with me."   He said, "I'd be delighted."   I said I'd
like to see two or three of the best episodes with him, and
he sent them.   Then Rick came out and he made a hell ...
he was <u>good</u>.   And I tell you one thing--the picture grossed
a million dollars more...

DW:  He's a lot like Montgomery Clift in RED RIVER.

HH:  Well, I showed him a lot of those things.

DW:  I've seen one early script of The THING, and
when they find the flying saucer, they don't have the scene
where they stretch out to form a circle, which is really a
great scene.

HH:  What do you think a director does?  He's telling
a story.  You can't sit up in a room and write a thing like
The THING.  You don't know what it's going to be like.  If
I remember rightly, that was phony ice.  We went up north
to get some snow and ice, and there wasn't any.  We had to
create our own.  We got sued for the salt we used.  It
melted and ran down and spoiled some people's vegetation.
Any director who's any good, when he gets on the set that
he's going to work with, he's going to change things.  Leo
McCarey, who I thought was a great director, because of
the little touches, the funny things, that he put in, would
play the piano and talk and fool around until noon time, then
say, "Let's start working."  Then they'd work like the devil
all afternoon.  Then these directors who want to get the
scene in the can by ten minutes after nine and show a great
day...

DW:  When you worked under another producer, did
they rush you?

HH:  I don't think I ever worked under anybody like
that.

DW:  It seems like most films are shot that way.
They just want to get it over with.

HH:  Maybe today.  But they're making such lousy
pictures today.  I don't mean all of them.  I made quite a
little money betting on the result of the Academy Awards.
I bet The STING was going to win.  It's the only comedy in
two years that's any good--WHAT'S UP, DOC? was made
two years before that.  Jack Ford came down here to die.
And we used to talk about the things that I stole from him,
the things that he stole from me.  He used to remember all
kinds of things.  One day he was laughing like hell and he
said, "I remember one time when I had a lousy picture and
you had a real good one and I got the Academy Award and
you didn't."  And he laughed.  He had HOW GREEN WAS
MY VALLEY, which is a pretty pukey picture, and I had
SERGEANT YORK.

AA:  You knew John Ford from the beginning?

HH:  Oh, yeah.  The owner-directors at Fox got
angry at the fact that the first five pictures I made were
really good.  They said, "Why does that guy think ... you
know."  Ford said, "Because he can read."  The head of

Fox doubled my salary in the second picture and doubled it again the next picture.

DW: A lot of I WAS A MALE WAR BRIDE was almost silent...

HH: Almost every picture that I make is first funny silent. It doesn't depend on lines. Peter Bogdanovich learned visual comedy from me. He did a very, very fine job of WHAT'S UP, DOC? Because he didn't have funny people to work with.

DW: I think WHAT'S UP, DOC? also takes from Frank Tashlin.

AA: A friend of mine was looking at the pictures in this book [Gili's Howard Hawks] and he saw this still here [from the restaurant scene in BRINGING UP BABY] and he said, "Is this something like WHAT'S UP, DOC?" I said, "Stupid! That's the remake of it."

HH: Well, that scene there--Bart Marshall, the actor, had a wooden leg, and we took two girls to a party. The hostess sent the girls upstairs to put their cloaks in the bedroom, and Bart put his wooden leg on the back of the girl's dress. It ripped the whole back of it...

AA: So this was not written by a writer. You just improvised on the set?

HH: "Improvising" is a bad word. Christ, I think people must think that directors don't contribute anything.

AA: Well, some of them don't.

HH: That's okay. Then just say it's "non-improvisation."

DW: I think Katharine Hepburn is so great in BRING-ING UP BABY...

HH: Well, it was the first time she played comedy, I believe. But she's so damn good. Give her the right idea, she's going to do it right. We had a marvelous little guy on that picture. He was a great comedian for Ziegfeld--the fellow who played the sheriff, Walter Catlett. I used to go and see him all the time. One day I said to Katie, "For

Christ's sake, can't I make it clear what I want to tell you?
I guess not, because I'm not getting it. " I said, "Wait a
minute. " I went over to Walter Catlett and I said, "Walter,
do me a favor, will you? Show Miss Hepburn how to do
this scene. " He said, "I'm not going to show her. She's
too good. " I said, "But what if she asked you?" "Then I'd
show her. " So I went back to Katie. I said, "Go over and
ask him how to do that scene. " And he did it, and she
said, "Oh! I see what you're doing. Now I know what's
wrong. Now I can do it. " She told me, "You've got to keep
that guy around. " So I'd write scenes for him for about
three weeks to keep him around. Hepburn was perfectly
serious being completely zany. If she'd tried to be funny or
cute, then it wouldn't have been any good. The only mistake
I made in that picture was that I had too many good comics.
I didn't have any sanity.

        DW: Like in I WAS A MALE WAR BRIDE--Cary
Grant is the center of sanity, and all these crazy things are
happening to him.

        HH: Katie--she's so good.

        DW: You didn't have a series of Hepburn films. You
had a series of Grant films.

        HH: Well, what comedies did I make after BRINGING
UP BABY that...

        DW: ...she could have been in?

        AA: HIS GIRL FRIDAY.

        HH: Don't you think the woman that was in that was
pretty good? I did try to get Hepburn for one other picture.
I've forgotten what it was. But a long time ago I gave up
trying to get women stars. In the first place, usually, a
woman star finds out that the left side of her face is better.
And she gets all the little cute tricks people like her for.
And she's afraid to do other things. It holds you back. You
can get men to do some new stuff.

        DW: Grant probably never did anything like ONLY
ANGELS HAVE WINGS before then.

        HH: I'm talking about girls. I used a great actress
in ONLY ANGELS HAVE WINGS, Jean Arthur. When the

picture was finished, I said, "Jean, I think you're the only
person that I ever worked with that I don't feel that I helped
one single bit. " I said, "Someday you're going to see, on
the screen, the girl that I wanted you to play. " About three
years later, I came home, and her car was in my front
driveway. She was waiting for me. She said, "I saw that
picture last night. I'll do any story that you want me to. "
That was one of the nicest things that was ever said to me.
You see, what I wanted was--when Cary Grant finds that
she has not taken the boat--I had a good scene written for
her where she's confused, bewildered. She doesn't know
why she's staying. She's embarrassed. She was eating
breakfast, and I told her to get all mixed up and stir the
coffee with a knife, you know, to try to cut with a spoon,
to finally start crying. "I can't do that, " she said. I said,
"Don't you want to try?" "No. It would just upset me. "
So what the hell. I just about gave up. And, you know,
she's good.

DW: I think she's good as she is in the picture.
But she's maybe too cute. I heard you had sort of a family
on that film. I've seen stills of the people on the set, and
it looks like you all have--somebody brought lunch one day,
somebody else brought it the next, or something.

HH: I don't remember.

AA: I'm sure it was shot according to the union
rules.

HH: We used to get a lot of ... Oh, I know! We
had a prop man whose father ran a delicatessen, if that's
what you mean. We all ate together. The food was much
better.

AA: That was shot on a stage mainly, wasn't it?

HH: Yeah, and we didn't have to listen to Harry
Cohn also.

DW: How much control did you have over the music
that was added to your films? Did you select the person
who did the music?

HH: Almost all films, unless I was trying to do somebody a favor, I had complete charge of, including the music.

DW:   ONLY ANGELS HAVE WINGS has hardly any
music, and when it does over, say, Thomas Mitchell's
death, it's very effective.

HH:   Now, the picture you're going to see [RED
RIVER] has a really good score.   Tiomkin was good.   And
also you had to keep musicians from playing too loud.

AA:   Right.   It's too loud in RED RIVER.

DW:   Oh, for that picture, I don't know.

HH:   Also, it depends on how the thing is re-recorded
for it.   I've fogotten whether it was RIO BRAVO or EL
DORADO.   I didn't want any violins or--I wanted hard
strings.   And when I went in to see it after they finished
mixing it, I couldn't hear the hard strings.   I made them
do it all over again and throw away the soft stuff and keep
the hard stuff.   HATARI! had some of the greatest music.
I came back and I talked with Dimi Tiomkin.   I said, "Now
look, Dimi.   I brought you back some native music.   Should
give you some ideas."   I brought back four or five instruments, like strange jew's-harps and that.   "I don't want one
violin, one cello, one woodwind, or any of those goddamn
things in the whole picture."   "Oh," he said, "that's a great
idea, boss.   That's a good idea."   He went home and he
thought it over and he came over to see me.   He said, "You
were fooling, weren't you?"   I said, "You're fired, Dimi."
"Oh, no..."   "You're fired.   You told me it was a great
idea, and I want anybody to want to do this without those
goddamn silly instruments."   I called up--I had seen a little
TV show...

AA:   "Peter Gunn"?

HH:   Yeah.   I told Mancini, "Do your worst, but no
violins, no woodwinds, none of that orchestral bunk."   Because the musical directors had been for years copying,
stealing from, playing operatic and concert music.   You
know, and doing a lousy job of it too.   The first time I
really liked something was THIRD MAN.   I like source music.   I'm not a musician.   I played in an orchestra once, in
a Dixieland--played a banjo.

AA:   Do you enjoy the music in John Ford pictures?

HH:   Sometimes.

DW:   Like, for instance, The SEARCHERS.

AA:   Everything he does is taken from the old American ... something that nobody touches.   "Oh, this is just a
lot of cornball. "  He takes about 20 songs and gives them to
the composer.

HH:   John took the corniest stuff in the world.   He
admitted it.   He said, "I can't do the kind of comedy you
make at all.   I can only do this corn. "   But he made awful
good corn.

AA:   The SEARCHERS, I think his best work, in
terms of the Western, started as a very tragic story, but
he kept on putting comedy into it because the middle was
sagging.

HH:   Well, we used to discuss that.   You're telling
the same old story, and the only way you can change it is
by getting different characters.   And the only different characters you can get are funny ones.   Now, I was very pleased
with EL DORADO.   Jim Caan didn't realize that he was
playing a funny role.   Thank God!   He played it seriously,
and I knew they were going to laugh.

DW:   Weren't there some people who said you better
try somebody that's already established, opposite Bogart in
TO HAVE AND HAVE NOT?

HH:   I had two scripts.

DW:   And you showed them the other one?

HH:   I didn't show anybody ... if they chanced to
read it, they wouldn't think that the girl's part was very
much.

AA:   All my friends are doing imitations of John
Wayne in RIO BRAVO.

HH:   Every once in a while, Sugar Ray Robinson and
Sammy Davis come over.   And they know all the dialogue,
of RED RIVER, RIO BRAVO, and everything.   And they put
on their version of it for me....   Goldwyn said, "There has
to be some way that you could remake BALL OF FIRE. "   I
said, "Probably could.   For $25,000 a week I probably
could. "   He said, "You made a deal. "   Oh, what the hell!

Then he wouldn't let me do anything.  Then he was so mad
at himself for making such a silly deal that he wouldn't let
me do anything.  One of the things that I said was, "I don't
have to use that--what's her name?--Mayo."  Not only did
I have to use Virginia Mayo--I didn't have a contract that
said that she--but he had her run and work and run on all
the scenes that Stanwyck did.  Well, she wasn't Stanwyck.
That girl couldn't do 'em.  They were messed up, they were
awful.  The more I got into it, the nastier I got because I
couldn't direct her.  Because he had seen to it that she was
going to copy Stanwyck.

AA:  It looked like it was forced acting.

HH:  It was completely awful.  It was the most un-
pleasant picture you'd ever known.  One picture that I made
called LAND OF THE PHARAOHS I didn't like at all.  We
ended up with a lot of characters--you didn't like one single
character in the whole picture.  I broke all my own rules,
because you hadn't something to root for.

DW:  I think the best parts of it were documentary--
how do you build a pyramid?

HH:  Oh, I know it.  We had some really good stuff
in that.  But, occasionally, you run off ... I got the idea
of taking these three stories and putting them together into
one.  I made RED LINE 7000, and it doesn't work.  Because
you just get interested in one story and you drop it and go
to another story.  You forget what's happened in the other
and you go to another one.  And, taken individually, for instance ... over in England, they think it's a classic, they
think it's one of the best pictures...

DW:  Robin Wood.

HH:  ... Yeah.  I think it's lousy.

AA:  I enjoyed it--the relations between men and
women.

HH:  Well, there were some interesting things--
because, you see, those were really true.  I knew a girl
who thought that she was bad luck to everybody.  She
wouldn't sleep with anybody because they may die.  The little
French girl was very good.  They were all pretty good.

DW:  Wasn't Barbara [Hawks' daughter] in The BIG SKY?

HH:  I don't think so.

AA:  It says here [in Gili's book], "Barbara Hawks, an Indian girl."

HH:  Oh!  I know one thing--she was the only one who had enough nerve to go in the water swimming.  It was ice water.

DW:  How did you decide what to shoot of the novel The Big Sky and what not to shoot?

HH:  I can't remember that, but in working on a story like that, you can't possibly tell the whole story.  Dudley Nichols and I used to get baggage tags.  For the first four or five days, we would write out scenes that we knew belonged in the picture.  We'd put those up on a big board.  Then we started hooking them together.  AIR FORCE was a hell of a job--to try and get that all in the picture.  We had red baggage tags, some yellow, then we had a code that said that love scenes will be in such and such a thing, funny scenes in such and such ... You could tell what it looked like.

DW:  Is the Barrymore character in TWENTIETH CENTURY modeled on any particular figure, personality?

HH:  The play was done by a very stylized Russian actress, the wife of Gregory Ratoff.

AA:  Oh, yeah.  She was my teacher--Leontovich, Madame Leontovich.

HH:  Yeah.  It was written for a very stylized--written for somebody to read lines like that.  It was played by a very dull actor, who just didn't seem to have any character.  When I decided to do it, I said the girl is going to be Sadie Glutz, from anywhere.  None of this stylized Russian stuff.  And I'm going to see if I can get John Barrymore.  I called him up and told him the story.  He'd seen the play, I think, and he said, "What makes you think that I'm any good for this?"  I said, "Well, it's the story of the greatest ham in the world, and God knows you fit that...."  I had never been

backstage.  So I told Barrymore he'd have to help me on all
that.  Carole Lombard was a second cousin of mine and the
worst actress in the world.  Nobody could possibly have been
as bad as she was.  She came from the same little town that
I did.  Marvellous gal, crazy as a bedbug.  I thought if she
could just be herself, she'd be great for the part.  I said to
Barrymore, "Look.  We've got a new girl.  I don't want to
hear one goddamn word from you until four o'clock in the
afternoon. "  "Well, why?"  I said, "Now promise that. "  He
promised.  "You'll learn why I want you to do it. "

     And they started the rehearsal.  This first scene was
a long scene, 12 pages.  And he looked at her and he could-
n't believe anybody could be so lousy.  He was holding his
stomach like this, looking at me.  I said, "Shut up!"  So I
told the cameraman to find something and announce that it
would be 15 minutes before we could do anything.  I took
Lombard for a walk around the stage and I said, "You've
been working hard on this. "  She said, "I'm glad it shows. "
And I said, "Really?  What do you get paid for the picture?"
And she said, "$5,000. "  I said, "What do you get paid
for?"  She said, "Well, acting, of course. "  I said, "Suppose I tell you you've already earned the $5,000. "  She
just stared at me.  I told her, "Just be yourself.  Now we're
going to go back in there.  And if you don't go and do any
goddamn thing that you feel like doing, I'm going to fire you
and get another girl. "  We went back, and I said, "Let's
make a tape. "  And Barrymore said, "We're not ready. "
I said, "Who is running this show?"  He said, "You are, "
and I said, "Okay.  Get in there and act. "  And they started
this scene, and she kicked at him like this, and he jumped
back.  I said, "Cut!  Print!"  He came back and he said,
"That was magnificent!  Have you been kidding me all this
time?"  And she broke into tears and ran off the stage.
And he said, "Howard, what the hell goes on around here?"
I said, "What you saw was just a girl.  She wasn't acting. "
We made the picture in three weeks time.  He was a great
actor if you got his attention, and she was a great personality.

     AA:  John Wayne is like that too...

     HH:  Oh, I get a kick out of Wayne.  When we started
to do RED RIVER, he was trying a little too hard.  I said,
"You do three good scenes and don't annoy the audience the
rest of the time and you'll be a big star. "  So he'd say to
me, "What is this we're gonna do?"  Now, it's very funny
when we're making a movie.  I can hear him off talking to

some actress, saying, "Now, hey, look.  The boss says this
is one of those scenes where you're not supposed to annoy
anybody...."  RED RIVER made Wayne a good actor, because
he does not try too hard, to do things that he's not capable
of doing.  He's a hell of a lot better than most people think
he is.

      I had a great girl for RED RIVER.  She got pregnant
two days before we left.  Maggie Sheridan had more promise
than almost anybody I ever knew.  But she married a very
nice, dull man, and after five years she wasn't the same
girl.  I tried her in another picture, The THING, and she
photographed beautifully.  And she was perfectly good, but
she didn't have that marvellous zest that she had beforehand.
Now, the little girl who did it really should have done musical comedy.  Light stuff.  She did a very good job for what
there was ... but I couldn't find anybody else.  I just
learned this at the last minute.  We had all the clothes
ready for Margaret Sheridan.

      DW:  Did you rewrite all her scenes?

      HH:  We wrote some of them because she worked with
cards.  My theory was that she was so good with cards that
she didn't have to be a whore.  Maggie worked for, oh, two
months, beforehand.  She could deal anything, flip cards all
around and do anything with them.

      AA:  Jane Russell plays the same character in The
TALL MEN.

      HH:  Well, my brother made that.  He asked me
what to make.  I said, "Take RED RIVER and do it up in
the snow."  I thought that was kind of pukey.  I like Jane,
but I don't think that she was very interesting in that picture.
She was just standard, just stock.  My brother hadn't any
training for writing.

      DW:  Did you edit out several scenes from The
THING?  Because they were too gory?

      HH:  I think that's just talk.

      DW:  Didn't you try to get Grant for MAN'S FAVOR-
ITE SPORT??

      HH:  Grant read the script, but he didn't want to do
it.  Rock Hudson read it and called and said he wanted to

do it.  I didn't know that he'd been in those <u>word</u> comedies
with that 42-year-old virgin.  When I started working with
Rock, he was very nice.  He tried very hard, but he wasn't
funny.  Paula Prentiss was good, but she couldn't remember
what she was doing from one shot to the next.  Her shots
never matched.

Some critic said that in ONLY ANGELS HAVE WINGS
I went way beyond reality.  I wrote the guy and I said,
"Every goddamn thing that was in ONLY ANGELS HAVE
WINGS is based on exact truth."  I was coming back from
Santa Barbara and I saw a big bomber up in the air.  Black
smoke started to come out of it.  Then I saw a chute come
out.  I knew somebody had to be in the airplane.  There
had to be two guys in there, and I only saw one chute.  The
guy that had jumped out was the pilot and he'd left the guy
behind.  He spent the rest of his life and was killed trying
to redeem himself for that.  Every time he'd walk into a
hangar on a rainy afternoon, and a bunch of guys were talking, the talk would stop.  So that wasn't any exaggeration.

DW:  And the way you did it in the movie, with the
acceptance of Barthelmess at the end--in the background you
see John Carroll, who earlier refused to fly...

AA:  Directors today don't go through all those experiences.

HH:  Hollywood--that's one of the worst places in the
world to live.  I've never been part of Hollywood because I
never cared about all that stuff.  I raised race horses.  The
people I liked would come over and ride.  I'd go hunting with
jockeys, anything except to hang around Hollywood people.
Listen to 'em talk about pictures.  Christ, I hate to talk
about pictures.

DW:  Did you see PAPER MOON?

HH:  I told Peter I hated kids in movies.  Made him
really mad.

DW:  Bogdanovich gets most of his ideas from other
films.

HH:  For years Peter sat on my set when I made a
movie.  He's learned.  Peter is pretty smart.  But I told
him, "There's one thing where you're not smart--comedy,
action, gangster ... You'd like to do all of that.  I have a

hunch you haven't lived long enough to do all that.    You're
not knowledgeable enough. "

--Palm Springs, August 14, 1974

## CREDITS

The ROAD TO GLORY   Fox   1926   70 minutes
Director: Howard Hawks. Screenplay: L. G. Rigby.
Story: Hawks. Photography: Joseph August. Assistant
Director: James Tinling.
Cast: May McAvoy (Judith Allen), Rockliffe Fellowes
(Del Cole), Leslie Fenton (David Hale), Ford Sterling (James
Allen), Milla Davenport (Aunt Selma).

FIG LEAVES   Fox   1926   72 minutes
Director: Howard Hawks. Screenplay: Hope Loring, Louis
D. Lighton. Story: Hawks. Photography: Joseph August.
(Technicolor sequence) Art Directors: William Cameron
Menzies, William S. Darling. Editor: Rose Smith. Cos-
tumes: Adrian. Supervision: Winfield R. Sheehan. Assist-
ant Director: James Tinling.
Cast: George O'Brien (Adam Smith), Olive Borden
(Eve Smith), André de Béranger (Josef André), Phyllis Haver
(Alice Atkins), Heinie Conklin (Eddie McSwiggen), William
Austin, Eulalie Jensen.

The CRADLE SNATCHERS   Fox   1927   70 minutes
Director: Howard Hawks. Screenplay: Sarah Y. Mason,
from the play by Russell Medcraft and Norma Mitchell.
Photography: L. William O'Connell. Titles: Malcolm Stu-
art Boylan. Assistant Director: James Tinling.
Cast: Arthur Lake, Sally Eilers, Nick Stuart, Louise
Fazenda, Ethel Wales, Joseph Striker, Dorothy Phillips, J.
Farrell MacDonald, Franklin Pangborn, William Davidson.

PAID TO LOVE   Fox   1927   80 minutes
Director: Howard Hawks. Screenplay: William M. Consel-
man, Seton I. Miller. Story: Harry Carr. Photography:
L. William O'Connell. Titles: Malcolm Stuart Boylan.
Adaptation: Benjamin Glazer. Art Director: William S.
Darling. Editor: Ralph Dixon. Assistant Director: James
Tinling.

Cast: Virginia Valli, George O'Brien, William Powell, J. Farrell MacDonald, Thomas Jefferson, Hank Mann.

A GIRL IN EVERY PORT   Fox   1928   90 minutes
Director: Howard Hawks. Screenplay: Seton I. Miller. Story: Hawks. Screen Story: James K. McGuinness. Photography: L. William O'Connell, R. J. Berquist. Titles: Malcolm Stuart Boylan. Art Director: William S. Darling. Assistant Director: William Tummel. Editor: Ralph Dixon.
Cast: Victor McLaglen (Spike Madden), Robert Armstrong (Bill), Louise Brooks (Marie), Greta Yoltz, Natalie Joyce, Maria Casajuana (Chiquita), Dorothy Mathews, Elena Jurado, Phalba Morgan (Lena), Leila Hyams (sailor's wife), Sally Rand (girl in Bombay), Natalie Kingston, Myrna Loy (Jetta), William Demarest (man in Bombay).

FAZIL   Fox   1928   95 minutes   musical score-sound effects and silent versions
Director: Howard Hawks. Screenplay: Seton I. Miller, Philip Klein, from the play, "L'Insoumise," by Pierre Frondaie and the English adaptation, "Prince Fazil." Photography: L. William O'Connell. Editor: Ralph Dixon. Assistant Director: James Tinling.
Cast: Charles Farrell, Greta Nissen, John Boles, Mae Busch, Eddie Sturgis, Vadim Uraneff, Hank Mann, Josephine Borio, Erville Alderson.

The AIR CIRCUS   Fox   1928   100 minutes   talking sequences, sound effects, musical score
Directors: Howard Hawks, Lewis B. Seiler. Screenplay: Seton I. Miller, Norman Z. McLeod. Story: Graham Baker, Andrew Bennison. Dialogue Director: Charles Judels. Photography: Dan Clark(e). Titles: William Kernell. Dialogue: Hugh Herbert. Editor: Ralph Dixon. Assistant Director: William Tummel.
Cast: Arthur Lake, Sue Carol, David Rollins, Charles Delaney, Heinie Conklin, Louise Dresser.

TRENT'S LAST CASE   Fox   1929   90 minutes
musical score-sound effects and silent versions
Director: Howard Hawks. Screenplay: Scott Darling, from the novel by E. C. Bentley. Adaptation: Beulah Marie Dix. Photography: Harold Rosson. Titles: Malcolm Stuart Boylan. Supervision: Bertram Millhauser. Assistant Director: E. D. Leshin.
Cast: Raymond Griffith (Philip Trent), Marceline Day, Raymond Hatton, Lawrence Gray, Donald Crisp, Edgar Kennedy, Nicholas Soussanin.

The DAWN PATROL    First National    1930   105 minutes
(FLIGHT COMMANDER)
Director:  Howard Hawks.   Screenplay:  Hawks, Dan Tothe-
roh, Seton I.  Miller, from the story, "Flight Commander,"
by John Monk Saunders.   Photography:  Ernest Haller.
Aerial sequences:  Leo Nomis.   Assistant:  Elmer Dyer.
Art Director:  Jack Okey.   Music:  Leo F. Forbstein.   Edi-
tor:  Ray Curtiss.   Special Technical Effects:  Fred Jackman.
Producer:  Robert North.
        Cast:  Richard Barthelmess (Dick Courtney), Douglas
Fairbanks, Jr. (Douglas Scott), Neil Hamilton (Major Brand),
William Janney (Gordon Scott), James Finlayson (field ser-
geant), Clyde Cook (Bott), Gardner James (Ralph Hollister),
Edmond Breon, Frank McHugh (Flaherty), Jack Ackroyd,
Harry Allen (mechanics).

The CRIMINAL CODE   Columbia   1931   94 minutes
Director:  Howard Hawks.   Screenplay:  Seton I. Miller,
Fred Niblo, Jr. , from the play by Martin Flavin.   Photogra-
phy:  James Wong Howe.   Editor:  Edward Curtiss.   Pro-
ducer:  Harry Cohn.
        Cast:  Walter Huston (Warden Brady), Phillips Holmes
(Robert Graham), Constance Cummings (Mary Brady), Mary
Doran (Gertrude Williams), DeWitt Jennings (Gleason), John
Sheehan (MacManus), Boris Karloff (Galloway), Otto Hoffman
(Fales), Clark Marshall (Runch), Arthur Hoyt, Ethel Wales
(Katie), John St. Polis (Dr. Rinewulf), Paul Porcasi (Spelvin),
Hugh Walker (Lew), Jack Vance, Andy Devine.

SCARFACE - SHAME OF THE NATION   United Artists/
Atlantic 1930  (released 1932)  90 minutes
Director:  Howard Hawks.   Screenplay:  Ben Hecht, from the
novel by Armitage Trail.   Adaptation and Dialogue:  Seton I.
Miller, John Lee Mahin, W. R. Burnett.   Photography:  Lee
Garmes, L. William O'Connell.   Music:  Adolph Tandler,
Gus Arnheim.   Settings:  Harry Oliver.   Editor:  Edward
Curtiss.   Supervising Editor:  Douglas Biggs.   Assistant
Director:  Richard Rosson.   Sound:  William Snyder.
        Cast:  Paul Muni (Tony Camonte), Ann Dvorak (Cesca),
Karen Morley (Poppy), Osgood Perkins (Johnny Lovo), Boris
Karloff (Gaffney), C. Henry Gordon (Guarino), George Raft
(Guino Rinaldo), Purnell Pratt (publisher), Vince Barnett
(Angelo), Inez Palange (Mrs. Camonte), Harry J. Vejar
(Costillo), Edwin Maxwell (Chief of Detectives), Tully Mar-
shall (managing editor), Henry Armetta (Pietro), Maurice
Black (Sullivan), Bert Starkey (Epstein).

The CROWD ROARS   Warner Brothers   1932   85 minutes
Director:  Howard Hawks.   Screenplay:  Kubec Glasmon,
John Bright, Seton I. Miller, Niven Busch.   Story:  Hawks.
Photography:  Sidney Hickox.   Music:  Leo F. Forbstein.
Art Director:  Jack Okey.   Editor:  John Stumar.   Technical Effects:  Fred Jackman.
Cast:  James Cagney (Joe Greer), Joan Blondell
(Anne), Ann Dvorak (Lee), Eric Linden (Eddie Greer), Guy
Kibbee (Dad Greer), Frank McHugh (Spud), William Arnold
(Bill), Leo Nomis, Charlotte Merriam (Spud's wife), Harry
Hartz, Ralph Hepburn, Fred Guisso, Phil Pardee, Spider
Matlock, Jack Brisko, Fred Frame (drivers).

TIGER SHARK   First National   1932   76 minutes
Director:  Howard Hawks.   Screenplay:  Wells Root, from
an original story, "Tuna," by Houston Branch.   Photography:
Tony Gaudio.   Music:  Leo F. Forbstein.   Art Director:
Jack Okey.   Editor:  Thomas Pratt.   Costumes:  Orry-Kelly.
Marine Supervision:  Captain Guy Silva.   Assistant Director:
Richard Rosson.
Cast:  Edward G. Robinson (Mike Mascarenhas),
Richard Arlen (Pipes Boley), Zita Johann (Quita Silva), Leila
Bennett (Muggsey, barber), Vince Barnett (engineer), J.
Carrol Naish (Tony), William Ricciardi (Manuel Silva), Edwin
Maxwell (doctor).

TODAY WE LIVE   MGM   1933   113 minutes
Producer, Director:  Howard Hawks.   Screenplay:  Edith
Fitzgerald, Dwight Taylor, from the story, "Turnabout," by
William Faulkner.   Dialogue:  Faulkner.   Photography:
Oliver T. Marsh.   Editor:  Edward Curtiss.
Cast:  Joan Crawford (Diana), Gary Cooper (Bogard),
Robert Young (Claude), Franchot Tone (Ronnie), Roscoe
Karns (McGinnis), Louise Closser Hale (Applegate), Rollo
Lloyd (major), Hilda Vaughn (Eleanor).

VIVA VILLA!   MGM   1934   112 minutes
Director:  Jack Conway (and, uncredited, Howard Hawks).
Screenplay:  Ben Hecht (and, uncredited, Hawks).   Story:
Edgcumb Pinchon, O. B. Stade.   Photography:  James Wong
Howe, Charles G. Clarke.   Music:  Herbert Stothart.   Musical supervision:  Juan Aguilar.   Art Director:  Harry
Oliver.   Sets:  Edwin B. Willis.   Producer:  David O. Selznick.   Assistant Director:  James D. Waters.   Editor:
Robert J. Kern.

Cast:  Wallace Beery (Pancho Villa), Leo Carrillo
(Sierra), Fay Wray (Teresa), Stuart Erwin (Johnny Sykes),
Donald Cook (Don Felipe), Henry B. Walthall (Madero),
Joseph Schildkraut (General Pascal), Katherine de Mille
(Rosita), George E. Stone (Chavito), Philip Cooper, Frank
Puglia, Francis X. Bushman, Jr., Henry Armetta, George
Regas, Harry Cording, Nigel de Brulier, Harry Semels,
Julian Rivero, Paul Stanton, Mischa Auer (attaché), Belle
Mitchell, Brandon Hurst, Arthur Treacher (English reporter),
Michael Visaroff, Arthur Thalasso, Chris Pin Martin, Emile
Chautard.

TWENTIETH CENTURY  Columbia  1934  91 minutes
Producer, Director: Howard Hawks. Screenplay: Charles
MacArthur, Ben Hecht, from their play, based on "Napoleon
on Broadway, " play by Charles Bruce Milholland. Photogra-
phy: Joseph August (and Joseph Walker?). Editor: Gene
Havlick.
Cast:  John Barrymore (Oscar Jaffe), Carole Lombard
(Lily Garland), Walter Connolly (Oliver Webb), Roscoe Karns
(Owen O'Malley), Charles Levison [Charles Lane] (Jacobs),
Etienne Girardot (Clark), Dale Fuller (Sadie), Ralph Forbes
(George Smith), Billie Seward, Clifford Thompson, James
Burtis, Gigi Parrish, Edgar Kennedy (McGonigle), Herman
Bing and Lee Kohlmar (bearded men), Ed Gargan, Fred
Kelsey, Pat Flaherty, Snowflake, Howard Hickman, Ed
Chandler, Lynton Brent, James Burke.

BARBARY COAST  United Artists  1935  91 minutes
Director: Howard Hawks. Screenplay: Ben Hecht, Charles
MacArthur (and Edward Chodorov?). Photography: Ray
June. Music: Alfred Newman. Art Director: Richard Day.
Producer: Samuel Goldwyn. Costumes: Omar Kiam. As-
sistant Director: Walter Mayo. Editor: Edward Curtiss.
Cast:  Miriam Hopkins (Swan), Edward G. Robinson
(Chamalis), Joel McCrea (Carmichael), Walter Brennan (Old
Atrocity), Frank Craven (Col. Cobb), Brian Donlevy (Knuck-
les), Harry Carey (Slocum), Clyde Cook, J. M. Kerrigan,
Donald Meek, Roger Gray, Rollo Lloyd, Matt McHugh, Otto
Hoffman, Frederick Vogeding, David Niven.

CEILING ZERO  First National/Cosmopolitan  1936
91 minutes
Director: Howard Hawks. Screenplay: Frank Wead, from
his play. Photography: Arthur Edeson. Music: Leo F.
Forbstein. Art Director: John Hughes. Editor: William
Holmes. Special Effects: Fred Jackman. Technical Adviser: Paul Mantz. Producer: Harry Joe Brown.

Cast: James Cagney (Dizzy Davis), Pat O'Brien (Jake Lee), June Travis (Tommy), Stuart Erwin (Texas Clarke), Isabel Jewell (Lou Clarke), Henry Wadsworth (Tay), Craig Reynolds (Joe Allen), Richard Purcell (Smiley), Robert Light, Garry Owen (Mike), Barton MacLane (Al Stone), Ed Gargan, Martha Tibbetts, Carlyle Moore, Jr. , Addison Richards, Pat West (Baldy), Mathilda Comont, Howard Allen, Frank McDonald.

The ROAD TO GLORY   Fox   1936   100 minutes
(WOODEN CROSSES.   ZERO HOUR)
Director: Howard Hawks. Screenplay: Joel Sayre, William Faulkner, from the film Les CROIX DE BOIS by Raymond Bernard and the book of the same name by Roland Dorgelès. Photography: Gregg Toland. Musical Director: Louis Silvers. Art Director: Hans Peters. Sets: Thomas Little. Editor: Edward Curtiss. Costumes: Gwen Wakeling. Producer: Darryl F. Zanuck. Associate Producer: Nunnally Johnson. Assistant Director: Ed O'Fearna.
Cast: Fredric March (Lt. Michel Denet), Warner Baxter (Capt. Paul Laroche), Lionel Barrymore (Papa Laroche), June Lang (Monique), Gregory Ratoff (Bouffiou), Victor Kilian (Regnier), Paul Stanton (relief captain), John Qualen (Duflous), Julius Tannen, Theodore von Eltz, Paul Fix, Leonid Kinskey, Jacques Vanaire, Edythe Raynore, George Warrington.

COME AND GET IT   United Artists   1936   99 minutes
Directors: Howard Hawks, William Wyler; logging sequences: Richard Rosson. Screenplay: Jane Murfin, Jules Furthman (and Robert Wyler?), from the book by Edna Ferber. Photography: Gregg Toland, Rudolph Maté. Music: Alfred Newman. Art Director: Richard Day. Sets: Julia Heron. Producer: Samuel Goldwyn. Special Effects: Ray Binger. Costumes: Omar Kiam. Assistant Director: Ross Lederman. Editor: Edward Curtiss.
Cast: Edward Arnold (Barney Glasgow), Frances Farmer (Lotta), Joel McCrea (Richard Glasgow), Walter Brennan (Swan Bostrom), Andrea Leeds (Evvie Glasgow), Frank Shields (Tony Schwerke), Mady Christians (Karie), Mary Nash (Emma Glasgow), Clem Bevans, Edwin Maxwell, Rollo Lloyd, Charles Halton, Jack Pennick.

BRINGING UP BABY   RKO   1938   100 minutes
Producer, Director: Howard Hawks. Screenplay: Dudley Nichols, Hagar Wilde (and, uncredited, Robert McGowan and Gertrude Purcell), from a story by Wilde. Photography: Russell Metty. Music: Roy Webb. Art Directors: Van

Nest Polglase, Perry Ferguson.  Sets: Darrell Silvera.
Editor: George Hively.  Special Effects: Vernon L. Walker.
Assistant Director: Edward Donahue.  Associate Producer:
Cliff Reid.

  Cast:  Cary Grant (David Huxley), Katharine Hepburn
(Susan),  Charles Ruggles (Major Horace Applegate), Walter
Catlett (Slocum),  Barry Fitzgerald (Gogarty), May Robson
(Aunt Elizabeth),  Fritz Feld (psychiatrist), Leona Roberts
(Mrs. Gogarty),  George Irving (Peabody), Tala Birell (psychi-
atrist's wife),  Virginia Walker (Alice Swallow), John Kelly,
Asta (George, the dog), Nissa (Baby), Ward Bond, Stanley
Blystone,  Edward Gargan and Buck Mack (zoo officials),
Geraldine Hall (maid), William Benedict and Buster Slaven
(caddies),  Jack Gardner, Pat West (Mac), Jack Carson
(roustabout),  Richard Lane (circus manager), Pat O'Malley
(deputy),  Billy Bevan (bartender), Frank M. Thomas (barker).

  **ONLY ANGELS HAVE WINGS**  Columbia  1939  121
minutes (PLANE NO. 4--pre-release title)
Producer, Director: Howard Hawks.  Screenplay: Jules
Furthman (and, uncredited, William Rankin, Eleanore Griffin).
Story:  Hawks.  Photography: Elmer Dyer, Joseph Walker.
Music: Dimitri Tiomkin, Morris Stoloff.  Art Director:
Lionel Banks.  Technical Adviser and Chief Pilot:  Paul
Mantz.  Special Effects:  E. Roy Davidson, Edwin C. Hahn.
Editor: Viola Lawrence.  Gowns: Kalloch.  Assistant
Director: Arthur Black.

  Cast:  Cary Grant (Jeff Carter), Jean Arthur (Bonnie
Lee),  Thomas Mitchell (Kid Dabb), Richard Barthelmess (Bat
MacPherson),  Sig Ruman (Dutchy), Rita Hayworth (Judith),
Victor Kilian (Sparks), John Carroll (Gent Shelton), Allyn
Joslyn (Les Peters), Donald Barry (Tex Gordon), Noah Beery,
Jr. (Joe Souther), Melissa [or Milissa] Sierra (Lily), Lucio
Villegas (Dr. Lagorio), Forbes Murray (Hartwood), James
Millican, Maciste (singer), Pat Flaherty (Mike), Pedro Regas
(Pancho),  Pat West (Baldy), Candy Candido (musician), Rafael
Corio (purser), Charles Moore, Vernon Dent (boat captain),
Ed Randolph, Stanley Brown (Hartwood, Jr. ), Sam Tong
(cook),  Bud Wolfe, Dick Botiller (tourist), Eddie Foster.

  **HIS GIRL FRIDAY**  Columbia  1940  92 minutes
Producer, Director: Howard Hawks.  Screenplay: Charles
Lederer, from the play, "The Front Page," by Ben Hecht
and Charles MacArthur.  Photography: Joseph Walker.
Music: Morris Stoloff.  Art Director: Lionel Banks.  Edi-
tor: Gene Havlick.  Gowns: Kalloch.  Assistant Director:
Clifton Broughton.

Cast:  Cary Grant (Walter Burns), Rosalind Russell
(Hildy Johnson), Ralph Bellamy (Bruce Baldwin), Gene Lock-
hart (Sheriff Hartwell), Abner Biberman (Diamond Louie),
Porter Hall (Murphy), Ernest Truex (Bensinger), Cliff Ed-
wards (Endicott), Clarence Kolb (Mayor), Roscoe Karns (Mc-
Cue), Frank Jenks (Wilson), Regis Toomey (Sanders), Frank
Orth (Duffy), John Qualen (Earl Williams), Helen Mack (Mol-
lie Malloy), Alma Kruger (Mrs. Baldwin), Billy Gilbert
(Joe Pettibone), Edwin Maxwell (Dr. Egelhoffer), Pat West
(Warden Cooley).

SERGEANT YORK   Warner Brothers   1941   134
minutes
Director:  Howard Hawks.  Screenplay:  Abem Finkel, Harry
Chandlee, Howard Koch, John Huston, from War Diary of
Sergeant York, edited by Tom Skeyhill, and Sergeant York--
Last of the Long Hunters by Skeyhill.  Photography:  Sol
Polito, Arthur Edeson.  Music:  Max Steiner.  Musical Di-
rector:  Leo F. Forbstein.  Art Director:  John Hughes.
Sets:  Fred MacLean.  Producers:  Jesse L. Lasky, Hal B.
Wallis.  Makeup:  Perc Westmore.
Cast:  Gary Cooper (Alvin C. York), Walter Brennan
(Pastor Rosier Pile), Joan Leslie (Gracie Williams), George
Tobias (Pusher Rose), Stanley Ridges (Major Buxton), Mar-
garet Wycherley (Mother York), Ward Bond (Ike Botkin),
Noah Beery, Jr. (Buck Lipscomb), June Lockhart (Rosie
York), Dickie Moore (George York), Clem Bevans (Zeke),
Howard da Silva (Lem), Charles Trowbridge (Cordell Hull),
Harvey Stevens, David Bruce (Bert Thomas), Charles Esmond,
Joe Sawyer (Sgt. Early), Pat Flaherty (Sgt. Parsons), Er-
ville Alderson (Nate), Elisha Cook, Jr., Ray Teal, Jack Pen-
nick, Tully Marshall, Don Douglas, Lane Chandler, Guy Wil-
kerson, Si Jenks, Eddy Waller, Henry Hall, William Haade,
Kay Sutton, Charles Middleton, Frank McGlynn, Victor Kilian
(Andrews), Sonny Bupp, Pat West, Frank Faylen, Murray
Alper, Charles Drake, Clyde Cook, William Forrest, Theo-
dore von Eltz, Jean Del Val, Russell Hicks, Joseph Girard,
Selmer Jackson, Edwin Stanley, Jack Mower, George Irving,
John Dilson, Walter Sande.

BALL OF FIRE   RKO   1941   111 minutes
Director:  Howard Hawks.  Screenplay:  Billy Wilder, Charles
Brackett, from the story, "From A to Z," by Wilder and
Thomas Monroe.  Photography:  Gregg Toland.  Music:
Alfred Newman.  Art Director:  Perry Ferguson.  Assistant:
McClure Claps.  Sets:  Howard Bristol.  Producer:  Samuel
Goldwyn.  Editor:  Daniel Mandell.  Assistant Director:
William Tummel.  Miss Stanwyck's Costumes:  Edith Head.

Cast:   Gary Cooper (Bertram Potts), Barbara Stan-
wyck (Sugarpuss O'Shea), Richard Haydn (Professor Oddly),
Oscar Homolka (Prof. Gurkakoff), Dana Andrews (Joe Lilac),
Dan Duryea (Duke Pastrami), Henry Travers (Prof. Jerome),
Allen Jenkins (garbage man), S. Z. Sakall (Prof. Magen-
bruch), Tully Marshall (Prof. Robinson), Leonid Kinskey
(Prof. Quintana), Aubrey Mather (Prof. Peagram), Gene
Krupa and his Band, Elisha Cook, Jr. (waiter), Mary Field
(Miss Totten), Kathleen Howard (Miss Bragg), Addison
Richards (D. A. ), Charles Lane, Tim Ryan, Ralph Peters,
Charles Arnt, Pat West, Otto Hoffman, Ed Chandler, Dick
Rush.

AIR FORCE   Warner Brothers   1943   124 minutes
Director:  Howard Hawks.   Screenplay:  Dudley Nichols (and,
uncredited, Arthur Horman).   Dialogue:  William Faulkner.
Photography:  James Wong Howe.   Music:  Franz Waxman.
Musical Director:  Leo F. Forbstein.   Art Director:  John
Hughes.   Sets:  Walter F. Tilford.   Producer:  Hal B. Wal-
lis.   Aerial Photography:  Elmer Dyer, Charles Marshall.
Special Effects:   E. Roy Davidson, Rex Wimpy, H. F. Koe-
nekamp.   Technical Adviser and Chief Pilot:   Paul Mantz.
Assistant Director:  Jack Sullivan.   Editor:  George Amy.
Cast:   John Garfield (Sgt. Winocki), John Ridgely
(Capt. Quincannon), George Tobias (Corp. Weinberg), Harry
Carey (Sgt. White), Gig Young (Lt. Williams), Arthur Ken-
nedy (Lt. McMartin), Charles Drake (Lt. Hauser), James
Brown (Lt. Tex Rader), Ed Brophy, Ward Wood, Ray Mont-
gomery, Stanley Ridges, Willard Robertson, Moroni Olsen,
Richard Lane, Bill Crago, Faye Emerson, Addison Richards,
James Flavin, Ann Doran, Dorothy Peterson, William For-
rest, Bill Hopper, Murray Alper, Walter Sande, Theodore
von Eltz, Edwin Stanley, Tom Neal, Bill Kennedy, Allan
Lane, Rand Brooks, James Millican.

TO HAVE AND HAVE NOT   Warner Brothers   1944
97 minutes
Producer, Director:  Howard Hawks.   Screenplay:  Jules
Furthman, William Faulkner, from the novel by Ernest
Hemingway.   Photography:  Sidney Hickox.   Music:  Leo F.
Forbstein.   Original Song, "How Little We Know," by Hoagy
Carmichael and Johnny Mercer.   Art Director:  Charles
Novi.   Sets:  Casey Roberts.   Editor:  Christian Nyby.
Assistant Director:  Jack Sullivan.   Special Effects:  E. Roy
Davidson, Rex Wimpy.   Technical Adviser:  Louis Comien.
Makeup:  Perc Westmore.   Gowns:  Milo Anderson.
Cast:   Humphrey Bogart (Harry Morgan), Walter

Brennan (Eddie), Lauren Bacall (Marie), Hoagy Carmichael
(Crickett), Marcel Dalio (Frenchy), Walter Sande (Johnson),
Dan Seymour (Capt. Renard), Walter Molnar (Paul de Bursac),
Dolores Moran (Helène de Bursac), Sheldon Leonard (Lt.
Coyo), Aldo Nadi (bodyguard), Paul Marion (Beauclerc), Pa-
tricia Shay (Mrs. Beauclerc), Pat West (bartender), Emmet
Smith (Emil), Sir Lancelot (Horatio), Eugene Borden, Crane
Whitley, Maurice Marsac.

The BIG SLEEP  Warner Brothers  1946  114 minutes
Producer, Director: Howard Hawks.  Screenplay: William
Faulkner, Jules Furthman, Leigh Brackett, from the novel
by Raymond Chandler.  Photography: Sidney Hickox.  Music:
Max Steiner.  Musical Director: Leo F. Forbstein.  Art
Director: Carl Jules Weyl.  Sets: Fred MacLean.  Editor:
Christian Nyby.  Special Effects: E. Roy Davidson, Warren
E. Lynch.  Assistant Director: Chuck Hansen.  Wardrobe:
Leah Rhodes.
      Cast:  Humphrey Bogart (Philip Marlowe), Lauren
Bacall (Vivian), John Ridgely (Eddie Mars), Louis Jean Heydt
(Joe Brody), Elisha Cook, Jr. (Jones), Regis Toomey (Bernie
Ohls), Sonia Darren (Agnes), Bob Steele (Canino), Martha
Vickers (Carmen), Tom Rafferty (Carol Lundgren), Dorothy
Malone (girl in bookshop), Charles Waldren (General Stern-
wood), Charles D. Brown (Norris), Tom Fadden (Sidney),
Ben Welden (Pete), Trevor Bardette (Art Huck), James Fla-
vin (Cronjager), Joy Barlowe (cab driver), Thomas Jackson
(Wilde), Peggy Knudsen (Mona Mars), Theodore von Eltz
(Geiger), Carole Douglas (librarian), Dan Wallace (Owen Tay-
lor), Tanis Chandler and Deannie Best (waitresses), Lorraine
Miller (hat-check girl), Shelby Payne (cigarette girl), Forbes
Murray, Joseph Crehan, Emmett Vogan.

RED RIVER  United Artists/Monterey  1948  125
minutes
Producer, Director: Howard Hawks.  Screenplay: Borden
Chase, Charles Schnee, from the book, Blazing Guns on the
Chisholm Trail, by Chase.  Photography: Russell Harlan.
Music: Dimitri Tiomkin.  Art Director: John Datu Arensma.
Editor: Christian Nyby.  Second Unit Director: Arthur Ros-
son.  Assistant Director: William McGarry.  Special Effects:
Don Steward.  Special Photographic Effects: Allan Thompson.
Makeup: Lee Greenway.  Executive Producer: Charles K.
Feldman.
      Cast:  John Wayne (Tom Dunson), Montgomery Clift
(Matthew Garth), Walter Brennan (Groot), John Ireland
(Cherry Valance), Joanne Dru (Tess Millay), Noah Beery, Jr.

(Buster), Chief Yowlachie (Quo), Paul Fix (Teeler), Hank
Worden (Sims), Harry Carey, Jr. (Dan Latimer), Ivan Parry
(Bunk Kenneally or Kennelly), Harry Carey, Sr. (Melville),
Coleen Gray (Fen), Mickey Kuhn (Matthew as a boy), Hal
Taliaferro (Old Leather), Paul Fiero (Fernandez), Ray Hyke,
William Self (wounded wrangler), Dan White (Laredo), Shelley
Winters, Glenn Strange, Tom Tyler.

A SONG IS BORN   RKO   1948   113 minutes (THAT'S
LIFE)
Director: Howard Hawks. Screenplay: Harry Tugend, based
on the film BALL OF FIRE. Photography (Technicolor):
Gregg Toland. Producer: Samuel Goldwyn. Music: Emil
Newman, Hugo Friedhofer. Songs: Don Raye, Gene DePaul.
Editor: Daniel Mandell. Special Photographic Effects: John
P. Fulton. Assistant Director: Joseph Boyle. Makeup:
Robert Stephanoff. Art Directors: George Jenkins, Perry
Ferguson.
    Cast: Danny Kaye (Prof. Robert Frisbee), Virginia
Mayo (Honey Swanson), Benny Goodman (Prof. Magenbruch),
Hugh Herbert (Prof. Twingle), Steve Cochran (Tony Crow),
J. Edward Bromberg (Dr. Elfini), Felix Bressart (Prof.
Gurkakoff), Ludwig Stossel (Prof. Traumer), O. Z. White-
head (Prof. Oddly), Esther Dale (Miss Bragg), Mary Field
(Miss Totten), Ben Welden (Monte), Sidney Blackmer (Ad-
ams), Paul Langton (Joe), Donald Kerr (waiter), Lane Chand-
ler (policeman), William Haade, Joseph Crehan, Joe Devlin,
and Tommy Dorsey, Louis Armstrong, Lionel Hampton,
Charlie Barnett, Mel Powell, Buck and Bubbles, The Page
Cavanagh Trio, and Louis Bellson.

I WAS A MALE WAR BRIDE   Fox   1949   105 minutes
(YOU CAN'T SLEEP HERE)
Director: Howard Hawks. Screenplay: Charles Lederer,
Leonard Spiegelgass, Hagar Wilde, from the magazine story
by Henri Rochard. Photography: Norbert Brodine, O. H.
Borrodaile. Music: Cyril Mockridge. Musical Director:
Lionel Newman. Art Directors: Lyle Wheeler, Albert Hog-
sett. Producer: Sol C. Siegel. Editor: James B. Clark.
Sets: Thomas Little, Walter M. Scott. Special Photographic
Effects: Fred Sersen. Makeup: Ben Nye. Assistant Di-
rector: Arthur Jacobson.
    Cast: Cary Grant (Henri Rochard), Ann Sheridan
(Catherine Gates), William Neff (Capt. Jack Rumsey), Eugene
Gericke (Warrant Officer Tony Jowitt), Marion Marshall and
Randy Stuart (WAACs), Kenneth Tobey (Red), Reuben Wen-
dorf (innkeeper's assistant), Lester Sharpe, Robert Stevenson,

David McMahon (chaplain), Joe Haworth, Harry Lauter,
William Self, Russ Conway, Martin Miller (Schindler), Paul
Hardmuth.

The THING   RKO/Winchester   1951   85 minutes
(The THING FROM ANOTHER WORLD)
Producer: Howard Hawks. Directors: Hawks and Christian
Nyby. Screenplay: Charles Lederer (and, uncredited, Ben
Hecht?), from the story, "Who Goes There?", by John W.
Campbell, Jr. (aka Don Stuart). Photography: Russell Har-
lan. Special Effects: Donald Steward. Special Photographic
Effects: Linwood Dunn. Special Photography: Lee Nelows.
Music: Dimitri Tiomkin. Art Directors: Albert S. D'Agos-
tino, John Hughes. Sets: Darrell Silvera, William Stevens.
Editor: Roland Cross. Makeup: Lee Greenway. Associate
Producer: Edward Lasker. Assistant Directors: Arthur
Siteman, Max Henry. Sound: Phil Brigandi, Clem Portman.
        Cast: Kenneth Tobey (Capt. Patrick Hendry), Marga-
ret Sheridan (Nikki Nicholson), Douglas Spencer (Scotty),
Dewey Martin (Bob), Robert Cornthwaite (Prof. Carrington),
James Young (Lt. Eddie Dykes), Robert Nichols (Lt. Mac-
Pherson), William Self (Barnes), John Dierkes (Dr. Chapman),
James Arness (The Thing), Eduard Franz (Dr. Stern), Sally
Creighton (Mrs. Chapman), Paul Frees (Dr. Voorhees),
George Fenneman (Dr. Redding), Norbert Schiller (Dr. Lau-
renz), David McMahon (Gen. Fogarty), Ted Cooper, Robert
Bray, Edmond Breon (Dr. Ambrose), Everett Glass (Dr.
Wilson), William Neff (Olson), Lee Tung Foo and Walter Ng
(cooks), Robert Stevenson (Capt. Smith), Robert Gutknecht
(Corp. Hauser), Allan Ray, Nicholas Byron.

The BIG SKY   RKO/Winchester   1952   120 minutes
Producer, Director: Howard Hawks. Screenplay: Dudley
Nichols, from the novel by A. B. Guthrie, Jr. Photography:
Russell Harlan. Music: Dimitri Tiomkin. Art Directors:
Albert S. D'Agostino, Perry Ferguson. Sets: Darrell Sil-
vera, William Stevens. Editor: Christian Nyby. Special
Effects: Donald Steward. Second Unit Director: Arthur
Rosson. Assistant Director: William McGarry. Associate
Producer: Edward Lasker. Makeup: Mel Burns, Don Cash.
Costumes: Dorothy Jeakins.
        Cast: Kirk Douglas (Jim Deakins), Dewey Martin
(Boone), Arthur Hunnicutt (Zeb), Elizabeth Threatt (Teal Eye),
Hank Worden (Poordevil), Jim Davis (Streak), Buddy Baer
(Romaine), Steven Geray (Jourdonnais), Henri Letondal
(Labadie), Robert Hunter (Chouquette), Booth Colman (Pascal),
Paul Frees (McMasters), Frank de Cova (Moleface), Guy

Wilkerson (Longface), Don Beddoe (horse trader), Barbara
Hawks, George Wallace, Max Wagner, Sam Ash, Frank
Lackteen, Jay Novello, William Self.

O. HENRY'S FULL HOUSE   Fox   1952   (The FULL
HOUSE. BAGDAD OF THE SUBWAY. O. HENRY'S BAGDAD
OF THE SUBWAY)
     "The Ransom of Red Chief" episode:  25 minutes
Director:  Howard Hawks.  Screenplay:  Nunnally Johnson,
from the short story by O. Henry.  Photography:  Milton
Krasner.  Music:  Alfred Newman.  Art Director:  Chester
Goce.  Editor:  William B. Murphy.  Narrator:  John Stein-
beck.  Producer:  André Hakim.
     Cast:  Fred Allen (Sam), Oscar Levant (Bill), Lee
Aaker (J. B. ), Kathleen Freeman (J. B. 's mother), Alfred
Mizner (J. B. 's father), Robert Easton.

MONKEY BUSINESS   Fox   1952   97 minutes   (DAR-
LING, I AM GROWING YOUNGER)
Director:  Howard Hawks.  Screenplay:  Ben Hecht, I. A. L.
Diamond, Charles Lederer, from a story by Harry Segall.
Photography:  Milton Krasner.  Music:  Leigh Harline.
Musical Director:  Lionel Newman.  Art Directors:  Lyle
Wheeler, George Patrick.  Sets:  Thomas Little, Walter M.
Scott.  Editor:  William B. Murphy.  Special Photographic
Effects:  Ray Kellogg.  Producer:  Sol C. Siegel.  Makeup:
Ben Nye.
     Cast:  Cary Grant (Prof. Barnaby Fulton), Ginger
Rogers (Edwina Fulton), Charles Coburn (Oliver Oxly), Mar-
ilyn Monroe (Lois Laurel), Hugh Marlowe (Hank Entwhistle),
Henri Letondal (Dr. Kitzel), Robert Cornthwaite (Dr. Zol-
deck), Larry Keating (G. J. Gulverly), Douglas Spencer
(Dr. Brunner), Esther Dale, George Winslow, Emmett Lynn,
Kathleen Freeman (nurse), Jerry Sheldon, Harry Carey, Jr.,
George Eldredge (car salesman), Heinie Conklin, Forbes
Murray, Olan Soule (hotel clerk), Joseph Mell (barber),
Jerry Paris, Roger Moore, Olive Carey, Ruth Warren, Dabbs
Greer (cabbie), Ray Montgomery, Melinda Plowman, Robert
Nichols (garage man).

GENTLEMEN PREFER BLONDES   Fox   1953   91
minutes
Director:  Howard Hawks.  Screenplay:  Charles Lederer,
from the play by Anita Loos and Joseph Fields.  Photography
(Technicolor):  Harry J. Wild.  Songs:  Jule Styne, Leo
Robin, Hoagy Carmichael, Harold Adamson.  Musical Director:  Lionel Newman.  Art Directors:  Lyle Wheeler,

Joseph C. Wright.   Choreography:   Jack Cole.   Editor:   Hugh
S. Fowler.   Sets:   Claude Carpenter.   Costumes:   Travilla.
Producer:   Sol C. Siegel.   Special Photographic Effects:
Ray Kellogg.   Makeup:   Ben Nye.   Assistant Director:   Paul
Helmick.
        Cast:   Marilyn Monroe (Lorelei),   Jane Russell (Doro-
thy),  Charles Coburn (Sir Francis Beekman),  Elliott Reid
(Malone),  Tommy Noonan (Gus),  George Winslow (Henry Spof-
ford III),  Marcel Dalio (magistrate),  Taylor Holmes,  Norma
Varden,  Howard Wendell,  Steven Geray (hotel manager),
Henri Letondal,  Alvy Moore,  Harry Carey, Jr. (Winslow),
George Chakiris,  Jean Del Val,  Ray Montgomery,  Charles
Tannen.

        LAND OF THE PHARAOHS   Warner Brothers/Conti-
nental Company   1955   101 minutes   (VALLEY OF THE
PHARAOHS)
Producer, Director:  Howard Hawks.   Screenplay:  William
Faulkner,  Harry Kurnitz,  Harold Jack Bloom.   Photography
(Warnercolor/Cinemascope):   Lee Garmes,  Russell Harlan.
Music:  Dimitri Tiomkin.   Art Director:  Alexandre Trauner.
Costumes:  Mayo.   Editors:  Rudi Fehr,  V. Sagovsky.
Special Effects:  Don Steward.   Associate Producer:  Arthur
Siteman.   Makeup:  Emile Lavigne.   Assistant Director:
Paul Helmick.   Second Unit Director:  Noel Howard.
        Cast:  Jack Hawkins (Pharaoh),  Joan Collins (Princess
Nellifer),  Dewey Martin (Senta),  Alexis Minotis (Hamar),
James Robertson Justice (Vashtar),  Luisa Boni (Kyra),  Syd-
ney Chaplin (Treneh),  James Hayter,  Kerima (Queen Nailla),
Piero Giagnoni.

        RIO BRAVO   Warner Brothers/Armada   1959   140
minutes   (BULL BY THE TAIL)
Producer, Director:  Howard Hawks.   Screenplay:  Jules
Furthman,  Leigh Brackett,  from a short story by B. H.
McCampbell.   Photography (Technicolor):  Russell Harlan.
Music:  Dimitri Tiomkin.   Songs:  Tiomkin,  Paul Francis
Webster.   Art Director:  Leo K. Kuter.   Sets:  Ralph S.
Hurst.   Editor:  Folmar Blangsted.   Costumes:  Marjorie
Best.   Assistant Director:  Paul Helmick.
        Cast:  John Wayne (John T. Chance),  Dean Martin
(Dude),  Walter Brennan (Stumpy),  Angie Dickinson (Feathers),
Ricky Nelson (Colorado),  Ward Bond (Pat Wheeler),  John
Russell (Nathan Burdett),  Pedro Gonzalez-Gonzalez (Carlos),
Estelita Rodriguez (Consuela),  Claude Akins (Joe Burdett),
Harry Carey, Jr. (Harold),  Malcolm Atterbury,  Bob Steele
(Matt Harris),  Bob Terhune (bartender),  Ted White (Bart),
Myron Healey?

HATARI! Paramount/Malabar  1962  155 minutes
(The AFRICAN STORY)
Producer, Director: Howard Hawks. Screenplay: Leigh
Brackett. Story: Harry Kurnitz. Photography (Technicolor):
Russell Harlan, Joseph Brun. Music: Henry Mancini.
Song, "Just for Tonight," by Johnny Mercer and Hoagy Car-
michael. Art Directors: Hal Pereira, Carl Anderson.
Sets: Sam Comer, Claude Carpenter. Editor: Stuart Gil-
more. Special Effects: John P. Fulton. Special Mechanical
Effects: Richard Parker. Technical Adviser: Willy deBeer.
Associate Producer, Second Unit Director: Paul Helmick.
Assistant Directors: Tom Connors, Russ Saunders.
    Cast: John Wayne (Sean Mercer), Elsa Martinelli
(Dallas), Hardy Kruger (Kurt), Gérard Blain (Chips), Red
Buttons (Pockets), Michèle Girardon (Brandy), Bruce Cabot
(Indian), Valentin de Vargas (Luis), Eduard Franz (Dr. San-
derson), Eric Rungren (Stan), Queenie Leonard (nurse), Jon
Chevron (Joseph), Jack Williams.

    MAN'S FAVORITE SPORT? Universal/Gibraltar/Lau-
rel  1964  120 minutes
Producer, Director: Howard Hawks. Screenplay: John Fen-
ton Murray, Steve McNeil (and, uncredited, Leigh Brackett?),
based on the story, "The Girl Who Almost Got Away," by
Pat Frank. Photography (Technicolor): Russell Harlan.
Music: Henry Mancini. Art Directors: Alexander Golitzen,
Tambi Larsen. Editor: Stuart Gilmore. Special Effects:
Ben McMahon. Assistant Director: Tom Connors, Jr.
Associate Producer: Paul Helmick. Makeup: Bud Westmore.
    Cast: Rock Hudson (Roger Willoughby), Paula Pren-
tiss (Abigail Page), Maria Perschy (Isolde "Easy" Mueller),
John McGiver (William Cadwalader), Charlene Holt (Tex Con-
nors), Roscoe Karns (Major Phipps), James Westerfield
(policeman), Norman Alden (John Screaming Eagle), Forrest
Lewis (Skaggs), Regis Toomey (Bagley), Tyler McVey, Kathie
Browne (Marcia), Don Allen (Tom), Edy Williams, Margaret
Sheridan (Cadwalader's secretary), Paul Langton (Mr. Stern),
John Zaremba, Jim Bannon, Chuck Courtney.

    RED LINE 7000 Paramount/Laurel  1965  110 minutes
Producer, Director: Howard Hawks. Screenplay: Hawks,
George Kirgo. Photography (Technicolor): Milton Krasner.
Music: Nelson Riddle. Art Directors: Hal Pereira, Arthur
Lonergan. Editors: Stuart Gilmore, Bill Brame. Special
Effects: Paul K. Lerpae. Second Unit Director: Bruce Kes-
sler. Assistant Director: Dick Moder. Makeup: Wally
Westmore.

Cast: James Caan (Mike Marsh), Laura Devon (Julie Kazarian), Gail Hire (Holly MacGregor), Charlene Holt (Lindy), John Robert Crawford (Ned Arp), Marianna Hill (Gabrielle), James Ward (Dan McCall), Norman Alden (Pat Kazarian), George Takei (Kato), Diane Strom, Carol Connors, Cissy Wellman, Forrest Lewis, Edy Williams, Robert Osterloh, Robert Donner (Leroy).

EL DORADO Paramount/Laurel 1967 122 minutes Producer, Director: Howard Hawks. Screenplay: Leigh Brackett, from the novel, The Stars in Their Courses, by Harry Brown. Photography (Technicolor): Harold Rosson. Music: Nelson Riddle. Art Directors: Hal Pereira, Carl Anderson. Editor: John Woodcock. Special Photographic Effects: Paul K. Lerpae. Makeup: Wally Westmore. Assistant Director: Andrew J. Durkus.

Cast: John Wayne (Cole Thornton), Robert Mitchum (J. P. Harrah), James Caan (Alan Bourdillon Traherne), Charlene Holt (Maudie), Michele Carey (Joey MacDonald), Arthur Hunnicutt (Bull Harris), Christopher George (Nelse McLeod), R. G. Armstrong (Kevin MacDonald), Edward Asner (Bart Jason), Paul Fix (Doc Miller), Robert Donner (Milt), Jim Davis (Jason's foreman), Johnny Crawford (Luke), Anne Newman, Adam Roarke (Matt), Charles Courtney, Diane Strom, Victoria George, Olaf Wieghorst (Swedish gunsmith), Charlita, Rodolfo Hoyos, Lee Powell.

RIO LOBO Cinema Center/Malabar 1970 114 minutes (SAN TIMOTEO) Producer, Director: Howard Hawks. Screenplay: Leigh Brackett. Story: Burton Wohl. Photography (Technicolor): William Clothier. Music: Jerry Goldsmith. Production Design: Robert Smith. Sets: William Kiernan. Editor: John Woodcock. Second Unit Director: Yakima Canutt. Assistant Director: Mike Moder. Associate Producer: Paul Helmick. Special Effects: A. D. Flowers, Clifford P. Wenger.

Cast: John Wayne (Cord McNally), Jorge Rivero (Pierre Cordona), Chris Mitchum (Tuscarora), Jack Elam (Phillips), Jennifer O'Neill (Shasta), Susana Dosamantes (Maria), Sherry Lansing (Amelita), Victor French (Ketcham), David Huddleston (Dr. Jones), Mike Henry (Sheriff Hendricks), Bill Williams, Jim Davis (Riley), Robert Donner (Whitey), Dean Smith, George Plimpton, Chuck Courtney, Robert Rothwell, Edward Faulkner, Hank Worden.

## PERIPHERAL FILMS

The LITTLE PRINCESS                      1917
Director:  Marshall Neilan.
      Hawks directed several scenes.

QUICKSANDS                      1923
Director:  Jack Conway.  Screenplay:  Hawks.

TIGER LOVE                      1924
Director:  George Melford.  Screenplay:  Hawks.

The DRESSMAKER FROM PARIS                      1925
Director:  Paul Bern.  Screenplay:  Hawks.

HONESTY--THE BEST POLICY                      1926
Director:  Chester Bennett.  Screenplay:  Hawks.

UNDERWORLD                      1927
Director:  Josef von Sternberg.  Screenplay:  Hawks (uncredited) and others.

GENTLEMEN PREFER BLONDES  Paramount  1928
Director:  Mal St. Clair.  Adaptation:  Anita Loos, John Emerson.

EL CÓDIGO PENAL  Columbia  1931
Director:  David Shelman.
      Spanish-language version of The CRIMINAL CODE, with Maria Alba and Barry Norton.

RED DUST  MGM  1932
Director:  Victor Fleming.  Script:  Hawks and others.

The PRIZEFIGHTER AND THE LADY                      1933
Director:  W. S. Van Dyke, replacing Hawks.

STREAMLINE EXPRESS  Republic  1935

Director: Leonard Fields. Screenplay: Fields, David Silverstein.
        A combination of TWENTIETH CENTURY and GRAND HOTEL. Theatrical producer Victor Jory tries to recapture his show's star, Evelyn Venable, on a monorail train's first cross-country run.

SUTTER'S GOLD                           1936
Director: James Cruze, replacing Hawks.

PEPE LE MOKO                            1936
Director: Julien Duvivier.
        Draws some characters from SCARFACE, according to Pauline Kael.

CAPTAINS COURAGEOUS  MGM  1937
Director: Victor Fleming. Screenplay: Hawks and others.

TEST PILOT  MGM  1938
Director: Victor Fleming. Screenplay: Hawks and others.

GONE WITH THE WIND  MGM  1939
Director: Victor Fleming. Screenplay: Hawks and others.

GUNGA DIN                               1939
Director: George Stevens, replacing Hawks.

INTERNATIONAL SQUADRON  Warner Brothers  1941
Director: Lothar Mendes. Screenplay: Barry Trivers.
Story: Frank Wead.
        A remake of CEILING ZERO, with Ronald Reagan as Jimmy Grant.

FLYING TIGERS  Republic  1942
Director: David Miller. Screenplay: Barry Trivers, Kenneth Gamet.
        Borrows from ONLY ANGELS HAVE WINGS, according to Andrew Sarris.

The OUTLAW  RKO  1943
Director: Howard Hughes, replacing Hawks.

CORVETTE K-225  Universal  1943
Director: Richard Rosson. Producer: Howard Hawks.
        Undistinguished lost-a-few-men-but-we-made-it war drama. The dramatic high point is petulant sublieutenant James Brown's sudden, belated realization that it's he and

not Captain Randolph Scott who prevents them from playing cribbage (and incidentally winning the war) together.

Bacall to Arms  Warner Brothers Merrie Melodies cartoon 1946
        Takeoff on TO HAVE AND HAVE NOT.

KEY LARGO                              1948
Director:  John Huston.
        Borrows the ending of Hemingway's To Have and Have Not, according to Pauline Kael.

The BREAKING POINT                              1950
Director:  Michael Curtiz.
        Remake of TO HAVE AND HAVE NOT.

TRENT'S LAST CASE  Republic  1952
Director:  Herbert Wilcox.  From the book by E. C. Bentley.

The WINGS OF EAGLES  MGM  1957
Director:  John Ford.  Based on the life of Frank Wead.
        Features Broadway marquee of Wead's play Ceiling Zero.

The GUN RUNNERS  United Artists  1958
Director:  Don Siegel.  Based on Hemingway's short story "One Trip Across," which was the basis of To Have and Have Not.

The GEORGE RAFT STORY  Allied Artists  1961
Director:  Joseph M. Newman.
        George Raft's death scene in SCARFACE re-created.

BEFORE THE REVOLUTION  Iride Cinematografica  1964
Director, Screenplay:  Bernardo Bertolucci.
        "1946--summed up in The BIG SLEEP."

TARGETS  Paramount  1968
Director, Screenplay:  Peter Bogdanovich.
        Bogdanovich re:  Hawks' The CRIMINAL CODE on TV: "He really knows how to tell a story."

J. R. Brenner  1969  (aka WHO'S THAT KNOCKING AT MY DOOR?)
Director:  Martin Scorsese.
        RIO BRAVO double-billed with SCARAMOUCHE at theater.

The LAST PICTURE SHOW   Columbia   1971
Director:   Peter Bogdanovich.
        Scenes from RED RIVER on theatre screen.

WITHOUT APPARENT MOTIVE   Fox   1971
Director:   Philippe Labro.
        References to TO HAVE AND HAVE NOT, The BIG
SLEEP.

SHAMUS   Columbia   1972
Director:   Buzz Kulik
        Implicit references to scenes (bookstore, hothouse,
etc.) in The BIG SLEEP.

DEAD PIGEON ON BEETHOVEN STREET   Emerson   1973
Director, Screenplay:   Samuel Fuller.
        Hero sees RIO BRAVO dubbed, in German movie
theater.

# INDEX

231

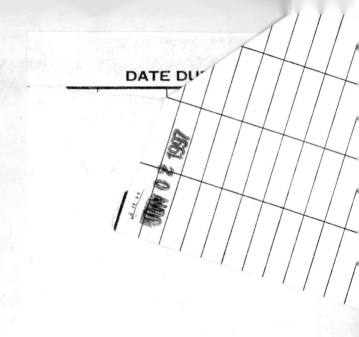